DIFFERENCE MAKER

Enacting systems theory in biology teaching

You can find me at cdmoore28@gmail.com
or @CMooreAnderson on social media.

Christian Moore-Anderson: Author & images
Blanca Martínez Valiente: Book design & cover design

1.
LAYING DOWN A PATH IN CONVERSING

The classroom forms a circular system

Hello, I'd like to talk to you about a different way of teaching, a different way of learning. Over the years, I've tried many things, including the teacher-led and student-led strategies. I'm not talking about new starters, plenaries, or other techniques. It was never just a matter of employing new tricks. Something more organic than rigorous structure was needed. Besides, my subject also required rethinking. Slipping into the abyss of biological details was always a danger on the cards. There needed to be something more integral than just knowing more content.

You probably know what I'm talking about. I'm sure you've felt – at some point – that to grasp biology was to master an encyclopaedia. If we've felt that way, what about our students? It's just facts and memorisation, I'd heard them say. And what about teaching biology if it isn't just delivering all that information? And then supplying questions for them to practise? I found myself tied to resource creation, maybe you have been too. My time was spent making detailed slide decks. It seemed to work well enough when I was in the classroom. But when we suddenly had to teach online during the coronavirus pandemic, my students learnt nothing. Something was amiss.

I sought new ideas and found systems theory. It provided my biology courses with unifying principles. Shielded from the abyss of content, my students understood more. Yet, as I continued reading, something else occurred. I hadn't expected it also to encompass my classroom and my teaching. More than just teaching about systems, I began *enacting* systems theory. Rather than being a resource maker and deliverer, lessons emerged from diagrams and dialogue. Freed from rigid structures and activities, my students and I laid a path together. It became more enjoyable and felt more real. In this book, I'm going to show you exactly how I do it, and also why I do it.

What's a system? Some people use the word system to refer to a set of procedures to follow, like a school's behaviour system. However, systems theory refers to something else: "A system is a set of things – people, cells, molecules, or whatever – interconnected in such a way that they produce their own pattern of behavior over time" (Meadows 2008, 2). Therefore, your school is a social system, in which a behaviour policy plays a role in the interactions. The classroom is a system of interacting students and teachers. Organisms are living systems of interacting cells, and humans are cognitive (thinking) systems. So, we teach in classrooms (a system), about living systems (organisms), to students (cognitive systems). Yet, despite this variety, I'll show you how they can all be understood with the same principles.

There will be two fundamental ideas that we'll constantly return to in this book. First, most of the interactions in systems happen in feedback loops. Feedback has become a common term in classrooms, we "give feedback" to students. However, feedback is a deeper idea that will help us think about teaching in a new light. These loops were studied by a field called cybernetics, which focused on how feedback loops (or circularity) led to adaptive behaviour. As I'll show you, this idea will be key to thinking about adapting to our students in the classroom as much as teaching about organisms.

The basic cybernetic idea of feedback began in the 1940s (Rosenblueth, Wiener and Bigelow 1943). It explained how regulation in a missile was analogous to someone reaching for a glass of water. When a missile moved slightly off track, the error was detected, and the thrusters were adjusted to bring it back in line. Equally, as a person reaches for a glass, they monitor the movement through sight. While the arm gets closer, any misalignment with the glass is corrected. This is a circular loop of information – from moving arm to eyes and brain, and from eyes and brain to moving arm.

This was referred to as a "negative" feedback loop, which allowed adaptation. The authors gave the example of someone with brain damage that inhibited this circular feedback mechanism. In this case, the arm didn't move towards the glass in a seemingly straight line. But from side to side in ever wider oscillations. The loop was severed, and self-control was lost.

What's this got to do with teaching? Teachers continually adapt to students through similar feedback loops. Norbert Wiener (1948/1961) likened cybernetics to steering – the art of steersmanship – and we could see teaching similarly. A steerer gives a boat its direction by regulating the rudder. But to keep its route, the steerer depends on receiving information from the boat itself and its orientation. Likewise, a teacher directs a lesson by constantly responding to the actions of their students. This way, they maintain a certain direction and act to avoid confusion or decreases in motivation. Steering uses a negative feedback loop and early cybernetics was about the continual regulation of systems using such loops.

Wiener often referred to the tools of humans as extensions of the human, connected through feedback loops. For example, a pilot can't fly without a plane, and the plane can't fly without its pilot (Rid 2016). Gregory Bateson, someone we'll return to often in this book, would take this notion to its logical conclusion (1972). He envisioned a logger cutting down a tree with an axe. As the logger swings the axe and produces the first cut, they analyse the incision. This informs the position and angle of the axe for the next strike in an iterative process. If the axe was considered an extension of the logger, so must the tree, because it formed an indispensable part of the circularity. Bateson's logger didn't fell the tree alone, but the logger, axe, and tree did it together. This isn't to say that they are physically connected – each constitutes its own physical body – but the logger's actions were part of a larger circular system which went beyond the physical bodies themselves.

This is a key idea from cybernetics to consider:
The classroom forms a circular system consisting of multiple and endless feedback loops.

Like the logger, the teacher, the physical space they occupy, the resources they use, and the students' responses, all form part of a circular feedback loop of interactions. Sometimes teachers may take pride in their students' exam results as if they were their own. On the other hand, teachers may dispense all the credit to their students. Yet, learning emerges from the whole system of interactions. A teacher's pen or whiteboard is as much an extension of their actions as their students are – all depend on each other for the system to function.

However, continual adaptation isn't always present. Many systems we interact with have been designed to behave as anticipated. Televisions, ovens, and cars all come with a guarantee that they'll do solely what they're expected to do. In other words, they aren't supposed to surprise you; if they do, they're considered faulty. Think about a car, you quickly learn that by pressing the accelerator by a certain amount, the vehicle always responds in the same degree. By releasing the pedal the system returns to how it was and future interactions will produce the same responses. Cyberneticians would call this a trivial system (Foerster 2003) and the classroom is nothing like this.

If the classroom were trivial, we'd never be surprised. We'd be able to master a particular way of explaining a topic and know exactly what all students would learn. In other words, with precise teaching inputs, precise learning outputs would be knowable before we even teach the lesson.

In contrast, you can't precisely predict the behaviour of nontrivial systems because every interaction with one changes how it behaves. The nontriviality of classrooms is what makes them such interesting places. As we teach, our students' perceptions shift and their responses can surprise us. The lesson continually evolves as each interaction triggers a change in mind. While teachers have predictive powers gained from experience, any one lesson can unfold in unforeseeable ways – as every teacher who has taught the same content with different classes knows. This makes steering, regulation, and adaptation the necessary – and endless – processes of teaching.

As the field evolved, cyberneticians began applying these ideas to the brain and became concerned with constructing a general science of mind (Varela et al. 2016) (something continued today in enactive cognitive science). From cybernetics, we can learn as much about adapting in the classroom as our students' learning. Each of these perspectives will be useful for us in this book.

You may be starting to see why it takes a moment to get to the detailed examples of my teaching. If I gave you these examples too early, you'd probably interpret them according to ideas you already know, whereas I want you to perceive something distinct. To understand what this book is about, I'll need to show you a model of teaching that I've made. And to understand the model, I need you to consider two ideas from cybernetics, both underpinned by the fundamental concepts of feedback loops and variety. The first of these ideas is conversation theory. The second will be the law of requisite variety.

A teacher's explanation doesn't transmit meaning

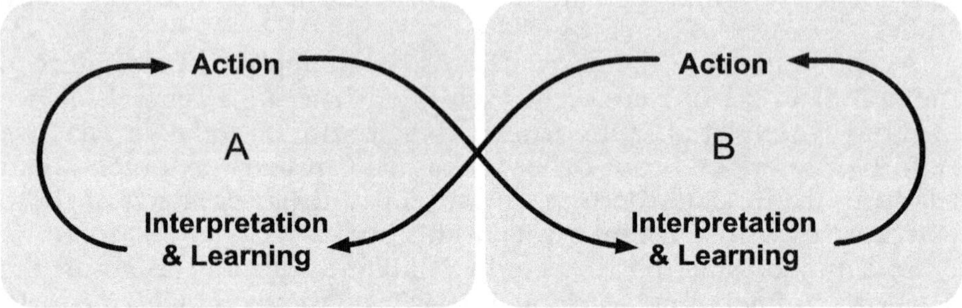

Figure 1: A simplified sketch of the basics of Pask's conversation theory (1975; 1976).

Key idea:
Meaning can't be transmitted to people, but we can reach a compatible meaning through conversation.

Gordon Pask's conversation theory (1975; 1976) was concerned with dialogical interaction. Conversation could be between two individuals, within an individual, or between groups of individuals. It was a process in which interactors adapted to each other. Similarly, cyberneticians saw learning as adaptive, which wasn't a coincidence. Both conversation and learning require active interpretation, decision-making, and response – whether that be with others or the self, through oral language, gestures, images, or via a machine.

Neither conversation, nor learning, is simply receipt of information, like passively obtaining and repeating an explanation. There's a biological reason for this; the nervous system only has direct access to itself and its own activity. Nerve impulses don't leave or enter the body, so the signals that give rise to our thoughts must occur in constant loops – neurons communicating with neurons. You can think of it as an *autonomous* system (Varela 1979) and the biological version of the proverb, "You can lead a horse to water, but you can't make it drink". Unlike a computer, information – such as a teacher's explanation – doesn't linearly enter the mind from the outside nor is processed step by step (Varela et al. 2016). Instead, a teacher's communication is "a gentle perturbation on an ongoing buzzing of internal activity" (Varela 1987, 66). I like this quote, so let me reword it: what we explain to students can trigger them to think, but not enter their mind to be stored.

Our lessons can't be a linear process of just telling information to students. Rather, lessons emerge as teachers and students exchange prompts and provocations that cause each other to interpret and act (Scott 2021). The diagram in Figure 1 shows a simple sketch of the theory, representing two interactants, or conversants, as A and B.

Pask addressed one of the most significant insights from information theory (Shannon 1948). Information theory revealed that *meaning* doesn't travel down a communication channel. Instead, it's *signals* that are sent between communicators. Signals can be, for example, electrical signals down a wire, notes on paper (e.g., writing), or modulations of sound (e.g., speech) (Glasersfeld 2003). A common example of the era is Morse code, which uses dots and dashes to represent the alphabet. If two people knew the code, they could communicate. But the most common examples are words themselves. In both examples, the receiver has to interpret the signals and make sense of them the best they can.

This is why for Heinz von Foerster – another cybernetician we'll return to often – it was the listener who determined the meaning of an utterance, not the speaker. He meant that: "Given the words a speaker has used, the listener can interpret the utterance only in terms of the meaning he, the listener, ascribes to these words" (Glasersfeld 2003, 1). A person can't receive a meaning like they can receive a parcel of contents. Instead, they perceive something new and then must make sense of it from the perspective of their own network of understandings. In other words, they make meaning with reference to their own history of experiences and prior knowledge.

This was seen in Bartlett's famous War of the Ghosts Experiment (1932). The participants in the study were asked to read a Native American story and recall it several times. As they recalled it, however, they tended to alter the story to fit their cultural background and experiences. Von Glasersfeld cites a transcript from a family therapy session that demonstrates the same phenomenon of the listener deciding the meaning of what they hear (Lax 1993, cited in Glasersfeld 1995, 143):

> Client (spontaneously): 'Do you remember what you said to me about X the last time?'
> Therapist: (waits and says nothing, because he is sure that he never mentioned X during the last session) ...
> Client: 'It was enormously helpful to me.'

Had the client misunderstood? Heinz von Foerster would argue that they hadn't:

> "... so-called misunderstandings, do not exist. There is only one understanding, namely, how I understood it. But maybe it is not

> what my counterpart had hoped I would understand. Then it is not a misunderstanding on my part. It's not as if I can misguess something. All that I have are his signs and what I have just heard." (2014, xxi).

In other words, students may not understand the way the curriculum had desired or write what the exam had demanded. But that doesn't mean there's some sort of error or failure of cognition; students can only think with the meaning they themselves perceive.

This inability to transmit meaning in communication makes planning precise explanations – and ensuring your students respond *correctly* – no failsafe solution for arriving at a compatible understanding. We can't simply tell students the meanings of things. A simple example is the use of words that have different meanings in the contexts of science and everyday life. "Energy" is one such word, as is "organic". And then, imagine what it's like to be a student trying to make sense of the word "mitochondria"? The teacher must somehow bring about a shared (compatible) understanding with their students of all these words. So what can we do about it?

Conversation theory proposes that a teacher and student can achieve compatible understandings through dialogue. By conversing until they mutually agree, or disagree, on the meaning of something. Conversation then acts like a negative feedback loop – correcting for differences in understanding. Daily conversations go this way. Conversants elaborate and rephrase in cycles, to ensure they are on the same page. People ask, "Do you see what I mean?" and confess, "Sorry, I thought you meant something else". Once a teacher explains a concept, they have to unveil what students think. Equally, students need to uncover what it means to the teacher to see if they understand similarly.

If we just ask students if they have understood – and if they say they have – who is to know if their understanding is compatible with ours? Pask advocated asking students to explain their understanding back to the teacher. He called it "Teachback" (1975). In Chapter 5, I'll discuss ways of obtaining frequent feedback from students in conversation.

Yet Pask (1980, 999) also warned that communication and conversation were not the same, because "very bad communication may admit very good conversation". What would this look like in the classroom? What immediately comes to mind is the talkative, confident, and articulate class that encounters a poor teacher explanation. A long discussion ensues in which students attempt to establish common ground with the teacher.

On the other hand, Pask argues that having perfect conditions for communication, "is no guarantee that any conversation will take place." (999). Here we have the opposite, interested and attentive students listening to a teacher's explanation, but no conversation between the two. And, hence, no feedback, circularity, or checking for compatible understanding. Pask's vision of conversation was one in which at least one of the conversants' views were changed or updated (Scott 2021). If not, it was just an exchange of messages.

I think the model I will propose is a step towards teaching that is both good communication (the exposition of ideas) and good conversation (the dialogic meaning-making). We're now a step closer to the model, next we need to consider the law of requisite variety.

The law of requisite variety gives insight into effective regulation of the classroom

Key idea:
Systems can maintain stability if their variety of responses (or options) matches the variety of situations they encounter, or, more concisely: Complexity of regulating system ≥ Complexity of system being regulated.

In the last section I gave a brief introduction to some of the ideas surrounding feedback loops, ideas I'll continue to elaborate on in practical classroom terms. Now I must introduce the second fundamental idea that will resurface throughout the book. Variety, as I'll show you, is essential for adapting to students and learning itself. Here I'll begin with the idea of adaptation, and in Chapter 2 I'll return to the idea to see how it's crucial for learning.

A major focus of cybernetics is the adaptation of a system to its environment. An environment is anything interacting with the system. For example, teachers must adapt to their students as much as schools must adapt to their communities. Yet, to do so, a system must be capable of responding to the changes it perceives in its environment, like a confused class or a community that desires a change in a school's policy.

When Ross Ashby developed the law of requisite variety (1956; 1958), he knew the capacity to adapt wasn't limitless. Just as species either persist or go extinct, systems can fail. The capacity to adapt depends on the variety of options you have at your disposal. This is as true for a teacher's ability to adapt to their students as it is for students to adapt and understand a new concept.

To simplify the idea, imagine a turn-based game, like chess, or American football. Let's say one American football team had a variety of set plays it could use. But the opponent team had exactly the right variety of set plays to counter them. The teams would be equal. Let's say a team introduced an innovative play that the opposing team hadn't seen before and had no counterplay. The opposing team wouldn't have the requisite variety of plays and would lose the game.

Adaptation is intertwined with the term "homeostasis". This literally means, "staying in the same place," or, in other words, "maintaining the same state" or even "maintaining stability". What, exactly, must be kept stable? Behaviour is adaptive if it can maintain the system's *essential variables* (Ashby 1952). Body temperature is the typical example. It's an essential variable – for birds and mammals – that must be maintained stable despite changing conditions in their environment. To do so, they must have a variety of responses available to them. For example, mammals may move to warmer or cooler habitats as a behavioural response. Equally, they may shiver or sweat, redistribute their blood to the surface or the innards, or erect their hair. If at any time their variety of responses is insufficient, they will suffer hypo-, or hyperthermia and possibly die. This point, therefore, is crucial. Stable systems are those that keep their essential variables within limits. When this doesn't happen, the survival of the system is in jeopardy.

We could see it this way in schools: to ensure the civil functioning of schools, teachers are often provided with a variety of responses. These range from verbal warnings, small sanctions, and restorative conversations to classroom or school expulsions. On the other hand, teachers often award students with merits or other tokens of praise. They can send congratulatory letters to parents or call home directly. We can also consider teachers adept at forming warm relationships with students as increasing the variety of the school system. Schools with too little variety (of responses/states) for the variety of situations they encounter in the school, may find it difficult to maintain stable conditions. One cybernetician considered the law of requisite variety to be so fundamental for the design of organisations, that it was the equivalent of Newton's laws for physics (Beer 1972).

The classroom is similar. Teachers act to maintain certain variables, such as their students' attention – or level of concentration – on what is being studied. We could also say that an essential variable is a dynamic, but relatively stable rate of learning. Teachers work to sustain these despite all types of disruptions to lessons. These perturbations might occur because the students are tired, the topic content is particularly tricky or any number of other variables. I'll return to this – and the requisite knowledge of the teacher – in Chapter 6.

This is cybernetics according to Ernst von Glasersfeld. He defines it as "the art of creating equilibrium in a world of possibilities and constraints." (1996, 495). The law of requisite variety states that a system can remain stable – or in equilibrium – if its variety of responses (or actions/options/states) match the variety of situations it encounters.

Ashby quantified the law by defining "variety" as the number of states a system can have. Every teacher knows the classroom is a complex system with innumerable possible states. This complexity partly stems from the variety of students, each with their personalities, moods, and understandings of the content of the course. For this reason, the law of requisite variety can also be expressed as the law of requisite complexity (Boisot & McKelvey 2011). This is the term you'll see below in my model of teaching (Figure 2).

If the classroom is complex – and it always is – you'll need a complex system (a teacher with a large variety of responses) to regulate it. What happens if the teacher doesn't have the requisite variety? Then those essential variables would fall below the viable limits more often. Learning would suffer.

The law of requisite variety is "the antithesis of the always attractive search for a silver bullet that will somehow make a complex problem go away" (Mobus & Kalton 2015, 43). So, here's the key idea again in its equation form:

Key idea:
Complexity of regulating system ≥ Complexity of system being regulated.

For any given situation, this equation gives two options. Either increase your complexity (e.g. a teacher's skill set and knowledge) or decrease the complexity of the other system (e.g. by adding routines to the classroom or setting students by attainment). Concerning the model I'll show you next, both the teacher and students need to experiment with this equation, raising and reducing complexity to ensure the intended learning happens.

When teachers present new ideas, they must reduce the complexity to avoid overwhelming their students. Equally, students must reduce the complexity of the content they are taught, to see what's important. But students must also explore complexity by following the ramifications of new ideas. To understand what I mean, let's look at the model.

An overview of the recursive teaching model and the rest of the book

By uniting the law of requisite variety with the simplified sketch of Pask's conversation, I created a model for thinking about classroom interactions. This recursive teaching model is shown in Figure 2, and following it, I'll give a quick overview of how it will form the structure of this book.

What does recursion mean? It's related to the word recurrent, which refers to repetition. But recursion includes the notion of something cycling back on itself, feeding back into itself, or referring to itself. Or simply: "Recursion is basically a turning, a 'rotation' in loops of feedback." (Harries-Jones 2016, 174).

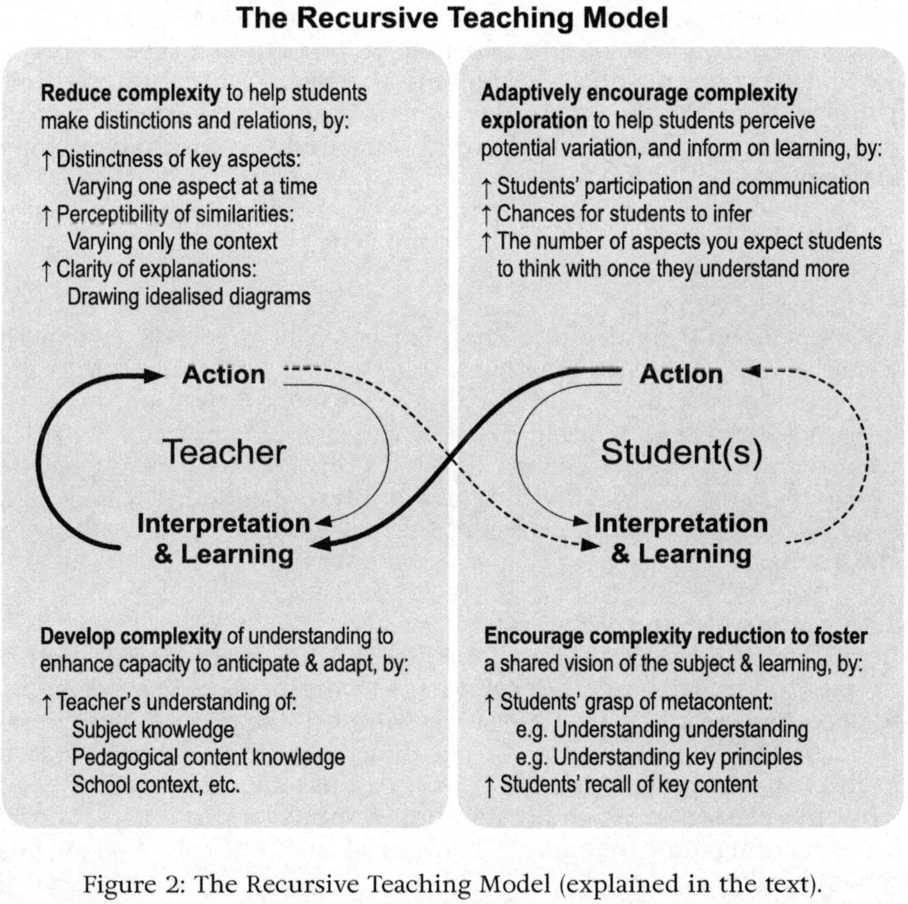

Figure 2: The Recursive Teaching Model (explained in the text).

Communication is often recursive and serves as a good example. As person A communicates with person B, they may use a certain word and meaning. Person B may then use it similarly with person C, who may then use it again with person A, and so on. In this case, the original word feeds back to the original speaker. These recursive loops bring a stable language into being (Foerster 2014) and can, therefore, bring about a shared way of seeing and talking about our subjects. This is something I'll discuss in Chapter 4.

In the classroom, we could see either recurrent or recursive activity. For example, in recurrent interaction, a teacher may explain a concept without conversation, then have students complete activities and move on with the lesson as each activity is finished, or students have uttered the correct (or wrong) answers. It's just a repetition of teachers and students alternating their actions. Recursive teaching, however, is based on conversation. Our discussions with students continually feed back into us, and we start talking about what we're talking about. We may rephrase previous utterances as students ask us questions. We may refer to what we're saying and to previous conversations in such a way that conversations continually build on each other (Maturana 2011). As we'll see in this book, these looping conversations trigger a sort of coordinated co-regulation – a coupling – between teacher and students. The class coevolves as both parties adapt to each other, ensuring mutual understanding before moving forward (something absent from teaching via recurrent activity).

The model is divided into four areas – each will be an explicit focus in the following chapters. Let me summarise the quadrants.

1. The teacher's action

Chapters 2 and 3 are dedicated to this part of the model. They're both about bringing clarity to what we teach. Chapter 2 focuses on learning according to cybernetics and teaching according to variation theory. It directly addresses the problem of ensuring students perceive what we want them to perceive. Chapter 3 follows this idea by focusing on the use of diagrams – especially the stock and flow diagram. The appendix is dedicated to a range of examples that I've designed and used in the classroom.

2. The student's interpretation

In Chapter 4 I'll introduce a new concept called metacontent, which helps students reduce complexity for themselves. Specifically, metacontent shares a way of seeing content – sharing fundamental patterns that repeat throughout a subject's concepts. There are two examples of metacontent that I will discuss and give examples of from my classroom: 1. understanding a subject's principles, and 2. understanding understanding. I'll also speak about how I help students remember key content.

3. The student's action

Students must explore the ramifications of new ideas to help them understand what is being taught. Having students explore ideas is also the only way that a teacher can receive rich feedback on how students think with what they know. Nevertheless, the responsibility lies on the teacher to (adaptively) regulate the complexity of tasks according to their students' performance. In Chapter 5 I'll show you how I manage this in conversation.

4. The teacher's interpretation

To match the complexity of the classroom – to be able to adapt – a teacher must develop a complex understanding. I'll take this idea beyond the law of requisite variety to look at Ashby's good regulator theorem. We'll come to this in Chapter 6.

Fundamentally, this is a model that is enacted over time. Nothing makes sense in biology, or the classroom, except through time. Because without time, the mutual responses that lead to adaptation can't occur. A person walking is never in balance Gregory Bateson would say, but constantly correcting for imbalance (1979). So, we could say that a classroom is never completely in harmony, but constantly correcting for dissonance of ideas.

Planning the skeleton of a lesson – what to show students, and in what order – is always important. But once the pieces begin moving, no one knows how the game will unfold. Davis et al. (2015, 221) see teaching as the interplay between the two: "It's never a trivial sequence of planning and implementing, but a complex, recursive process of anticipating and engaging." Much of the art of teaching is skilful anticipation and adept adaptation. I'll demonstrate how I do so in this book.

2. TO PERCEIVE, STUDENTS MUST MAKE THEIR OWN DISTINCTIONS

How can we teach new things to students if we can't transmit meanings? To answer this, we'll need to look at ideas from cybernetics and variation theory. I'll give examples from biology throughout, but the detailed lesson examples can only come after I've presented this distinct thought style. Had I done otherwise, you may have interpreted the detailed examples through a different lens. The first idea is drawing distinctions – a fundamental act of learning. Then, we'll have to look at what provokes students to draw those distinctions. Finally, we'll look at how to use variation theory – based on making distinctions – in biology teaching and detailed examples of my lessons.

Awareness begins with the distinctions students make

Key ideas:
Drawing a distinction is the fundamental cognitive act.
The distinctions we've made determine what we perceive.

George Spencer-Brown's *Laws of Form* (1979) had a major impact on the development of cybernetics. He wanted to show the first, and most fundamental act of cognition, is drawing distinctions. The book began like this: “We take as given the idea of distinction and the idea of indication, and that we cannot make an indication without drawing a distinction.” (1). Then, he developed a calculus of indications using the following symbol: ⏋ to represent a distinction (hence the symbol of the front cover). You can think of it as an abbreviated box □ denoting an inside and outside (Kaufmann 2017).

At first, we come into a world of oneness with little ability to indicate anything at all, a world of indistinguishable senses and feelings. Spencer-Brown referred to this idea as the void. A primal distinction we make is to distinguish between ourselves and the environment so that we become self-aware. From here, we continue separating the world – in our mind – into distinct parts. What had once been whole entities, became composites of distinct parts (Maturana & Varela 1980). For example, what had once been plants in your perception, became different species with distinct traits.

In our classes, we provoke students to make even more distinctions. To distinguish the cell types of leaves and their organisation; to make distinct organisms that produce their own food (autotrophs) from those that must obtain it (heterotrophs); to differentiate genetic adaptation over generations from bodily adaptations that are not inherited; to distinguish open vascular systems from closed ones; and to perceive explanation as distinct from description.

Without making distinctions, students can't perceive. They can't indicate, refer to, communicate, or converse. They can't participate. The exact moment we point into our environment to indicate something new we make a distinction. We mentally place it in a box, separated from everything else, and give it a name. We perceive it. This is Spencer-Brown's "law of calling", and its command, "Draw a distinction" can be considered a primal act of construction of a world (Foerster 1970a).

> "For example, to say, 'Let there be light' is also to say 'Let there be a distinction between light and something other than light – call it darkness'. Light must come forth in distinction from darkness; otherwise all would be light, in which brilliance nothing could be distinguished." (Clarke 2020, 204).

When Darwin and Wallace pointed out the effect of varying chances of death – depending on an organism's fit within its environment – selection was made distinct. Where once there had been just the idea of death in populations, selection came forth in people's minds. Suddenly it could be indicated and discussed by those who perceived the idea from Darwin and Wallace's work.

For this reason, Spencer-Brown argued that "the ideas of description, indication, name, and instruction can amount to the same thing." (1979, 81). They are all acts of distinguishing something from everything else. This reminds me of my son, who would tell us that he was "tired" when this could have meant hot, hungry, thirsty, or tired. The lack of distinctions between the different sensations inhibited mutual understanding. It also reminds me of how students often get confused because they haven't yet made the distinction between molecules – such as enzymes – and living cells.

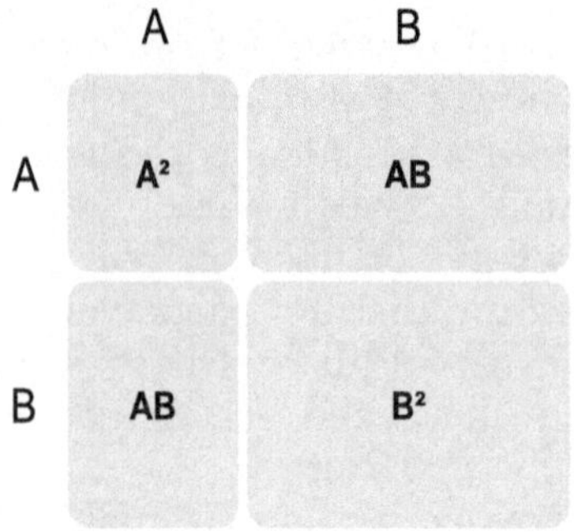

Figure 3: A geometric illustration of the expression $(a+b)^2 = a^2+2ab+b^2$.

Yet it isn't always about separating into more distinct parts, as I realised thanks to Gregory Bateson (1979). Bateson discussed how "every schoolboy knows that $(a+b)^2 = a^2+2ab+b^2$ ... but many schoolboys do not know that there is a geometric demonstration of the same binomial expansion" (73–74). The geometric version is shown in Figure 3.

This is a case of similarity, showing how two things are the same. But Bateson asks:

> "What has the schoolboy learned from our stating the same old equation in a new language? In a certain sense, nothing has been added. No new information has been generated or captured by my asserting that $(a+b)^2 = a^2+2ab+b^2$ in geometry as well as in algebra ... [but] the discovery (if it be discovery) that the two languages (of algebra and of geometry) are mutually translatable is itself an enlightenment" (74-75).

This enlightenment consisted of experiencing a sudden realisation that two things, once considered different, were the same. Their distinctions weren't coherent and required redrawing so two distinctions became one.

When reading the science education literature, I came across the same idea. Dykstra et al. (1992) drew from educational research and their own experience of teaching physics to develop three categories of conceptual change. I'll translate them into biological examples:

Differentiation (drawing distinctions). For example:

- Discerning density-dependent and density-independent factors affecting a population.
- Distinguishing between autotrophs and heterotrophs, or holozoic nutrition and saprotrophic nutrition.
- Differentiating between simple diffusion and osmosis.

- Discerning ventilation from gas exchange, the bulk transport due to pressure gradients, and the diffusion of gases due to concentration gradients.
- Seeing the difference between fast and slow life strategies in plants.

Class extension (redrawing distinctions that result in reclassification). For example:
- Realising that all species on Earth are made from the same fundamental molecules and are not "made from different stuff".
- Recognising that physiological homeostasis is analogous to population controls in ecosystems.
- Comprehending that what occurs in natural selection is the same as what occurs in tumours.
- Grasping that ultrafiltration in the kidney and somatic hypermutation in B cells are both ways of increasing an organism's variety (to match its environment).
- Realising that the digestive tract is as much the surface of you as your skin.
- Discerning that Neanderthals might be "us" after all.

Reconceptualisation (redrawing the relations between distinctions). For example:
- Seeing that selection is dependent on variation.
- Noticing that breathing is not "for the lungs" but "for all cells of the body".
- Realising that plants don't obtain organic molecules from the soil, just water and minerals.
- Grasping that carbon dioxide isn't just a waste product of organisms, but also the material source for building organic molecules.

These ideas are, in fact, deeply ingrained in the language we use. The English verb "to mistake" is to take something for what it is not. Likewise, in Spanish, the word for "to mistake" is "equivocarse". The Spanish verb traces its origins to Latin, which means "to make equal", or more colloquially, "to call something the same that is actually different". In English, we also see the word equivocal, which means ambiguous. In information theory, "equivocation" refers to the uncertainty, or lack of clarity, in a message that can lead to different interpretations (Krippendorff 2009). Similarly, the verbs to confuse, and to confound – also from Latin – literally mean "to mix with" or "to merge with". In other words "to mix or mingle things or ideas to make them indistinguishable" (Etymonline 2024).

Here's a vital point for teachers: distinctions and indications are *made* by someone. They aren't distinctions that are transmitted or gathered. The distinction emerges as a relationship between the distinction maker and their perceived environment. "The environment [itself] contains no information. The environment is as it is," von Foerster argued (1970b, 189).

In the same way that there is no colour in the world, "there is simply no one-to-one relationship between light flux at various wavelengths and the colours we perceive" (Varela et al. 2016, 160). Consequently, for von Foerster (2014):

> "This reminds me, incidentally, of that very funny saying: 'Seeing is believing.' I, however, would reverse this saying – 'Believing is seeing' – one only sees what one believes." (103). Because "the distinction is not 'there,' the distinction is here in me or from me" (28).

Thought and perception stem from our assumptions – our distinctions. Some distinctions are so obvious to us as humans – like the difference between a rock and a tree – that we don't question them. But others, such as whether plants obtain their nutrition from soil or air are more confusing.

Crucially, the distinctions students have made also determine what students *won't* perceive. If they've not made the distinction, they can't see it, indicate it, talk about it, or think with it. This means that teachers shouldn't be satisfied with just defining something in precise words.

"What is a definition? In order for a definition to be effective it must make a distinction." (Kauffman 2016, 491). A definition *is* a distinction. Firstly, we must provoke students to perceive the distinction. Otherwise, the definition we present to students may just add to their peculiar vocabulary. And repeating back to us that peculiar vocabulary is no guarantee of understanding.

For example, we can't just define the process of natural selection – or explain it precisely – and expect it to provoke any understanding. If we want students to understand, we have to provoke them to draw the critical distinctions of both variation and selection – as two parts of the whole concept of natural selection (more on this in a moment). Only then will they perceive those aspects of evolution and be able to think with the concept.

If making distinctions is key, our interest lies in how to bring them about. It was Bateson who realised that we draw distinctions when we perceive a difference that makes a difference. This is what I'll discuss next.

Students make distinctions when they perceive a difference that makes a difference to them

Key idea:
Information is a difference that makes a difference for the observer.

Bateson's interests lay in the cybernetics of communication and learning. He knew that any focus on the information sender was a distraction – it was the receiver, who needed consideration. As such, the term signal was inadequate because it referred to something sent, rather than discerned. Bateson redefined signal as "news" – something that meant something to a perceiver (Harries-Jones 1995). News suggests a change, a variation, or a difference, about a state of affairs. Bateson also explained how the human nervous system is a perceiver of such changes, variations, and differences:

> "Only news of a difference can enter into man's sense organs ... Only difference can affect and trigger an end organ – so all our information (our universe of perception) is built on differences." (unpublished notebook 1973, cited in Harries-Jones 1995, 176).

Accordingly, he defined nerve impulses as "news of a difference". This is because we become habituated – and stop sensing – a stimulus when we no longer perceive a change in it. Most teachers will have come into a classroom of students and been hit by a strong smell of humanity. Yet after several minutes, we stop noticing its presence – we're only reminded of it when we leave the room and reenter. This is a good example of how Bateson understood "difference" – not as an antonym of similarity, resemblance, or identity – but as change, or variation (Harries-Jones 2016).

Spencer-Brown's distinctions influenced Bateson's ideas, another influence was Alfred Korzybski's famous metaphor:

> "A map is not the territory it represents, but if correct, it has a similar structure to the territory, which accounts for its usefulness." (Harries-Jones 1995).

Korzybski was making the fundamental distinction between reality – like an actual territory – and the version of it we construct in our mind – like a map. Our role as teachers is to help students build their own maps of our subjects in a manner that is compatible with ours. Using this analogy, Bateson brought together Spencer-Brown's distinctions with his notion of difference (1972, 320):

> "We know the territory does not get onto the map. That is the central point about which we here are all agreed."

OK, sure, but what is it that ends up in our perception, what gets on the map? Bateson focuses on this next:

> "Now, if the territory were uniform, nothing would get onto the map except its boundaries, which are the points at which it ceases to be uniform ..."

So, the non-changing, the invariant, is categorised as one thing, without any distinctions whatsoever. What is it then, that gets on the map, what makes up our perception?

> "What gets onto the map, in fact, is difference, be it a difference in altitude, a difference in vegetation, a difference in population structure, difference in surface, or whatever. Differences are the things that get onto a map."

Differences are key then, but what if there are no perceptible differences? The answer, according to Bateson (1979) is that:

> "It takes at least two somethings to create a difference. To produce news of difference, i.e., information, there must be two entities (real or imagined) ..." (68).

Alone – a thing in itself – is like "a sound of one hand clapping." (69). Or more colloquially, he said that "it takes two to know one" (Nachmanovitch 1982, 35–36).

But what do differences consist of? Bateson knew that differences were not some sort of physical substance or anything that could be transferred from teacher to student. For example, in a relationship between two people, silence, or lack of interaction, can represent news of a difference. This brings us back to the key idea of this section:

Key idea:
Information is a difference that makes a difference for the observer.

In this sense, there is no information in a classroom except that which the student decides is information (Foerster 2003). What logically follows is that teachers can't simply transmit, give, or tell students their understanding and expect them to make the same distinctions. If ideas and concepts are assemblages of distinctions – as Bateson thought (1979, 228) – then this must also be the central concern of school pedagogy.

For this, we need to move on to the work of Ference Marton and colleagues, who developed a pedagogical theory fit for the classroom. And it is this theory that allows us to see exactly how to reduce the complexity of our teaching.

CHAPTER 2

Key ideas about distinction making – how cybernetics and variation theory converged

The history of variation theory is different to that of systems theory, but, in my opinion, they converged on key points. In this section, I'll bridge the gap between the two. To do this I'll show you how the ideas we've already visited – distinctions, differences, and dialogue – are also seen in variation theory. The motive is to help *see with* variation theory rather than perceiving it as just another teaching trick. After that, we'll be able to see it in detailed examples.

The beginning of variation theory can be traced to Marton and Booth's book, *Learning and Awareness* (1997). The authors brought a new way of thinking about learning that stemmed from previous research into how people saw phenomena. These studies were part of phenomenography. This wasn't experimental, it was a method for simply describing the different ways that people directly experienced – or saw – specific phenomena. What they found in this work aligns with Spencer-Brown's laws of form – people appeared to see phenomena in discretely different ways.

If learning were simply about the accrual of small knowledge tokens, then people's ways of seeing would be like human height. There are no categories for human height, just a continuous difference between shorter to taller people. The work Marton and Booth (1997) were building upon suggested that awareness was more like blood types – there were discrete categories of ways of understanding. And some were more powerful than others.

The difference between categories depended on awareness of certain, *critical* aspects (or distinctions), despite varying levels of knowledge. Let's look at a specific example discussed in *Learning and Awareness*. This study (Booth 1992) researched the distinct ways computer programmers understood the concept of recursion. It wasn't an intervention, the study simply looked at how they saw recursion as an idea. If you remember, recursion is similar to recurrent but includes the notion of something cycling back on itself, feeding back into itself, or referring to itself.

The students were learning about recursion so that they could program an application to repeat its own process until a certain function is completed. The study found just three distinct ways students saw recursion after studying the course. The first group saw it as a feature to be used in the programming language. The second group saw it as a programming feature and a repeating process. The third, while noting the programming feature and the repetitive process, also saw the aspect of self-reference. They discerned in the programming language that it wasn't just repeating itself recurrently. In circularity, the programming language referred to itself as an application and applied its own process to itself. This is recursion. This final group of students were able to develop the best programmes and transfer their knowledge to other contexts.

What was the difference that made the difference? From interpreting the findings of phenomenographic research, Marton and Booth (1997) saw learning as intimately connected to awareness. The students in the study on recursion (Booth 1992) could be separated into three groups depending on the distinctions they had drawn. The difference in perception of recursion in computer programming was the different distinctions they had in mind when thinking about the concept. Or, in the words of variation theory, the different aspects they had in their focal awareness.

The aspects (distinctions) people are aware of will always vary. But there appear to be important aspects that – once discerned – fundamentally change how people perceive a phenomenon in a powerful way. I'll return to these *critical* aspects in the next section where I exemplify variation theory in my teaching.

Fundamentally, the idea is similar to Spencer-Brown's distinctions (1979). Naming, describing – and ultimately therefore perception and awareness – come from the act of drawing distinctions. When we make a distinction, we draw a box around something and give it a name. Spencer-Brown (1979) simply referred to whatever was named as "marked" against a backdrop that was "unmarked". In a similar way, Marton and Booth (1997) refer to the term "aspect" as something that a person can become aware of (and therefore, perceive and experience).

When Marton and Booth use the term "aspect" they are referring to whatever we indicate in making a distinction – whatever is in that box we draw. Also, rather than discussing distinction-making, they use the verb, "to discern" and the noun, "discernment".

Marton et al. (2004) argue that how we go about ourselves in any given situation depends on our knowledge. But what knowledge we pull from depends on how we perceive the situation, according to the distinctions we've made. To show this, they give this example:

> "Someone is standing in a lake with the water up to his knees and aiming at a fish in the water with a harpoon. He might aim at the fish where it appears to be, that is, where he actually sees it, or at a slightly adjusted angle, that is, where he thinks it should actually be if he takes the refraction of the light into consideration. These two different ways of acting are based on two different ways of understanding the situation and the latter is more powerful than the former." (5).

This is my first key idea – shared by cybernetics and variation theory – that I want to share:

Key idea 1:
The distinctions we've made (and not made) determine what we perceive.

The second convergence is that of difference and variety. For Bateson, information was a difference that made a difference. And that can lead us to make a distinction. Marton and Booth (1997) use the term "variation" in a similar manner to Bateson's difference – a word that is safer from mistaking "difference" as an antonym of similarity. However, they also discuss variation in another manner that is important for teaching and learning.

Marton and Booth (1997) suggested that awareness depends on discerning – making distinct – an aspect in your mind. And you become aware of this aspect due to its "potential variation" (206). This potential variation means that to discern an aspect for what it is, someone must also be aware that it could be different. To illustrate this idea, the cybernetician Ross Ashby (1956) depicted the dilemma of a prisoner attempting to communicate with his wife. Before imprisonment, he and his wife had agreed on a code of communication through the delivery of different cakes. Each cake would have a different meaning about what had occurred to the prisoner's accomplices. Whether they had been caught, sentenced, or let free would be indicated by a distinct cake. There was then, a variety of possible meanings, from which the prisoner would discern a meaning when the cake arrived.

Nevertheless, the prison guards somehow become aware of the scheme. They then act to prevent the communication between the two and convince the prisoner that they will only allow his wife to bring one type of cake. When a cake finally arrives, the prisoner is confused rather than informed. Did she deliver the cake as a message, or not? Was it simply because she couldn't let any other cake in? Did she bring more than one cake – to give more than one message – but only one was allowed through? Did she know about the rule and just wanted to bring me a gift? With no variety of messages, the meaning was lost. Ashby gave another example (1956, 124):

> "Two soldiers are taken prisoner by two enemy countries A and B, one by each; and their two wives later each receive the brief message 'I am well'. It is known, however, that country A allows the prisoner a choice from 1. I am well, 2. I am slightly ill, or 3. I am seriously ill.
>
> While country B allows only the message of 1. I am well ... The two wives will certainly be aware that though each has received the same phrase, the information that they have received are by no means identical."

For Ashby information was variety – it's with a variety of possibilities that something can have meaning. This idea of *potential variation* gives us something precise to work with as teachers. Think about it this way: an aspect is something that can vary, is perceptible because it can vary, and its meaning comes from this variability. This is key idea two, which we'll explore in the next section.

Key idea 2:
We make distinctions due to an awareness of variation (variety, a difference, or change).

However, with Bateson's example above, we also saw that distinctions can be redrawn if we perceive similarity where we once had a distinction.

This leads us to the third similarity. Like cybernetics, variation theory assumes that distinctions and meanings aren't transmissible to other people (Lo 2012; Marton 2015). A distinction is a relationship that an individual has formed with its environment. This is key idea three:

Key idea 3:
Distinctions can't be transmitted to students, so students must be provoked into making their own distinctions.

Finally, there is one last convergence that I want to mention. After teachers provoke students to make meaning, teachers must probe to see what students have understood. We must converse with students, just as conversation theory suggests. This assumption is also found in variation theory (Lo 2012; Marton 2015). This is key idea four:

Key idea 4:
We must converse (written or spoken) with students to see what meaning they have discerned, and to work towards a compatible meaning.

With this, we're ready to consider variation theory applied directly to teaching and see detailed examples from my classroom. Before we go there, I'll leave you with a table (Table 1) of the approximate compatibilities that I perceive in vocabulary between cybernetics and variation theory. Bateson's notion of difference was sometimes quite general and loose; he spoke of differences and difference makers. But also differences between differences and resemblances between differences. For the teacher, variation theory's terminology is clearer.

Terminology found in cybernetics	Terminology found in variation theory
Spencer-Brown **Make a distinction**	Marton & Booth **Discern**
Spencer-Brown **Marked (by a distinction)**	Marton & Booth **Aspect (that which is discerned)**
Bateson **Difference**	Marton & Booth **Variation**
Bateson **Difference that makes a difference** "It takes two to know one" (Bateson's common phrase cited in Nachmanovitch 1982, 35–36).	Marton & Booth **Showing different "features" (of an aspect)** "The learner must simultaneously be aware of at least two features and the difference between them, in order to discern any of them" (Marton 2015, 48).
Bateson **Conceptions are aggregates of differences or distinctions** "The smallest unit of mental process is a difference or distinction or news of a difference. What is called an idea in popular speech seems to be a complex aggregate of such units." (1979, 228)	Marton & Booth **Conceptions are complexes of aspects** "The variation in how a certain phenomenon is experienced, between or within individuals, can thus be understood in terms of ... different complexes of [aspects]." (1997)

Table 1: Approximate compatibilities I see in the terminology between cybernetics and variation theory.

Variation theory provides an explicit model for designing classroom teaching

Key idea:
Students are unlikely to learn if shown many examples of the thing itself. Varying an aspect first is key.

One of the problems that variation theory points to is the abundant use of sameness, rather than difference, in teaching. In the classroom, it's common for a teacher to explain a novel concept by showing examples of it in varying contexts. Like showing the same patterns of exchange surfaces in the lungs, intestines, and placenta. What's the problem? The context varies, while the concept to be learnt doesn't. Think about it this way, “If an aspect of a phenomenon, as far as it has been experienced by the person, has never varied, why should the person be concerned about it?” (Pang et al. 2017, 65).

It reminds me of when I was honing the knives of my in-laws (with a honing rod), and I commented on the bad shape they were in. I had my wife sense it with the honing rod, but she couldn't perceive it. Instead, I had to seek out a variety of knives in the kitchen in better and worse shape so she could note the difference. Variation in an aspect allowed her to become aware of that aspect. She had to perceive how it could be different – its potential variation.

This example is like Ashby's story of the prisoner and his single cake, or Bateson's sound of one hand clapping. If a teacher only gives one example with no variety – even if the same example is presented in different contexts – what meaning does it have? If I'd had my wife hone different knives in different houses, but all with the same level of deformation, she'd have never perceived the aspect of blade deformation. If you can't perceive it in one example, then you aren't going to perceive it in several more showing the same thing. Only through perceiving variety within an aspect can that aspect be discerned.

But hold on, variation theory is a theory of learning, not a theory of the lesson. Therefore, it's perfectly possible to have a lesson focused on similarity and analogy. It's possible to spend much of a lesson drawing on analogies from everyday life – or previous topics – before presenting a difference.

Variation theory sees learning (not a lesson) as broadly composed of two steps: separation and fusion (Kullberg et al. 2024). Separation is the process of discerning, distinguishing, or making a distinction. Separating, because it becomes apparent among other things. Fusion, because you bring together distinctions in your mind – simultaneously – to think with. Let me define them, and then we'll look at examples.

Separation:

- Contrast – using examples of difference (variety) so that a critical aspect varies while everything else doesn't. The goal here is discernment, making a distinction. This would be like having students discern the aspect of genetic variation by showing examples of varying levels of genetic variation in a population. Or varying the degree of selection experienced by a population so they can discern the aspect of selection.
- Generalisation – examples of similarity in different contexts, so that a critical aspect stays invariant, and everything else varies. The goal here is transfer – seeing the aspect under different guises and separating it from other contexts. This would be like generalising the idea of selection to other examples. Such as somatic selection of lymphocytes in the immune system, or cells within a tumour. But this phase should always come after students have discerned those aspects. Difference should come before similarity.

Fusion:

- Simultaneity – examples in which several aspects vary. If an object of learning is to discern two critical aspects, a final step in the process is simultaneously perceiving them together as they vary. Just like when learning about natural selection students must discern the aspects of genetic variation and selection individually. But once done, you bring them together and think with them simultaneously to understand natural selection – bringing together aspects and seeing how they relate. I'll come back to this step in the next chapter. There I'll show you how I build stock and flow models and provoke students to see a system functioning as a whole after we've discerned its parts.

What we perceive – and therefore think about – results from the assembly of aspects that we bring to mind. Or, in other words, the complexes of aspects that are brought into our focal awareness (Marton & Booth 1997). But we must first discern those aspects for them to be available to our mind.

To visualise the process of separation, imagine an isolated settlement. The people living there have been told that they speak Russian. But they've never encountered – heard or heard of – any other language. What idea do they have of language? Oral language to them probably equates to the word Russian without distinction – such that the word Russian meant exactly the same thing as oral language. No matter how many times they hear Russian, they don't differentiate between language and Russian. One day, however, some nomads happen across the settlement. Immediately, they perceive that the nomads speak a different language. At this very moment, oral language becomes an aspect they are aware of and a distinction is made. "Russian is a type of oral language." The discernment of "language" as a concept, required language itself to vary. The people needed to experience a difference – to know that it could be different.

In variation theory, meaning-making occurs the moment someone discerns a new aspect – the moment a distinction is made and separated from other things. In this example, oral language and Russian were previously non-distinct ideas for the people. But they drew a distinction around oral language and another distinction around the idea of "Russian". The meanings of the word Russian, and the meaning of oral language were no longer the same – they became separated, made distinct. And, therefore, they were then able to perceive them separately. The moment this occurs, the part-whole relationship becomes apparent – Russian is a type of oral language, a more general idea.

Keep this in mind for later, as it's a core idea of variation theory. The meanings of the whole aspect (in this case oral language), and its parts (in this case Russian & the foreign language) are discerned simultaneously. Like Ashby's (1956) example of the prisoner and his cakes, they couldn't have made meaning of the whole aspect *before* becoming aware of variation within it. Discernment of parts occurs in tandem with discernment of their whole aspect.

What about generalisation and seeing similarity? After discerning an aspect, seeing more examples of it in new contexts – seeing similarity – allows people to generalise it. That is to see it in other examples or apply it to new situations. For example, the Russian speakers in the example above could later come to see similarities in speaking a language with other things, such as sign language, braille, or programming language. With every new example, the concept becomes less abstract and more concrete.

But this is the caveat: before being able to generalise students must first be aware of the aspect, otherwise they wouldn't know what they're looking for in the other examples. When teaching something new, difference must come before similarity.

It is often at this point that people I talk to get confused. They mistake variation theory for a pedagogical activity of showing students what something is and isn't. In teaching, this is called "examples and non-examples" (or positive and negative examples) and is discussed in the work of Engelmann and Carnine (1991). There are similarities between their work and variation theory, but we must discern the difference. So, here's my take.

What are the similarities? Engelmann and Carnine (1991) argue that it's impossible to learn from a single example. And they state that positive examples alone – just examples of similarity – won't cut it either. But the details need attention.

Engelmann and Carnine don't discuss sequencing as a key aspect of learning. Let's say we showed examples first, and then non-examples after. This means the sequence would begin with examples of similarity. Something variation theory warns against because variation – difference – is required for students to discern something new.

What if then, we reversed the sequence so that non-examples came first? Or interweaved examples with non-examples? But here's the other issue. Non-examples – as their name suggests – are antonyms. They supposedly show what something is not. Exactly what that means is then open to debate – it's ambiguous and offers little guidance for teachers on what constitutes a non-example. Engelmann and Carnine (1991) only refer to them as "minimally different" (35), and despite this minimality, they discuss them in terms of "this is X" and "this is not X".

What is a "non-example" exactly? Let's have a closer look. It was Ludwig Wittgenstein who suggested that a proposition and its negation are talking about the same thing (Wittgenstein 1922; Foerster 2014). When republicans call for "no king", as opposed to having "a king", they are still discussing the idea of a king – they're discussing the aspect of monarchy. There is more to consider than the two values of examples and non-examples, more than true or false; there are three values (Günther 1962). There is a whole aspect, like monarchy, and then two parts of the possible variety along a continuum. For example, from the all-powerful king to no king. Noting these two values – perceiving the difference between them – causes the aspect of monarchy to come forth. Just as Bateson often said, "It takes two to know one" (Nachmanovitch 1982, 35–36). In other words, perceiving a difference between two parts of the same aspect, causes that aspect to come forth in your awareness and to be made distinct.

Variation theory builds on this idea: it posits that to see an aspect, to perceive, distinguish, indicate, and experience it, you need two parts that denote the possible variety. Spencer-Brown's *law of calling* came with the injunction: *Make a distinction.* To provoke students to do just that, the *law of variation* comes with its own injunction: *Show variation in the aspect that you want students to perceive.*

If we want students to perceive genetic mutation, show varied examples of mutation. This isn't showing mutation and non-mutation – it's showing differences within the idea of mutation. If it's natural selection, show examples of varying degrees of selection, which could include an absence of selective pressure up to a strong pressure. Selection is a single continuum.

If it's coronary heart disease, show variations of plaque size, location, and their relative consequences. But you may be asking: What if you contrasted a heart attack (caused by coronary heart disease) with cardiac arrest (caused by an electrical malfunction) – wouldn't this be a non-example? No, it would be shifting the students' awareness to variation within the aspect of heart failure – a more general concept. (Something you may also want to show, depending on your goals). Rather than examples and non-examples, variation theory impels you to show the aspects you want to show, but vary them, have them change, show differences, make them discernible.

Here's an example of the same thing in my classes. When I recently taught about stem cells, I began by drawing a zygote (a single fertilised egg cell) and telling the students that they all started life that way. But that has little meaning to them – just details to know, a curiosity perhaps. I said they were now a system of maybe 20 trillion cells and we discussed development through cell division. I then drew a sperm cell with a little stick man inside the nucleus and told them about preformation theory. This had proposed that a preformed animal was brought inside a sperm cell to an egg cell and then just got bigger. I asked what difference that would make.

So, what had I done? Wasn't preformation theory a non-example? It wasn't. I contrasted an undetermined, plastic development (epigenesis) with a predetermined, non-plastic development (preformation). The contrast presented variety in the aspect of developmental plasticity. With the help of some discussion and prompts, students could discern this aspect – in the context of stem cells – that hadn't been apparent to them before. In other words, by varying only this aspect, they could separate it from the rest – making a distinction.

Before we move on to the examples, I want to point out a crucial distinction. There is an assumption of Engelmann and Carnine's "examples and non-examples" (1991) that is incompatible with both cybernetics and variation theory. The authors argue that "communication should be faultless", and when it's designed to be so, it's "faultless for any learner" (40). This is the idea that if you know the information inputs to students, you can entirely predict – with precision – their learning outputs. If you remember, this was von Foerster's definition of a trivial system (1971). In this view, if teaching doesn't work out as planned, it's seen as an *error* in the students' processing of the transmitted information.

A cybernetic (and enactive) view wouldn't recognise any errors, because students are nontrivial *autonomous* systems (Varela 1979). Their nervous activity – their perception and understanding – isn't controllable from without. The external world only nudges the ongoing buzz of activity in the nervous system (Varela 1987, 60). Put another way, the mind isn't defined by external inputs but by internal dynamics, such that external stimuli can only trigger the mind to respond in some way (Maturana 2011). This means that students can only think with what they themselves perceive. It isn't an error of cognition that drives the divergence in sense-making, but simply, a difference in perception.

Next, I offer two examples from my classroom. In Example Box 1, I'll show an example of a lesson that typically begins with differences and moves towards generalisation with examples of similarity. This is the order proposed by variation theory in which we learn new aspects. Marton (2015) admits that in practice, cycles of discernment and generalisation occur all the time. Where you begin in the cycle will depend on the students you have in front of you.

Often, lessons spend considerable time – at the beginning and throughout – building on similarity. Frequently, we may first work with ideas students already know via analogy (similarity) of some foundational knowledge to set the scene for the presentation of a difference to show something new. Therefore, a lesson doesn't often go in the order of difference to similarity – contrast to comparison, variation to analogy – when considering everything that goes on. But, if we consider a novel aspect in isolation, examples should be shown in the order of difference to similarity. This is the purpose of Example Box 2, which shows a lesson on natural selection with mixed use of difference and similarity.

Example Box 1

Showing difference before similarity when teaching bioaccumulation and biomagnification

The purpose of this example is not a detailed view of how I teach the lesson, but to focus on how I use difference and similarity. I won't elaborate on how I conduct discussions until Chapter 5. This is an example of a lesson I've taught to 14–16-year-olds (Figure 4).

The key to understanding biomagnification is the mass balance principle: What enters a system must either leave the system or accumulate within it. This is the critical aspect. Therefore, I began the lesson by drawing a small box. Below the box, I drew some dots and named them “phytoplankton”. You can see this in the diagram (Figure 4) on the left-hand side. I showed them some pictures of phytoplankton and explained that they are photosynthetic organisms. I then pulled on my students' prior knowledge by asking them what substances were likely to enter phytoplankton. This draws on their idea of autotrophy and photosynthesis. To make my comparison as clear as possible, I encouraged the students to whittle down to the basics. I settled on oxygen, carbon dioxide, water, and minerals, and added them to the diagram.

I then asked students what substances they expected would leave the phytoplankton. This draws on conceptual knowledge about respiration and excretion. I helped the students by writing out the equation of photosynthesis and respiration as shown in the diagram. The choice of phytoplankton for this lesson was deliberate so that I could have students think about inputs and outputs in simple terms of photosynthesis and respiration. Again, I asked students to reduce their examples to the basics, and I settled again on oxygen, carbon dioxide, water, and minerals. I added these to the diagram to highlight that they are, in fact, the same.

I wanted to explore this idea to make the mass balance principle explicit. I asked students what would happen to a cell if more substances enter than leave, as the photosynthesis rate is faster than the respiration rate. It would, of course, gain mass. I reversed the question, and students recognised that the phytoplankton would lose mass. And if the rates were equal on average, their mass would remain the same on average.

Next, I told them about methylmercury, a toxin, which tends to be taken up by phytoplankton but not excreted. Or at least the potential rate of excretion is slow compared to potential uptake rates. I asked, “What's the difference between mercury and the examples we've just added to the diagram?”

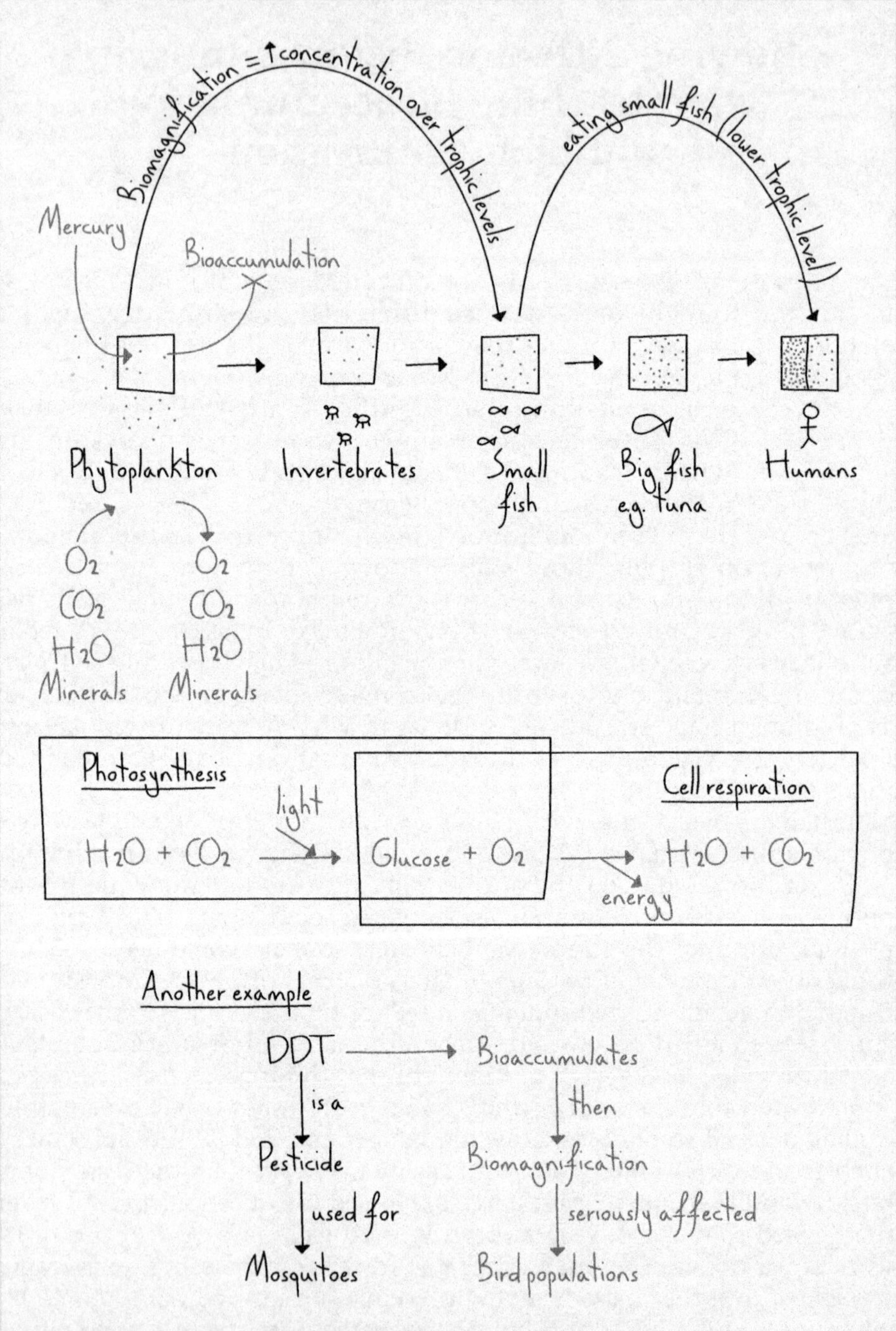

Figure 4: The complete diagram that I co-constructed with students to teach biomagnification, explained in the main text.

The students saw that what entered the system also left it, but mercury entered and accumulated. I added a few dots in the box to represent the mercury, and I told the students that this is called bioaccumulation. With this contrast, I varied a critical aspect. This provoked my students to bring the aspect into their focal awareness and discern the idea of bioaccumulation.

Next, I wanted to explore the ramifications of the concept – biomagnification. So, I drew another box with little animals below, which I labelled invertebrates. I drew an arrow from the phytoplankton box to the invertebrate box and told students that the invertebrates consume the phytoplankton. I asked the students what would happen to an invertebrate if it consumed large amounts of phytoplankton over its lifespan. What would happen to the mercury if it continued entering – but not leaving – the invertebrate? Students saw that the mercury would accumulate in the invertebrates in a higher concentration than in the phytoplankton. I added more dots in the box to represent this higher concentration. I then asked what would happen if the lifespan of the invertebrates was shorter or longer. The longer the lifespan, the more time there would be to accumulate mercury. This contrast helped students bring forth the time aspect of bioaccumulation and biomagnification. I then repeated the process for "small fish", "large fish", and then the human. At this point, I asked students what the difference would be if a human ate primarily smaller fish compared to larger fish. They saw that humans would accumulate more mercury if they ate larger fish more often. And here I explained to them the problems associated with frequently eating tuna – a large fish high in the food chain.

This was another contrast for discerning a critical aspect. By varying the trophic level of humans, while keeping the rest invariant, students could perceive the aspect of biomagnification across trophic levels. I emphasised that it's not necessarily the size of the fish, but its trophic level.

Up to this point, the lesson had focused mainly on differences to help students understand the concept. However, it was now a good time to generalise the concept via examples of similarity. According to variation theory, ideal generalisation would involve keeping the concept the same while allowing everything else to vary. Therefore, other examples of bioaccumulation and biomagnification will work well. The example I used was the use of DDT as a pesticide for mosquito and malaria control. DDT, like methylmercury, bioaccumulates in fat tissue and causes problems for populations high in the food chain.

Example Box 2

Showing difference & similarity when teaching natural selection

In my experience, natural selection is often taught as a sequence of steps to be remembered. After which (and sometimes before), several examples of natural selection are shown. Little time is given to exploring potential variation, so it's often just content with no discernment of critical aspects. The purpose of this example is not to show exactly how I teach something, but to show how I have employed difference (variation) and similarity with my classes. Either of these can come at any time in the lesson depending on what is needed and how dialogue with students develops. If I need an analogy to pull on my students' prior knowledge, I'll give examples of similarity. The examples of difference to provoke discernment do not necessarily have to come at the beginning of a lesson, just at the beginning of discernment. This is how I've explored similarity and difference when teaching natural selection to 14-year-olds over two fifty-minute lessons (Figure 5).

In natural selection, in my view, the critical aspects are 1. inheritable (genetic) variation, and 2. selection. So, rather than just telling students about them, together we had to explore what genetic variation and selection were. To do that, I had to show examples in which these aspects varied.

Assumptions of genetic variation

I began this class by pointing out something students already knew – we have varying traits between us. I also asked students about their siblings, "Are they the same as you, despite coming from the same parents?"

From here, I asked why siblings are different, and students typically knew that they had inherited only part of their mother's DNA and part of their father's. This was pulling on the knowledge they had learnt earlier in secondary school.

I was now ready to begin the diagram. I drew the (lower) arrow between "population with less variation" and "population with more variation". I then asked the students why the variation had increased. My students referred to what we'd just discussed, and I added sexual reproduction to the diagram. I also added mutation and its description. I told the students that the process was called inheritable variation, and I labelled the arrow of the diagram. When doing so, I asked, "Why have I written 'inheritable variation', why not simply 'variation'? What does that word mean?".

Here I wanted to make the distinction between somatic variation and genetic variation. Both of which are parts of the aspect of organismal variation. My students may have known the word inheritance but needed help in this context. Giving them an example, I referred to variation in muscle growth due to weight training. To get them thinking I followed it with a question, "If I had a child before weight training, and then another after becoming a bodybuilder, would the second child inherit larger muscles?"

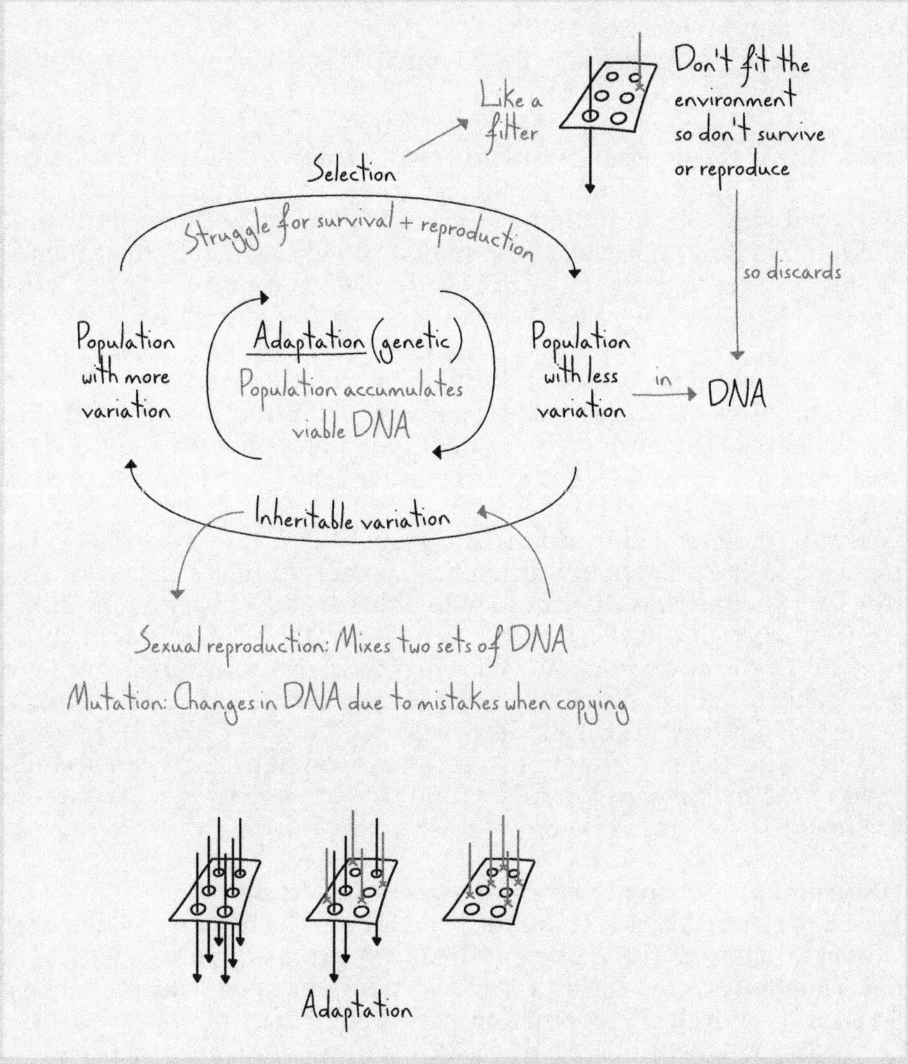

Figure 5: The complete diagram that I co-constructed with my students to teach natural selection. Explained in the main text.

After discussing this I provoked them again, "So, by weight training could it cause a precise change in your own DNA for building larger muscles? And could that weight training cause that precise DNA mutation in the DNA of sperm and egg cells?"

I continued the dialogue until I felt the students were happy with the distinction between non-heritable and heritable variation. It was time to move on because the ramifications of genetic variation are only seen in the light of selection. Varying this critical aspect would have to come later, after describing the full system.

Assumptions of selection

I drew the (upper) arrow from "population with more variation" to "population with less variation". I gave it the name of selection and told students it was something that acted like a filter. I then drew the filter on the diagram with only two arrows – one that doesn't get through the filter, and one that does. This is an example of difference – a key distinction in natural selection is precisely *differential* survival and reproduction. I provoked the students to consider the consequence of this difference, "What happens to the DNA of those that don't get through the filter – who don't survive to reproduce? And what happens to those that do get through the filter by surviving and reproducing?"

I then asked what caused this difference, in other words what caused selection. After some discussion, I gave my definition, which I added to the diagram. The cause is the struggle for survival and reproduction. So, then, I asked, "What's the difference between those that get through the filter and those that don't?"

Some students had heard of "survival of the fittest" but others also mentioned the adjective "stronger". I suggested that a better way of thinking about it was that those who didn't fit the environment didn't get through the filter. Their DNA was discarded but not that of those that did fit the environment. Those that fit their environment well are better able to gain resources, survive, grow, and reproduce. Fitness then, is the level of fit with the environment.

With this, the description of a set of assumptions had been set, and it was time to explore its ramifications. It was time to vary its parts to see how the system worked.

Discernment: varying the critical aspect of selection

I drew the three filters seen on the left. One in which no arrow managed to get through the filter, one in which some did, and one in which all did. These filters vary the aspect of selection – or, you could say, varying levels of how well the population fits its environment.

"So, what's the difference?" I asked. "All die, some die, none die" a student replied. Many had similar answers, which represented what they saw on the surface. To get them thinking I had to remind them that nothing in systems, or biology, makes sense except over time.

"That's a difference, but what difference does it make?" The students saw quickly that one was an example of extinction. How about the other two? They saw them as distinct from extinction but found any further distinction more elusive.

"Remember, systems happen over time. What would it mean – not for individuals – but for a species over generations? Put your finger on the diagram and follow it around for each situation – and think about the accumulation of variation." I gave them time to discuss the idea in pairs. A student answered that, in one example, the genetic variation would remain at a similar level, while in the other it would rise. This was because they'd followed the diagram around over time. I asked the class if they agreed or not. To answer, I followed the system around – using my finger – while narrating my view. "Think about it this way: as we go round the systems, one system adds and removes genetic variation, while the other just adds."

Then I asked, "Which example would lead to a species fitting their environment more and which less?" I listened to some answers and asked for justifications (how I do this is discussed in Chapter 5).

I then gave an example in which the aspect of selection had varied. The example – in which selection isn't observed – was the use of caesarean sections instead of natural births. Previously a mother and their child were likely to die if their child's head did not match the pelvis size of their mother. This selective pressure kept the foetal head size within certain limits. Any child with a head too big was likely to die and their alleles were lost from the population. In contrast, now that caesarean sections are becoming more common, these alleles remain in the population. Due to advances in technology – which is now our environment – all these mothers and babies fit their environment without distinction for this trait.

Therefore, selection is no longer discarding the associated alleles from the population, genetic variation in those associated alleles will increase. There is diversity, but no death, and therefore no adaptive direction for this trait. I explained that, in many thousands of years, humans may not be able to give natural birth. This example varied selection by contrasting the cases of it acting strongly and weakly, on a population (i.e. before and after the introduction of caesarean sections).

Discernment: varying the critical aspect of genetic variation

It was time to focus on the important interplay between variation and selection. Only with selection (without extinction) will a population continue to adapt. To have my students see this, I kept selection invariant while varying the aspect of genetic variation.

I asked my students, "What if we had selection, but no genetic variation?" After giving them a moment to ponder this, I gave the example of banana plantations which are genetic clones and provoked students with some questions:

"What if a fungus arrived and infected a banana tree on a plantation? What'd be the likely fate of the plantation?" I let students discuss in pairs, and afterwards, they generally agreed that there were only two choices. Either they all survive, or they all die.

"With this fungus, what would be the difference between a plantation of cloned bananas, and one next to it that had a lot of genetic variation between its bananas?" With this, I had varied the aspect of genetic variation but kept the aspect of selection – the fungal pathogen – invariant. The students saw that with genetic variation, some may survive while others will not. Through death, the population would lose the less resistant alleles and retain the more resistant ones. And so, only with both – genetic variation and selection – can adaptation emerge. Without differences, there is no distinguishing.

Generalisation: an analogy with card games

Having varied the critical aspects – variation and selection – I now returned to using similarity by drawing an analogy with card games and poker. My students were familiar with card games of many types. I asked them about the card games they'd played and if there were any similarities with natural selection.

I provoked them with some scenarios, "What if you were all dealt the exact same cards, would the game work? What if you all won, or you all lost, would the game work?" Here's the analogy: for a card game to work, you must all be dealt different cards, there must be variation.

"Can you change your cards if you don't like them?" I asked. Some students mentioned the games in which this was possible but agreed that it wasn't the norm.

"What does winning or losing depend on?" I asked. They agreed that a large part of it was the luck of the deal – and then you had to play your cards the best you could considering the other players and their cards. I asked them if this was similar to a population, "Do the individuals choose their alleles, or are they able to swap them?" No, we don't, and we can't. Instead, we're all dealt the alleles we have, and we just have to play them the best we can during our lives.

Finally, I went back to the analogy of winners and losers. I asked what was needed to ensure that some players won and some lost. The variation in cards and how well they're played. And so I pointed out that for some to win, others had to lose. For a card game to work, there must be losers. And the same is true of populations. For them to adapt, there must be variation and selection – there must be some individuals with sets of alleles that don't fit the environment as well as others. And when those individuals die without reproducing, they take those alleles with them.

You may be wondering why I didn't begin the lesson with the analogy of card games. Because card games are not exactly the same as natural selection. If you begin with enticing students into thinking one concept is the same as one, they already know, they may not go on to perceive anything new – the crucial aspects that make them distinct. Therefore, I didn't evoke the analogy until I had explored the new aspects via variation. I also made sure that we explored the differences with card games before the lesson was over. Card games, for example, return losing cards to the deck, whereas in natural selection alleles selected for elimination do not return.

Here we've seen both phases of separation – contrasting and generalising. But what about fusion? Fusion represents seeing the critical aspects together, which, in this case, is natural selection. As you'll see in Chapter 4, "variation and selection" is a principle that I embed into my course and discuss often. Therefore, students get ample practice with thinking with these two aspects simultaneously. We'll return to fusion in the next chapter. Finally, I also have a stock and flow model for teaching natural selection, which is found in the appendix.

CHAPTER 2

A heuristic for teaching systems – vary one aspect and ask what difference it makes over time

Key idea:
Vary a key structure or process – one at a time – by asking “What if?”

The key to planning with variation theory is the distinction that Marton (2015) draws between the things that are taught in a lesson. Firstly, there is the content – the details and facts – and secondly, there is what students are expected to do with them, such as explain or describe. Yet, Marton argues, these tell us little about what students are expected to learn. Because, when he uses the word learn, he means discern. It's the moment you discern the part-whole relationship of the aspects. We've seen (in Example Box 2), that to discern the aspect of genetic variation (the whole), I had to show varying examples – from clones to diverse populations – of genetic variation (the parts). Once discerned, the critical aspects of genetic variation and selection could be thought about simultaneously to understand natural selection. In a lesson plan, the “object of learning” is what you want students to become aware of, and consists of the critical aspects you'll focus on.

There are two key steps to take during teaching. The first is to contextualise the aspects because the object of learning is always situated in a bigger context (Marton et al. 2004). This step comes naturally to teachers. We don't tend to begin lessons by attacking the key ideas without first discussing what we're generally talking about. In biology, it's often a case of contextualising within the whole organism, or a whole ecosystem (Moore-Anderson 2023). It may involve showing images, diagrams, real specimens, or physical equipment. The next step is to vary the critical aspects, and this is what I'll focus on in this section.

Some lessons naturally fall into using variation theory, as I'm sure many of you are thinking. For example, when teaching wind-pollinated and insect-pollinated flowers you inevitably vary the parts by contrasting the two. However, with other concepts, you have to decide what to vary. To get you started, I've got a pragmatic idea that works out well in biology – a subject of systems.

Most of our lessons in biology are focused on describing and explaining systems. Meadows defines a system as “a set of things – people, cells, molecules, or whatever – interconnected in such a way that they produce their own pattern of behaviour over time” (2008, 2). There is a key distinction here: the parts, and the behaviour of the whole system.

Describing the system and its usual dynamics involves discussing the parts, and what they do. You can consider this the content – the details that students need to know. Beyond this are the how and why of the content – the explanation. How the system carries out its behaviour as a whole, and why it does so – the *understanding* of the content. For this, we need students to see how the system could be different. We want them to grasp the "potential variation" that could be observed in the system, because, as Kurt Lewin said, "You cannot understand a system until you try to change it" (quoted by Schein 1996).

Therefore, here's a heuristic to follow and trial when teaching biological systems:

Identify and vary key aspects of the system.

Think about the content you'll teach and what is important to understand.

- If it's a structure (e.g. leaf structure, or intestinal structure) then physically vary the key structures. For example, for leaf structure, you'd vary things like the orientation of palisade cells, or the number of stomata. I discuss this in Example Box 3.
- If it's a process (e.g. bioaccumulation, natural selection), then vary rates or accumulations. For example, for bioaccumulation (Example Box 1) I varied the rate of accumulation. I contrasted a zero accumulation rate with a non-zero accumulation rate. For natural selection (Example Box 2), I varied the rate of selection and the accumulation of genetic variation in a population. I'll elaborate more on varying rates and accumulations in the next chapter.
- If it's a structure and a process (e.g. the nephron and its mechanism), then you vary both physical structures, and rates and accumulations – depending on what you want to show. For example, you could vary the physical length of the loop of Henle or make the physical fenestrations of the glomerulus larger. You could vary the rate of active transport of glucose in the proximal tubule, or the accumulation of solutes in the medulla.

How to vary a key aspect

Vary a key aspect of the system – by asking "What if?" – and keep the rest invariant (at time zero). Then have students mentally simulate how the process or mechanism will unfold differently over time. Do this for any key aspect – avoid varying an aspect such that it utterly breaks the system and leaves little to think about. The extent to which you have students mentally simulate is something I'll discuss in Chapter 5 on adaptively regulating complexity production.

With this, we expect students to follow the ramifications for the system's parts and as a whole over time. This type of variation is something that Tan and colleagues (2013; 2020) have called "sequential variation", which traces the "cascading effects" of variations. Because, after time zero, the other parts of the system will also vary.

If the system is the alveolus, I want to show how the diffusion distance, surface area, and concentration gradient could vary. The first two are about structure, and the third is an accumulation. For the structure, I could add variation by asking "What if the capillaries in the alveolus were located slightly further away?". I could vary the physical surface area by asking "What if the alveoli lost their folds to become one large sack (as in emphysema)?". To show how the accumulation of a concentration gradient can vary, I can ask "What if the blood flow rate were much slower?".

For community biodiversity, the key is to see how species biodiversity can vary. Biodiversity is not a structure, but an accumulation within a process. Therefore, I'll give examples to students in which I vary that accumulation; by keeping one species invariant while varying the number of other species.

Here's the key idea again:
Vary a key structure or process – one at a time – by asking "What if?"

To see this idea in more depth, in Example Box 3 and 4 I give examples from my classroom of planning for discernment according to the heuristic given above.

Example Box 3

Planning for discernment during a lesson on leaf structure

In this lesson, with my 14-year-old biology students, I wanted them to make sense of the structure of a typical dicot leaf. This example discusses how I planned and used examples of variation but not other factors of the lesson. The lesson diagram can be found in Figure 6. I also teach this lesson using a stock and flow diagram which can be found in the appendix.

Using the heuristic I gave above for planning for discernment, this is how I did it. First, I thought about the overall behaviour of the system and its holistic significance. In this case, a leaf carries out gas exchange (including water) and absorbs light for photosynthesis. Therefore, I need to present variation in these aspects. Next, I thought about the parts of the system that I could vary to show how the behaviour of the system could be different.

There are two principal structures involved in gas exchange. The spongy mesophyll allows diffusion inside the leaf and stomata allow diffusion in and out of the leaf. Therefore, I thought of these questions to provoke students:

- What if the leaf were upside down?
- What if the leaf had no spongy mesophyll layer?

For the absorption of light, the component of main importance is the palisade layer. Therefore, I thought of these questions to provoke students:

- What if the palisade cells were oriented horizontally instead of vertically?
- What if the palisade cells had fewer chloroplasts than normal?

Let's see how the lesson unfolded in time. Firstly, I drew a simple cross-section of a dicot leaf. This can be seen as the rectangle at the top of the page. Here, I give students a descriptive overview of the system, including the key processes of gas exchange, water evaporation, and light absorption. I then drew the same diagram to the right and asked, "What would happen if – for some reason – the leaf started to grow upside down?"

This variation allows students to see why the palisade layer is at the top of a leaf, and why stomata are clustered at the bottom. Water evaporation would increase in this situation due to more sunlight

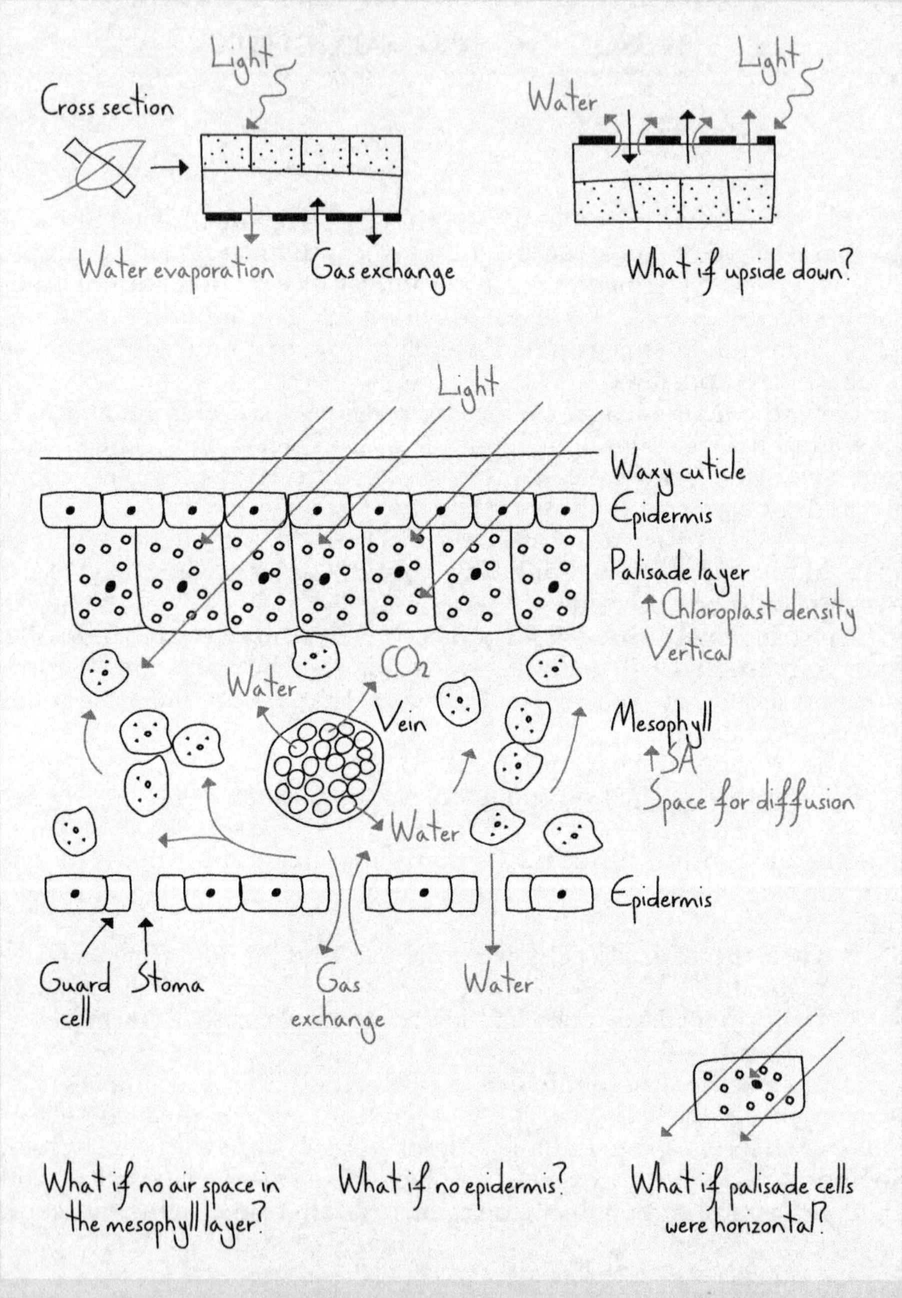

Figure 6: The complete diagram of a dicot leaf that I co-constructed with my students, explained in the main text.

exposure increasing the temperature of the upper surface. Light absorption by chloroplasts would decrease.

Next, I began drawing the detailed leaf diagram, starting with the upper layers. The waxy cuticle, the epidermis, which prevents water loss, could be understood thanks to the previous example.

"What if there was no waxy cuticle?" I had collected some leaves from the school grounds and had them feel the waxy layer. In general, they found this bit easy.

Next, I added the palisade layer and drew another palisade cell, in a horizontal orientation next to the diagram. I asked the students, "What would happen if the cells developed to be like this instead of vertically?"

After asking the question – which focused their attention on this difference – I added the rays of light to show how fewer photons are absorbed in the horizontal palisade cell as there are fewer layers of chloroplasts.

The quantity of chloroplasts in palisade cells is a key adaptation. I varied this also, "What would happen if these palisade cells had fewer chloroplasts?"

This was easy enough for the students to think about, so I reversed the idea, "So, why don't they pack in even more chloroplasts?"

This question pulled on their evolutionary thinking and the trade-offs of energy investment. "It wouldn't be worth it." a student replied. Through discussion, my students agreed that there would eventually be too much energy cost of maintaining chloroplasts considering the quantity of light absorbed.

I moved on to draw the spongy mesophyll layer – making explicit the large air spaces, and the lower concentration of chloroplasts. But this is just a description. I pointed out the difference and asked, "Why are there fewer chloroplasts in the mesophyll cells compared with the palisade cells?"

I like this question. Notice how it pulls on the idea of a trade-off I put to the students earlier. In this case, my students found it intuitively – maybe because they'd had the chance to think before. There isn't much light left to absorb underneath the palisade layer.

I then added the lower epidermis to the diagram and discussed the presence of guard cells and stomata. I told them that the air space allows quick diffusion of gases to and from all cells, including the palisade layer. To vary this aspect, I asked them, "What would happen if the mesophyll were full of cells with no air space?"

But this is just an extreme, so after bringing their attention to this aspect, I asked them something more nuanced, "Which plants do you think would grow quicker, those with more cells in the mesophyll, or those with less?"

This gave us ample discussion, as I also prompted students to think about examples, such as slow-growing cacti, and fast-growing weeds.

To find meaning in the lower epidermis, I provoked students by asking them, "What would happen if a leaf didn't grow a mesophyll layer and just developed a lower epidermis joining to the palisade?"

After varying all the key structures and discussing the differences they would make, it was time to generalise. To do this, I showed them cross sections of leaves from other plants, with other structures (for example pine leaves). And had the students identify the parts. Finally, to vary the system, and have students reason with what they have learnt, I asked students to answer a written "What if?" question, according to the taxonomy of understanding (discussed in Chapter 4). This was the question: What would happen if a plant in a population developed leaves that were twice as thick as normal?

When I teach this lesson, I also develop a stock and flow model, which you can find in the appendix. Stock and flow models are explained in the next chapter.

Example Box 4

Planning for discernment during a lesson on fermentation biotechnology

When teaching students about fermentation in biotechnology there are several steps in the process for which I need to generate variation. This is because it's quite an isolated topic for many students. This example discusses how I planned and used examples of variation but does not discuss other factors of the lesson such as how I carried out discussions. The lesson diagram can be found in Figure 7.

Using the heuristic I gave above for planning for discernment, this is how I did it for a class of 14-year-olds. First, I thought about the overall behaviour of the system and its holistic significance. In this case, the key is the population of living cells consuming nutrients and producing waste products. Therefore, I needed to present variation in these aspects. Next, I thought about the parts of the system that I could vary to show how the behaviour of the system could be different.

For the population of living cells, I planned these examples:

- Contrasting bacteria in a beaker of nutrients to viruses in an identical beaker of nutrients.
- Contrasting population size over time in a closed system (a beaker) and in a fermenter with continuous input of nutrients and output of products.

For the nutrients and waste products, I planned these examples:

- Contrasting nutrients and products in a closed system (a beaker) and in a fermenter with continuous input of nutrients and output of products.

For the open system:

- Contrasting functional parts with those that stop functioning as they should.

Let's see how the lesson unfolded over time. Firstly, I drew the two beakers in the top-left and told students that they were identical in nutrient contents and sterile, except that in one I added a single species of bacteria, and in the other, I added a single species of viruses. I then asked the students to draw a graph of population size over time. Students generally saw that the virus population wouldn't increase, but there was some variation in answers with regard to the bacterial population. Some saw that it would decline eventually, others thought it'd plateau only. After a discussion of their ideas, I gave them my graph. And I asked them to draw another graph below showing the nutrients and waste products in the same system over time. I drew my versions of the graph, and we discussed the differences between mine and theirs.

Next, I moved on to discuss with my students some fermentation technologies that work in this manner. Such as yoghurt from milk, soy sauce from soybeans, and wine from grape juice. In these cases, the whole system is desirable as a product. This is giving students examples of similarity after difference.

Following this I moved on to (continuous) bioreactors, or fermenters. I showed some images of them before I drew a diagram of the system. I annotated and discussed the functions – building a description of the system. Now the key difference is between the closed systems – that we'd just discussed – and open systems. Therefore, I asked them to draw the same graphs as before but now for this type of open-system fermentation.

We compared my student's answers with mine in a discussion. This discussion led me to vary the parts of the open system, "So, what would happen if the stirring and mixing of the system stopped? What would happen if the outflow became blocked? What if the filter on the inflow was faulty and allowed other microorganisms in?"

Concluding the discussion of these variations, I gave examples of similarity, such as the use of bioreactors in the production of insulin, or antibiotics.

Finally, I asked students a question to think through more thoroughly and give a written answer according to the taxonomy of understanding (discussed in Chapter 4). Here's a question I asked, "What if a fermenter was contaminated by a different species that used the same nutrients but produced different waste products?"

Figure 7: The complete diagram that I co-constructed with my students to teach them about fermentation.

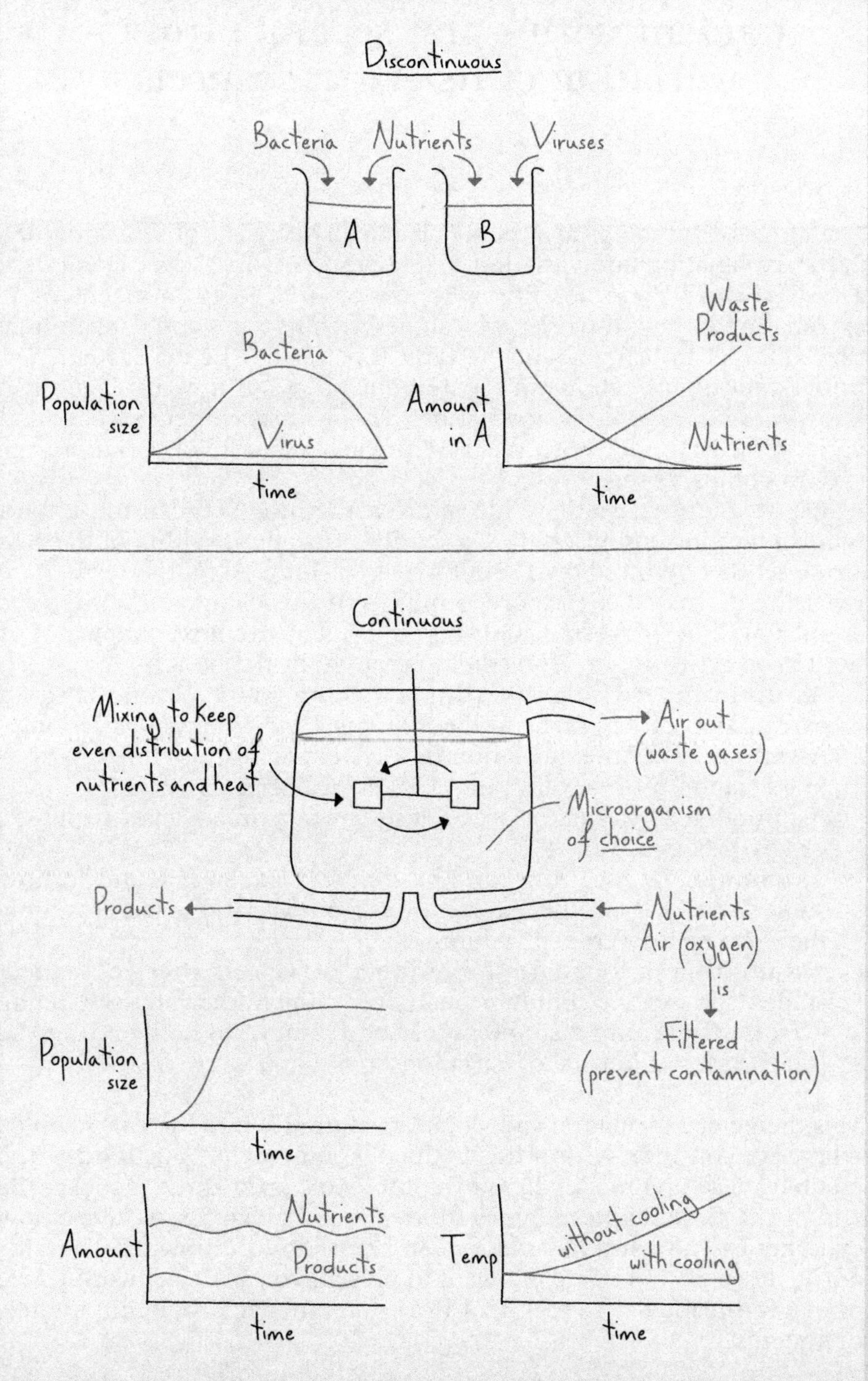
Discontinuous
Bacteria
Nutrients
Viruses
A
B
Bacteria
Population size
Virus
time
Waste Products
Amount in A
Nutrients
time
Continuous
Mixing to keep even distribution of nutrients and heat
Air out (waste gases)
Microorganism of choice
Products
Nutrients
Air (oxygen)
is
Filtered (prevent contamination)
Population size
time
Nutrients
Amount
Products
time
without cooling
Temp
with cooling
time

CHAPTER 2

An explanation of a system arises in tandem with – not separate from – variation of its critical aspects

Teaching about biological systems principally consists of two entwined parts: explanation and variation. Explanation involves portraying how a system works, and possibly why it is as it is. To get a mechanistic explanation of how it works, we can describe its parts and explain how they interact to bring about the typical behaviour of the system. Yet, understanding a system isn't just about knowing how it is, but also knowing how it could be (or not be). This is discernment of potential variation (Marton & Booth 1997). With each example of variation, the system comes forth.

Let me summarise these ideas into something you can think with whilst planning and teaching – a set of assumptions. Think of these as a rule set that defines how I think when teaching. Assumptions 1–3 are what I've discussed with more emphasis in this chapter. Assumptions 4 and 5 will be addressed with more focus in the next chapters. But we'll keep returning to all of them throughout the book.

- **Assumption 1:** Understanding a system involves knowing an explanation of its parts and whole, plus their potential variation.
- **Assumption 2:** An explanation of a system arises in tandem with – not separate from – variation of its critical aspects.
- **Assumption 3:** Vary one aspect of a system at a time – a key structure, or key process.
- **Assumption 4:** Meaning can't be transmitted, so respond to how students infer their own explanations from variation – not just how they restate a given explanation.
- **Assumption 5:** Regulate the number of aspects that you expect students to explore simultaneously according to their understanding – from discerning a single aspect of a system to deliberating the interconnected effects of variation on a whole system.

This theme of explanation and variation continues into the next chapter, where we continue within the "reducing complexity" quadrant of the recursive teaching model. If you want to, look again at the model at the end of the first chapter (Figure 2). In the next chapter, we'll see how cybernetics and variation theory can be used with drawing diagrams during lessons. In particular, I want to present you with a powerful style of diagram called the stock and flow diagram for producing models of systems.

3.
TO INDICATE THEIR DISTINCTIONS, TEACHERS CAN DRAW DIAGRAMS WITH STUDENTS

When sharing our understandings, the distinctions we've made, and what things mean to us, nothing is better than pointing directly to something and saying, "This is what I mean". This chapter is all about using diagrams to share meanings, and I want to show you a special diagram that has utterly transformed my classroom – the stock and flow diagram.

Advantages of drawing diagrams live: clarity of connections, stepwise sense-making, less transient information

Diagrams allow clearer expression of differences that make a difference
Diagrams act like maps of a concept. Just as a map is not the territory, a diagram is not the concept. As Bateson expressed, what gets on the map is not similarity, but difference (1972). As such, diagrams help us explicitly show students the distinctions and relations that make a concept what it is to us.

Diagrams allow the expression of relationships in two dimensions
The problem we face as teachers was explained by systems thinker Donella Meadows (2008, 5):

> "Words and sentences must, by necessity, come only one at a time in linear, logical order. Systems happen all at once. They are connected not

> just in one direction, but in many directions simultaneously. To discuss them properly, it is necessary somehow to use a language that shares some of the same properties as the phenomena under discussion."

One of the advantages of the diagram is the ability to show an interlinked concept. In a moment, I'll show you a diagram that speaks the language of systems.

Diagram construction can occur in conjunction with conversation to reach shared meanings
Importantly, diagrams can be drawn section by section, with negotiation of meaning as each new section is elaborated. When students are suddenly shown complete diagrams, they often struggle to discern what's important. There may be too much information at once, too many differences to interpret, and students can be cognitively overloaded (Sweller 2011).

Instead, it's better to build diagrams section by section while discussing the meaning of each new addition. There is some evidence that supports this idea. Fiorella and Mayer (2016) found that students learnt more from a teacher who drew their explanations, rather than simply explaining ready-made diagrams. Interestingly, however, this was only the case when the students could see the teacher's body or hand, indicating the social dimension of co-constructing diagrams.

Building a diagram during a lesson can avoid transient information
Problems arise in lessons due to transient information, which occurs when information appears and then disappears (Wong et al. 2012). This is common with the presentation of slide decks. A crucial image is shown but vanishes when the teacher moves to the next slide. This puts pressure on the student to retain all the aspects in mind while connecting them to the information on the next slide.

Nevertheless, humans can exploit what Merlin Donald (1991) calls the external memory field. Donald argues that humans use symbolic material – diagrams in my classes – as a "temporary holding tank" of information (329). Therefore, building diagrams with students helps them consider relatively more aspects. And, as students differ in their cognitive capacity, we make our lessons more accessible to all. To avoid transient information, we can plan to keep diagrams and annotations visible throughout a lesson. In my case, a whole lesson (or concept) doesn't exceed the single page of A4 paper that I project for my students.

Practical advice on drawing diagrams during lessons

Key idea:
There are no serious logistical obstacles to drawing diagrams during lessons, and you'll get better at drawing quickly.

The slide deck is, for many, a security net. It provides diagrams, content, and ideas, because the teacher is worried about forgetting mid-lesson what to say, do, or what to cover. It lowers the teacher's cognitive load.

Teachers confess that they couldn't just teach without a collection of resources to help them. Yet, I too have my lesson resources, plans, and question banks. I plan the diagrams I want to draw and at the side, I make notes of the images or videos, I want to show and questions I may ask. They all go on one page of A4 paper, and I take a photo. During a lesson, I put this photo on my computer screen for me to see while I draw for students. At the end of the lesson, I may make extra notes for the future and take a new photo. All my other media – images and videos – is stored in one large folder on my computer with searchable names. When they are needed during a lesson, I use the search function on my computer or an internet search.

If you want to get drawing, here's some quick advice. Draw your lesson on one page, ensuring the whole diagram and annotations remain visible during that lesson. Take a photo, and then see what emerges during the lesson when you redraw it. Your illustration and composition abilities will improve quickly. If you don't have much time, plan a rough version and allow a better version to emerge during a lesson.

I prefer to draw on paper and use a document camera (visualiser) to project my diagram. I can face the students during the lesson while in conversation. I'm also much better at writing and drawing on paper than on a board. A tablet computer also works well. I have my paper in landscape orientation, so it matches the format of the projection or screen.

A rushed diagram often has writing that is harder to read, and figures that are less clear than they should be. Students have less time to follow the construction as it happens, and it's less satisfying to look at and learn from. My advice is to relax while drawing and enjoy producing something rewardingly clear.

A common question is whether students should copy the diagram with the teacher as they go along, or just watch. It seems that there is an unsolvable trade-off between the two options. The reality is that daydreaming is a natural human tendency, and interest varies. Asking students to draw with me, section by section helps keep their focus.

Many students comment that drawing helps them understand the diagram. As does tracing ideas in the diagram with their finger. This may be the sensorimotor connection with cognition (Varela et al. 2016). You can avoid slowing the lesson too much by keeping diagrams simple. Example Box 5 shows a good example of this.

Example Box 5

Diagrams and dialogue when teaching autopoiesis

The first biology lesson I teach to my 11-year-old students is an introduction to autopoiesis. Autopoiesis means self-creating. The concept originates from the work of Humberto Maturana and Francisco Varela (1980), two cyberneticians I've cited many times in this book. The cell was their paradigmatic case, and they showed how it acted as a network of processes that creates itself (an example of recursion). It contrasts with allopoiesis, in which one system creates another, for example, humans creating their machines.

Autopoiesis is about autonomy and the ability of organisms to maintain their own identity, despite the second law of thermodynamics acting against it. For example:

> "Every five days you get a new stomach lining. You get a new liver every two months. Your skin replaces itself every six weeks. Every year, ninety-eight per cent of the atoms in your body are replaced. This nonstop chemical replacement, metabolism, is a sure sign of life" (Margulis & Sagan 1995, 23).

"Life ... is reproducing autopoiesis. The autopoietic view of life is circular." (Margulis & Sagan 1997, 264). Reproducing autopoiesis means that life is a continual process of reproducing its ability to self-produce. This gives organisms innate purpose and a notion of what is good and bad for them – good is typically whatever keeps autopoiesis going (Thompson 2010).

There are two important points to consider. The first is self-production: an organism is organised to keep producing its own structure. The second is self-distinction: it brings itself forth and separates itself from its environment. Although, Razeto-Barry (2012) suggests that the workable definition is something like this:

- An autopoietic system is a network of processes, which produces some of its own components (some can be obtained directly from the environment).
- This network of processes also generates the conditions – a body – that maintain the network together as a discrete individual unit.

The object of learning for my lesson was autopoiesis, but this came with several critical aspects. I anticipated that the first had already been discerned by students aged eleven. My students had already discerned an aspect of the second law of thermodynamics, in the context of the decrease in the quality of energy over time. The example here, however, is a different aspect of this law. The others, I anticipated, would be new to them:

- Organisms are distinct from their environment
- Organisms on Earth are made from the same types of molecules.
- Organisms build and maintain themselves.
- Organisms obtain molecules and energy from their environment to build and maintain themselves.
- Things in the universe tend towards disorder – to disintegrate, degrade, or dissipate (the second law of thermodynamics).

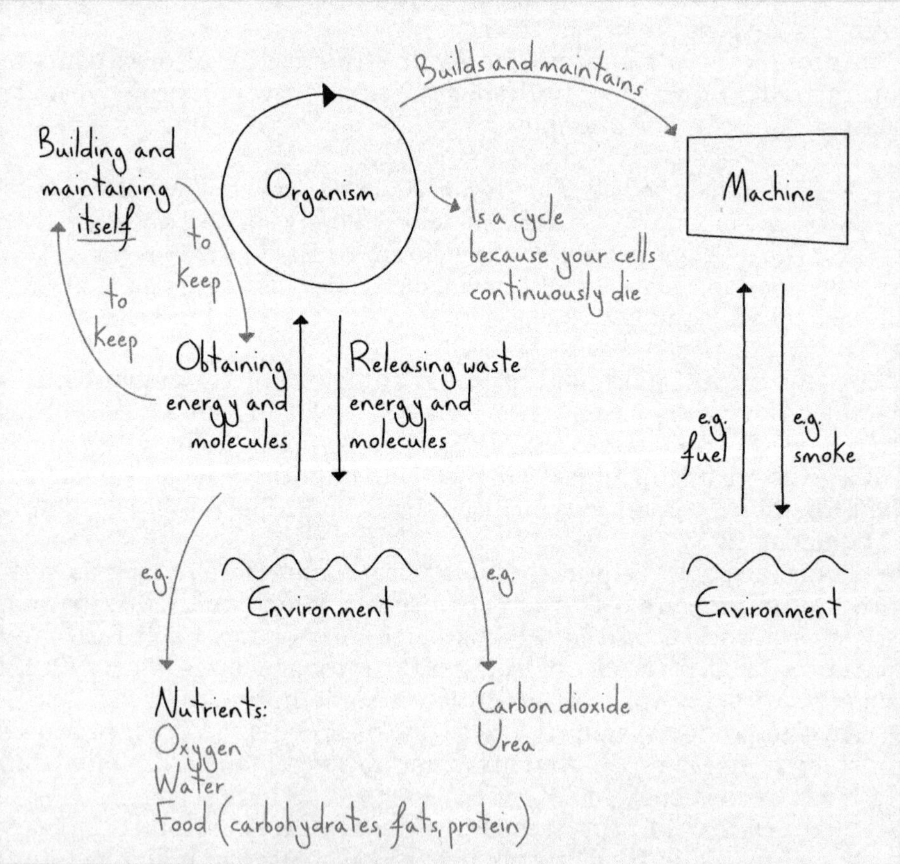

Figure 8: The complete diagram that I co-constructed with my students to teach them about autopoiesis.

These aspects would need contextualisation by drawing on all the prior knowledge that my young students already had of being an organism. Here's how I taught this recently.

I went into the lesson with the diagram in mind, which highlighted a number of distinctions. All of the components of the diagram (Figure 8) were familiar to the students at this age. But my goal was to provoke a mental redrawing of distinctions. I began by drawing the cycle of the organism and the squiggle of the environment. And I provoked the students by asking, "What do we mean when we say that organisms are different to their environment – where's the boundary?"

This distinction is key to understanding autopoiesis. But for my students, it was easy – as I had anticipated – because they have many years of experience living as an organism. We agreed that there is an edge to an organism, and what is beyond that can simply be called the environment. Organisms make themselves (ourselves) distinct from their environment.

Next, I drew the arrows of exchange with the environment. Here I was adding nuance to the previous distinction. We are distinct from the environment but we need to exchange with it in order to live. I provoked them again, "What do we get from the environment? And what do we give to it?"

We discussed food, water, oxygen, urine, etc. As anticipated, my students could identify the matter that was exchanged, and I added them to the diagram as examples.

But from here, I wanted to take my students into new territory and for them to see new things. I asked them, "What do we do with the nutrients we obtain?"

My students' knowledge was at its limit, and they tended to have little idea. Some just said "for energy", while others recognised that they didn't know. I told them that we build ourselves from them. But telling them is of little use alone – I had to provoke the students to act: "How much do you weigh? 30 kg, 40 kg? And when you were born, maybe 3 kg, or 4 kg? Where did all that mass come from?"

This question brought to their focal awareness the critical aspect of mass accumulation. The fact that they are somehow becoming more of something. The next step was for them to see this accumulation as directly tied to the input of molecules from the environment. I didn't solicit any answers to this question. Because, in my experience, students don't tend to know, and they tend not to have thought about it either. It's an aspect yet to be discerned. Therefore, I let them think for a moment before asking something else.

"What are you made from, then?" Some students replied that they were made from cells. "Good, but what are they made from?" I responded. As a class, we came to the answers of the typical organic molecules, and I added them to the diagram. Some students hadn't heard of carbohydrates before, so I gave examples of foods rich in these molecules. I then followed the line of reasoning, "So, if you're mainly made of proteins, fats, carbs, and water, where did that come from?"

It was time to establish that students are made from the molecules they eat. But I didn't move too quickly. There were lots of examples I wanted to discuss so that students could make this distinction. I started with a bit of fun. I was teaching Spanish children primarily, and in Spain it is traditional and common to eat cured ham. So, I asked, "If you built yourself from the molecules you eat, are you made mainly from ham?".

After more dialogue, I wanted to generalise the concept over more species. This was to ensure students draw the distinction around all forms of organisms on Earth.

"How about plants? Are they made, primarily, from the same molecules as us?" I had students vote with their hands. Some were confident that we weren't, others were unsure. So, I asked if they ate plant-based food. We identified examples, from spinach to beans. "Why do you eat them? Surely if you eat them, it's because you want to build yourself from their molecules?"

I entered into dialogue with the goal of having students redraw this distinction that we are somehow made from different molecules.

"If plants are made from the same principal molecules, how about other organisms? Bacteria? Whales? Fungi?" I referred to other foods they had eaten, like mushrooms. "And are you not food for a lion? What would a lion do with your molecules?"

Once I perceived – via their responses and gestures – that the students had begun redrawing their distinctions, I taught them that all life on Earth traces its family back to a single population of cells over four billion years ago. Hence, we're mainly made from the same molecules. "But," some students said, "we can't eat wood." A great objection to explore. The students had come up against an obstacle that prevented discernment. The idea hadn't yet fit their experience, so it was essential for them to grapple more with the concept.

I explained that we didn't have the right digestive system to process and absorb it, even though it is made of carbohydrates. Yet, other organisms could. I gave them examples of termites, but also cattle that consume grass. Grass is primarily made from the same carbohydrate, cellulose, which we can't digest. In the history of humanity, one solution to finding nutrients was to allow animals, such as cattle, to eat grass (which we can't digest). The cattle accumulate nutrients from the grass before humans then eat them.

It was time to move on to the core aspect of autopoiesis, "What's the purpose of building our structure?" Some students answered, "To live" and other ideas lacking distinction. I gave them the answer directly – we build our structure so that we can obtain nutrients from the environment. And we obtain those nutrients so we can build and maintain our structure. This is the inherent circularity of autopoiesis – of life.

This was an idea that was quite new to my students. It is the idea of persistence despite the odds. And it needed some discussion on the second law of thermodynamics – another of our critical aspects. I asked students, "What happens to your clothes after a long time?"

"They get old," a student replied. *Fantastic*, I thought, this was what I had been anticipating. My students were familiar with our universe by age eleven. They understood that, with time, things tend to disintegrate – from order to disorder. This is the second law of thermodynamics. My student had equated this law with time. For them, time and disorder were the same thing. I asked in response, "What if, in a different universe, objects didn't tend to break down over time? Somewhere those clothes just stayed like new. In that place, would it make sense to say that an object had gotten old?"

This is a key distinction to make, and I gave them a difference to help them see what I see – potential variation. "And so, what happens to us? The fact is that our cells are dying all the time."

The example I appealed to, for students of this age, was the skin. Skin as the barrier of dead cells that protects the living cells underneath. These dead cells constantly fall off the body, so must be replaced. How do we build new ones? Well, we need to consume more nutrients to build their parts. This is why autopoiesis is a continuous cycle, as I noted in the diagram. "You build yourself. No one builds you, you're autonomous" I said.

It was time to establish the distinction between organism and environment. So, I provoked students with a seemingly obvious question, "Okay then, what was the environment when you were inside your mother's uterus?"

I told them that their mothers hadn't built them at all. Their mothers had been their environment. One that was particularly adept at providing nutrients and removing waste. Some dialogue around this continued and continued the conversation until they seemed satisfied with this concept.

For a final contrast, I drew the section of the diagram representing a machine. I used common examples the students were familiar with, such as the combustion-engine car. We noted the similarities before focusing on the difference maker – we build ourselves, and we build machines. Machines depend on us for their persistence, we repair them. But we build, maintain, and heal ourselves.

Notice how, in this example, I built the diagram bit by bit. I didn't produce it ahead of time and project a finished and curated image. The students and I built the diagram together.

Stock and flow diagrams can explicitly share a teacher's mental distinctions and relations

Key idea:
Building stock and flow models makes your understanding clearer to your students and yourself.

Look at Figure 9 and you can find an interesting diagram. Unlike a concept map, which categorises and connects ideas, this one also shows what occurs over time. It shows how the system could vary over time. In other words, it speaks the language of systems and has become an indispensable tool in my classroom.

In the diagram, you can see a stock (the box) of wolves and one of rabbits. This stock represents an accumulation of individuals in a population. There is also an inflow to the populations. These are the births, which increase the population size. And an outflow from the populations. These are the deaths. The curved arrows show what affects the rates of flows.

There's a story to tell here. The more wolves there are, the more rabbits die. What will happen over time? Fewer rabbits cause fewer nutrients per wolf, which causes fewer births of wolves. This is circular causality: the wolves' hunting of rabbits, comes back to cause a change to their own population and hunting rate. Just talking it through with students doesn't do it justice. Clarity is lost in the linearisation of the model into sentences, and other diagram types can't capture time and circularity like these can. The transformation that these models have caused to my classroom has warranted them a chapter and appendix. I'll explain how to read, design, and build them with students.

Stock and flow diagrams originate from system dynamics, pioneered by the practical-minded Jay Forrester (1961; 1968). The payoff for learning the symbols is large for students and teachers, as communication of a teacher's ideas is vastly improved. Teachers already use many diagrams in biology lessons, but typically the format, symbols, and rules change with each example. Stock and flow diagrams allow all this to remain stable, while only the concept varies.

In biology, we have to teach about unknown systems (to students), so often we must first describe systems. We must discuss their structure and function, presenting diagrams like I have shown in Example Box 1 to 5. The danger is becoming trapped in the structure-function cycle, with every topic becoming a descriptive tour of biological parts. The usefulness (and joy) of knowing a system, is pondering its dynamics

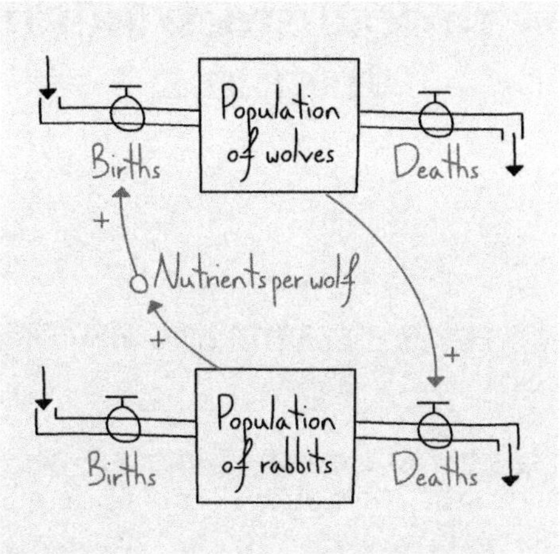

Figure 9: A stock and flow diagram showing predator-prey dynamics.

– how it performs. Stock and flow models allow you to escape the structure-function trap.

Nevertheless, it's not just because you can convey ideas more precisely in a stock and flow diagram. It's also because, by designing the model beforehand, you make your thoughts distinct to yourself. As Bertrand Russell said, “Everything is vague to a degree you do not realize till you have tried to make it precise.” (1918, 4).

The rest of this chapter is dedicated to how I use stock and flow diagrams in my classroom. You can think of the models I create as qualitative system dynamics. While I don't simulate them mathematically, we can simulate them via “mental walk-through”. (Richmond 1994, 143).

How to read stock and flow diagrams

Key idea:
Students only need to learn a handful of symbols to develop models over different topics.

Many symbols of stock and flow diagrams are easy to learn because they rely on the hydraulic metaphor – our understanding of the flow of water. Sometimes people even call it "bathtub dynamics". Here's a simple model of a bathtub, with an inflow and outflow of water (Figure 10). The first distinction the models make is the difference between accumulations and flows in a system. An accumulation is a perceived persistence of stuff, whereas flows are a process – or flow of stuff – that occurs over time.

To perceive the distinction you can carry out a "snapshot test" (Sterman 2000). You imagine the system paused in time and consider what can be measured and what can't. Something that accumulates can be counted, so this is a stock. Stocks are quantities. As processes occur over time, when you pause a system, you can't see it occurring, so you can't determine its rate. These are flows, which have units of rate. For example, entities per time, items per day, units per month. With the bathtub, we could pause time and quantify how much water is in the tub, but not know the rate of water coming in or out. In the same way that at any one moment, you can know how much money is in a bank account (a stock), but you can't tell if it is rising or falling unless you observe the inflows and outflows over time. At first glance, this can feel non-intuitive for specific instances. For example, the total glucose in the blood is a stock, even though it is flowing around the vascular system. The blood acts like a container of glucose, and by using the snapshot

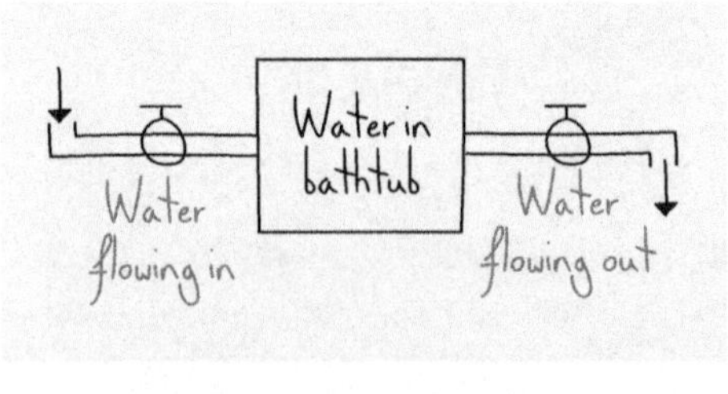

Figure 10: A stock and flow diagram representing the flow of water into, accumulating in, and flowing out of a bathtub.

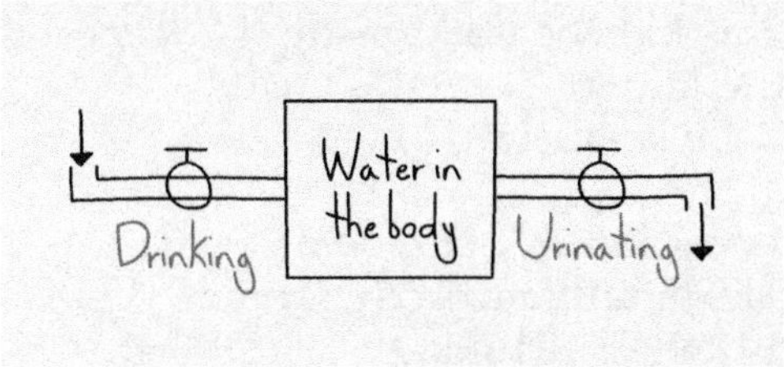

Figure 11: A stock and flow diagram representing the flow of water into, accumulating in, and flowing out of a human body.

test, we could quantify the glucose in the blood. I'll elaborate on this distinction, and its importance for coherent models, in a moment.

Using the hydraulic metaphor, the inflows and outflows can be regulated, just like a tap can regulate the flow of water into a bath. That's what those circles represent, taps. So, the model's focus is on three things: stocks (accumulations of stuff), flows (rates of stuff flowing), and what regulates the flows. At the beginning or end of some flows, there are holes with water draining in or out. These mark the edge of the model – the edge of what we're interested in – and don't affect anything within the model.

If we wanted, we could show the same model for water in a human body, as shown in Figure 11. This model suggests a constant rate of water entering and leaving the body. We all know that this isn't how it works. Sometimes we drink too much, which leads to losing our thirst and urinating much more. To have this model fit our experience, we must add something that regulates the inflows and outflows. Let's add some variables and connectors, as shown in Figure 12.

This model makes more sense than the previous one. Let me explain why. Notice the variable I've added, called "thirst". It has an arrow coming towards it from the stock, and a type of relation, or connection, is given as "–". What does this mean? It means that the stock "Water in the body" affects the level of thirst you experience. Think about it this way:

Negative signs mean that the relationship is "opposite", so either:
- the larger X, the smaller Y, or
- the smaller X, the larger Y.

Therefore the proposition in the model is:
- the more water in the body, the less thirst, or
- the less water in the body, the more thirst.

Thirst is a variable that connects to the inflow tap called "drinking". This time the connection is "+".

Positive signs mean that the relationship is "same", so either:
- the larger X, the larger Y, or
- the smaller X, the smaller Y.

Therefore the proposition in the model is:
- the more thirst, the more drinking, or
- the less thirst, the less drinking.

We now have a negative feedback loop. These are often easy to see in simple models, but to make sure, let's follow the loop around beginning with a low stock quantity. Less water in the body leads to more thirst, and more thirst leads to more drinking. This ultimately causes more water in the body.

Regulating the outflow, we have another negative feedback loop. This time, without specifying any variables that act in the loop. The level of detail you add, is, of course, part of the design and purpose of the model. In the model (Figure 12) there is a connector between the stock and the outflow. It has a "same" or "positive" connection. The proposition then, is then:
1. the more water in the body, the more you urinate, or
2. the less water in the body, the less you urinate.

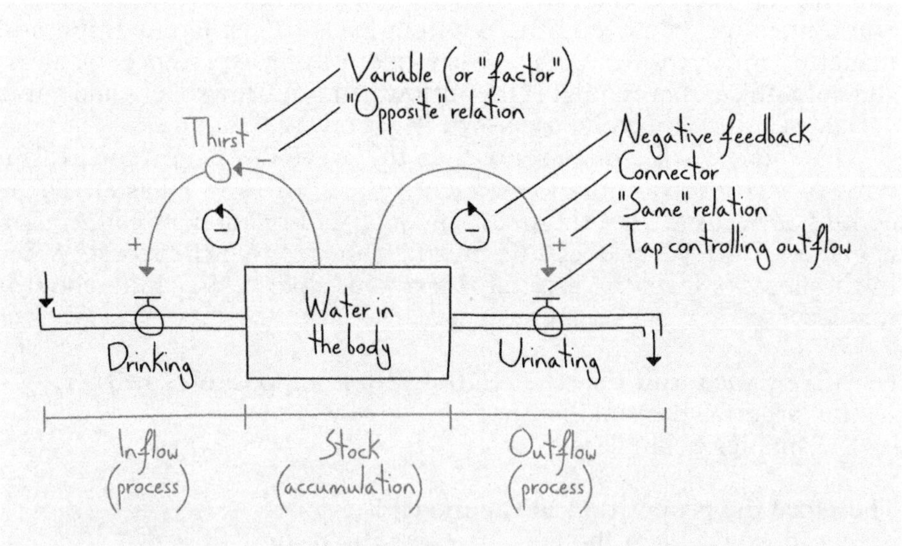

Figure 12: A stock and flow diagram representing the flow of water in a human body and how it is regulated via feedback loops.

Following the loop around: more water in the body causes more urination, which causes less water in the body. The only way to change the water accumulation is via inflows and outflows. Therefore, you can't have a connection going directly to a stock. You need to specify the process that affects the stock by connecting to its flows.

To contrast the two models – the water in the bathtub and the water in the body – here is an example of the dynamics of the system in graphical format (Figure 13).

In Figure 14, I contrast models with feedback loops from models without them. In Example Box 6, I'll explain how I've introduced these models to my youngest biology students.

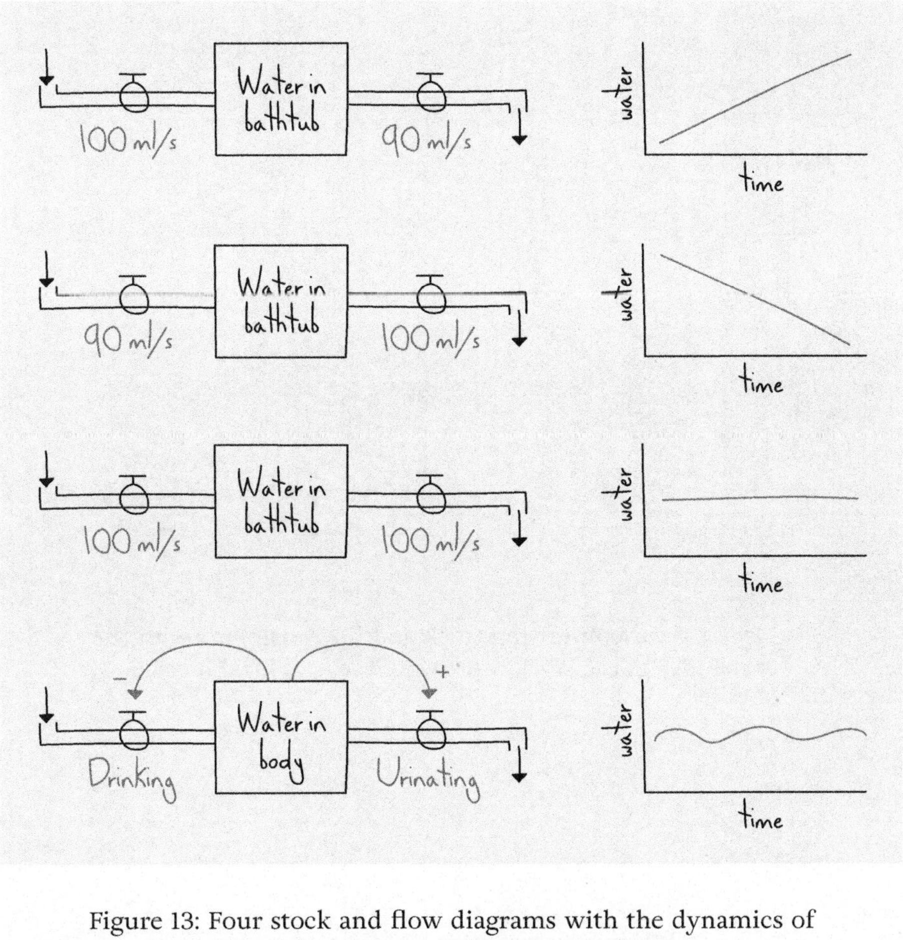

Figure 13: Four stock and flow diagrams with the dynamics of the stock represented in graphical format.

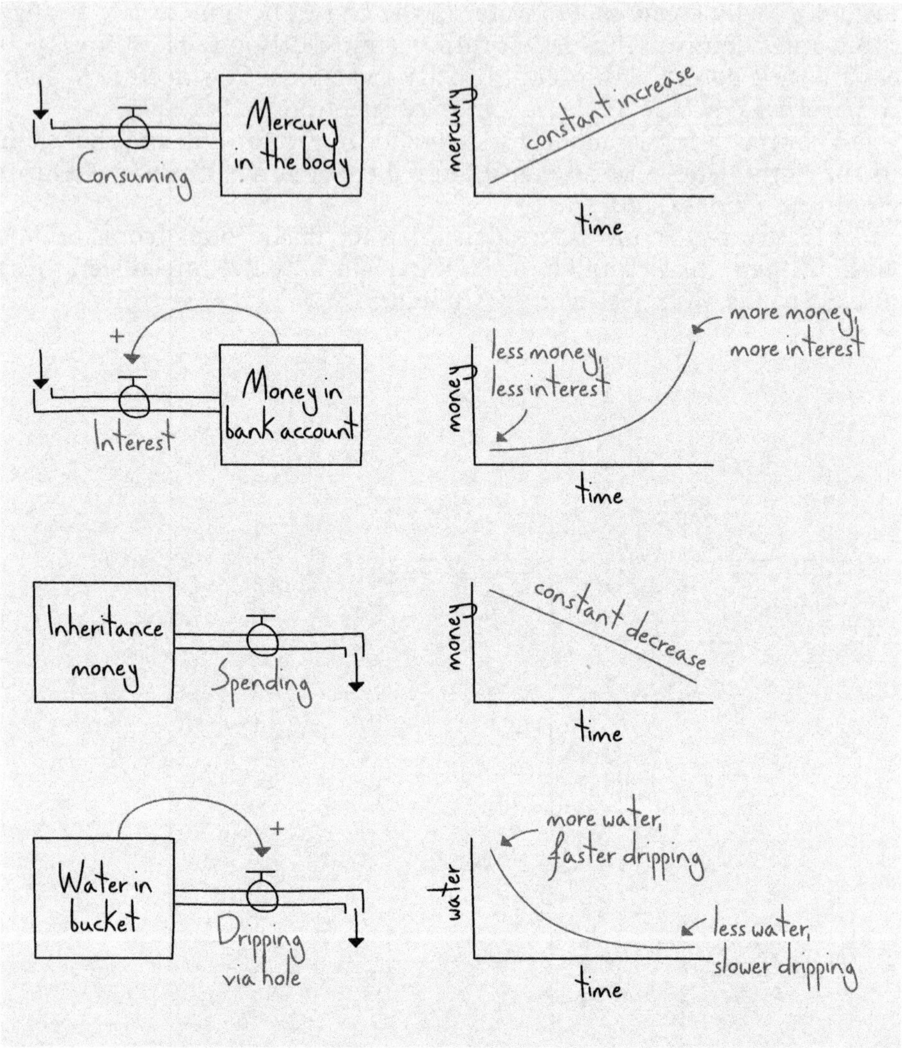

Figure 14: Four contrasting stock and flow diagrams with the dynamics of the stock represented in graphical format.

Example Box 6

Introducing the stock and flow concept for the first time

When I begin teaching my 11-year-olds I introduce them to stock and flow diagrams. In this example, I'll show you how I did it recently.

Introducing the flow and the stock symbols

I started with two graduated beakers and poured water from one into the other. As I was doing it, I asked a student to take a photo. While students were observing the photo, I asked them if they could tell, more or less, how much water was in the beaker. They agreed that they could. Then I asked if they could tell how fast the water was flowing and they agreed that they couldn't. Here I'd made explicit the difference between stocks and flows. I told the students that the difference is that one was an accumulation, whereas the other was a flow that only happened over time. I then drew the representation of the beakers as a stock and flow diagram (Figure 15).

Introducing the idea of regulating the flow rates

Now they'd seen the basic symbols, I asked them if a bathtub is similar to the diagram. They thought it was, but recognised that it needed an outflow. Therefore, I drew the stock and flow diagram representing a bathtub with an inflow and outflow (Figure 16). However, the outflow had a tap, and baths don't typically have a tap in their drain. To help students understand this, I asked them if there was any way they could regulate how fast water flowed out of a drain. They gave examples of

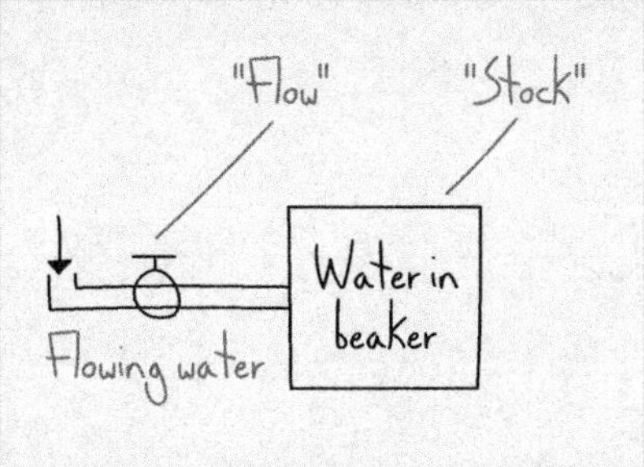

Figure 15: A stock and flow diagram representing water being poured from one beaker into another.

putting the plug only halfway over the hole, and I said that the tap symbol represented this – the regulation of the flow.

Introducing bathtub dynamics & mass balance

It was time to start thinking conceptually with the model. Firstly, I wanted my students to discern that accumulations are determined by inflow and outflow rates. I began by asking them what would happen to the water in the bathtub if the inflow rate was higher than the outflow. I gave them three choices to vote on: It would increase, stay the same, or decrease. I did this again for the following questions: if the inflow and outflow rates were equal, and if the outflow rate was higher than the inflow rate. To help visualise this, I used Jon Darkow's bathtub systems model online. With the help of this simulation, I also asked what would happen if the inflow rate was only slightly higher than the outflow rate compared to if it were much higher. I then introduced the mass balance principle: What enters a system must either leave the system or accumulate within it. This principle would help us later in the lesson when we got to the biological content.

Introducing feedback loops

To do this I used a vertical column with three small horizontal outlets, which teachers use to demonstrate how water pressure increases with depth. I plugged the two upper outlets with blue tack, leaving just the bottom outlet as a drain for water. (Any vessel with a drain for water can be used here). I filled the column with water while my finger plugged the only open outlet. I then let go, allowing the students to observe the outflow rate of water as it emptied. At first, the water shoots out, but as the water drains, the outflow slows. I asked the students why this might be, and many answered that the water pushed down (i.e. pressure). We returned to the diagram and I showed students how to represent it by adding a feedback loop (Figure 16). At this point, I also introduced students to the positive symbol and its meaning ("same").

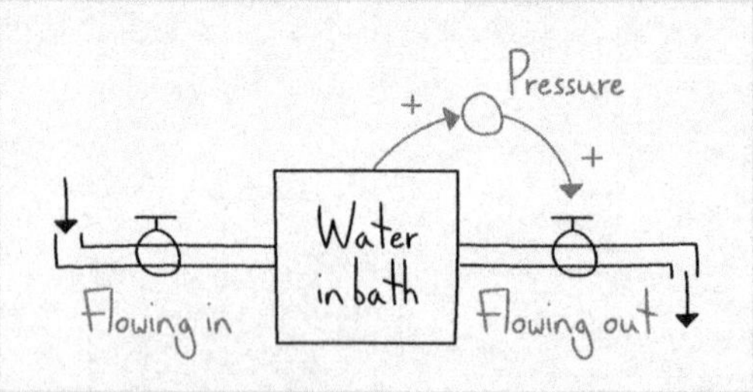

Figure 16: A stock and flow diagram with a feedback loop showing that the more water in a bath, the more pressure, and therefore the faster the water leaves.

Introducing stocks and flows with biological content

I told the students that since I was 18 I'd hardly changed weight despite eating every day. I was nudging the students to transfer their recently acquired idea of the mass balance principle to living organisms. However, many reasoned that it was because humans poop out mass to maintain a balance. So, I drew a diagram for them representing the human's boundaries plus its inputs and outputs (Figure 17). This was to distinguish between what is part of our body, and what is simply in a tube that runs through our body (e.g. faeces). This helped me show the distinction between the elimination of faeces and the excretion of waste products.

I then added a stock and flow diagram for a person's biomass and asked students to identify the inflow and outflow. It was time to return to how I maintained my body mass over time. I asked my students again, and they understood that the inflow and outflow rates must be equal. However, they generally needed more elaboration on how the outflow is mainly the breathing out of carbon dioxide.

Finally, I asked students how the model would be different for children their age. We discussed how their body mass was increasing so their inflow must be higher than their outflow. We also discussed how a fully grown adult lost biomass when on a diet – with an outflow rate higher than the inflow rate. And I asked students where the biomass went when someone was dieting. They were surprised that it is mainly breathed out.

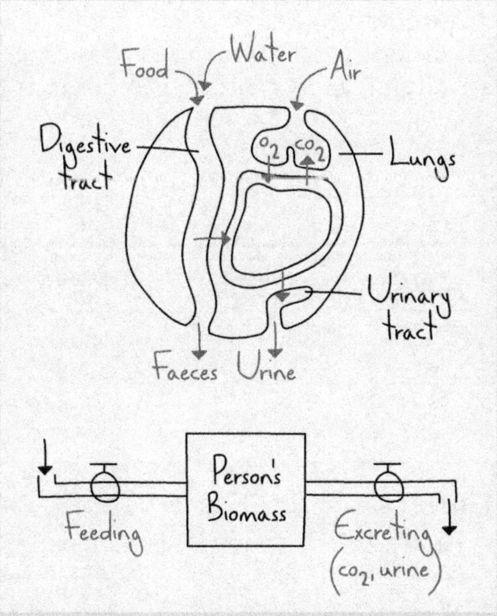

Figure 17: Two representations of inflows and outflows of molecules for the human body.

Stock and flow diagrams make distinctions clear and allow the exploration of possibilities

Key idea:
A single model conveys clearly what other variations of the system could be.

A stock and flow model isn't a single explanation, but many possible explanations. Consider the example in Figure 18a, a model of eutrophication. Let me build it up in parts.

Whenever you come to a new model, start by scanning the stocks and flows – these convey the structure of the system and the designer's motives. I have designed the model to distinguish two separate systems: the algae population, and the populations of the rest of the community. For now, I've removed all the other variables and connections.

A key feature of stock and flow diagrams is their consistency with the mass balance principle: what enters a system must either leave the system or accumulate within it. Mass balance reasoning is considered one of the important skills for developing a deep understanding of biological systems (Modell 2000).

How does this model follow the mass balance principle? Let's mentally simulate the algae system. Algae come into being via cell

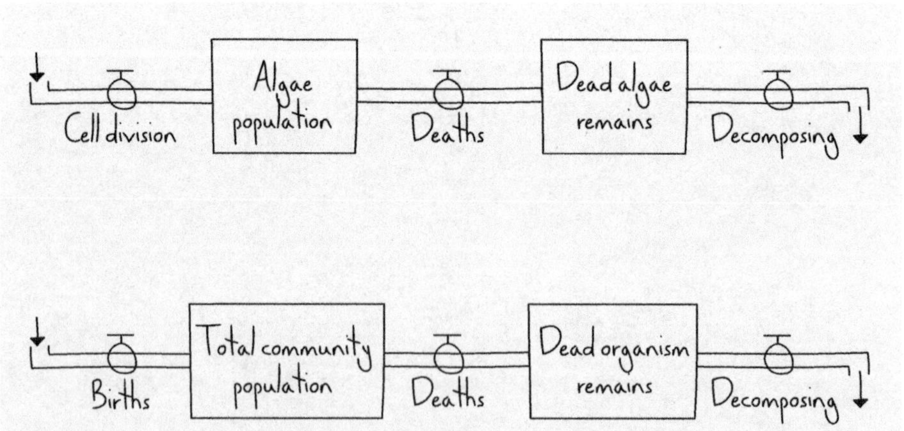

Figure 18a: The basic stock and flow structure of eutrophication that I've drawn for students prior to its explanation.

division and accumulate in the population. That's the first stock. When they die, their leftovers accumulate in the water. This is the second stock. Decomposition is then the process that removes these remains from the system. In stock and flow diagrams, what flows through a flow must be what accumulates in any connected stock. This is a fundamental rule for developing good models. Yet, it's mass balance, not "form balance". So, it's fine for the matter of the algae to flow through the tubes, and for there to be two stocks in which that matter is in different forms (i.e. alive and dead). Let's add some variables (Figure 18b).

The model shows that algae populations are constrained by a negative feedback loop. When populations become too high, competition for nutrients increases and there is less per individual. This limits any further population increase. However, when fertilisers leach into water bodies, available nutrients increase dramatically, and the population is released from the constraint. If we follow the model, fertiliser leaching increases the available nutrients, and this, in turn, increases the cell division rate. We'd say that the population "blooms" (creating an algal bloom).

However, the larger the population, the model suggests, the larger the mortality rate (deaths per unit of time – note the positive connection between the stock and outflow). As the algae die their remains

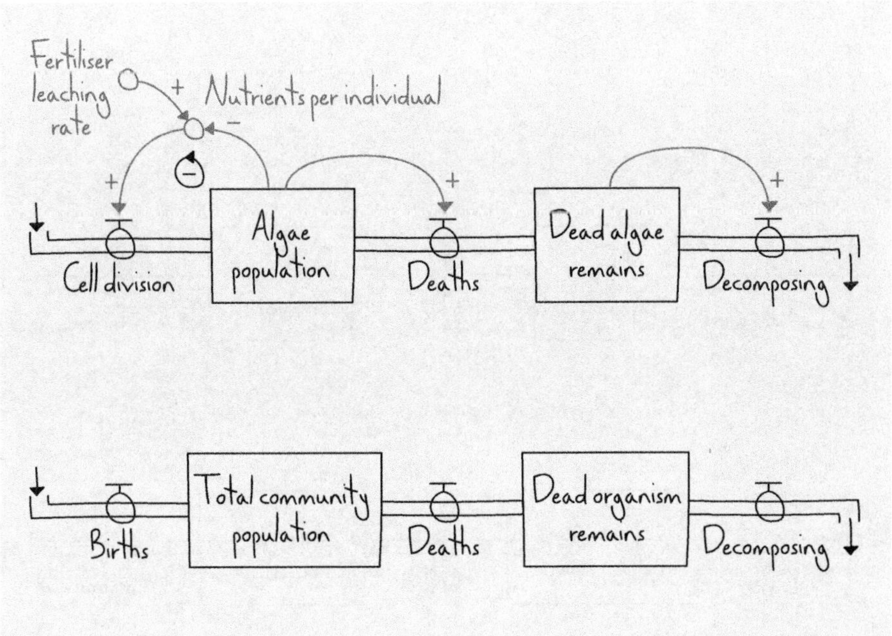

Figure 18b: The partially complete stock and flow diagram of eutrophication that I co-construct with students.

accumulate in the next stock (dead algae remains). And again, the larger this stock, the larger the outflow rate. So the rate of decomposition accelerates. Here's where the actions of algae, in my model, interact with the rest of the population. Let's add in more variables (Figure 18c).

What do the new variables and connections show? As mentioned, the decomposition of algae is now accelerating, and with it, the biological demand for oxygen rises. As the biological oxygen demand rises it has an "opposite" effect on the water's oxygen concentration. The organisms in the community that depend on oxygen begin to suffocate, and this leads to an increase in deaths. This is seen in the "opposite" effect of oxygen concentration on the mortality rate – the lower the oxygen, the higher the mortality rate. What happens next? A devastating positive feedback loop. Let's add in the final variables (Figure 18d).

As the oxygen concentration drops, the death rate increases for the rest of the community, and the bodies begin to pile up in the next stock. Notice the connections I've added between the stocks and the outflows. The larger the population, the higher the mortality rate. Which leads to more dead remains, and a faster decomposition rate. The oxygen concentration plummets evermore.

Here's the crucial link in the loop. Look at how the increase in decomposition rate also increases the oxygen demand – scrubbing the water of any oxygen left behind. The positive feedback loop begins

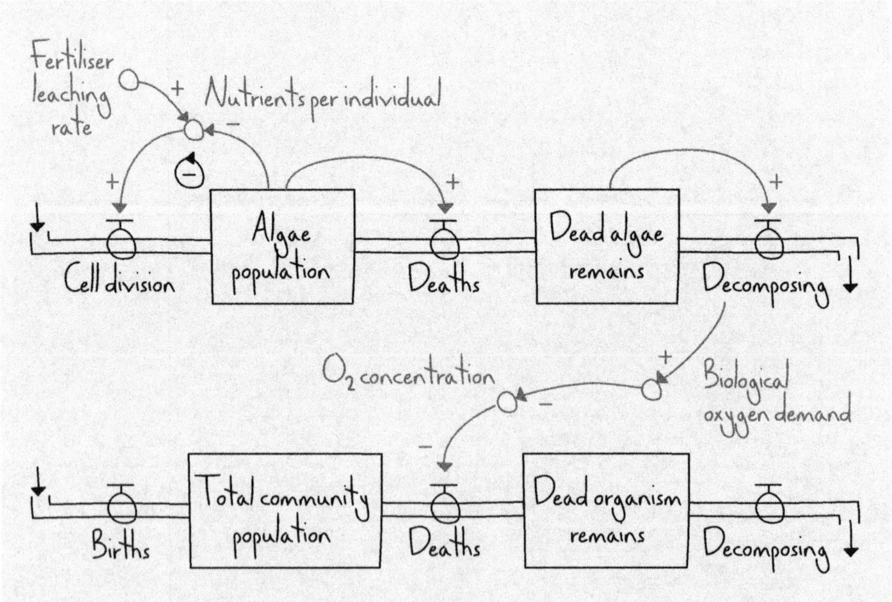

Figure 18c: The partially complete stock and flow diagram of eutrophication that I co-construct with students.

with an increase in a variable – biological oxygen demand – and then loops back on itself to further increase it again, and again. Ultimately, the positive feedback loop drives a change of state in the system. It only stops when the leaching stops and the dead remains return to their previous levels.

That's the story of the model. A story that can be built step by step with students. Each step makes a new aspect distinct, and each new addition to the model allows variation. With each section, I can ask, "What if X increased, and what if it decreased?" Students can ponder the differences as the story unfolds, and then as a whole system. The model allows students to see the dynamics of the system, not a linear, unchanging, step-by-step process. It helps them to see how it could be different.

In contrast, I often see eutrophication taught as a linear flow diagram that doesn't make explicit the mass balance principle or any circularity. These flowcharts may read something like this:

Fertiliser leaches into a lake → algae reproduce quickly and bloom → algae eventually die → decomposers use up oxygen to decompose the algae → oxygen concentration in the water decreases → other organisms die from lack of oxygen.

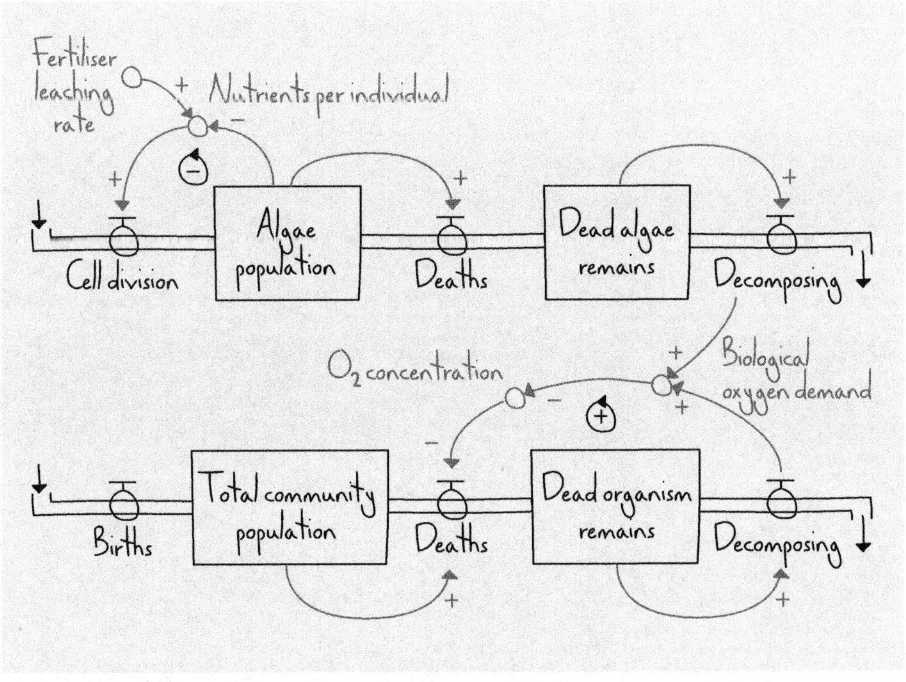

Figure 18d: The complete stock and flow diagram of eutrophication that I co-construct with students.

A problem with flowcharts is the lack of differentiation. When there is an arrow, does it mean that something converts into something else, something flows into something else, or something causes something else? In stock and flow diagrams there are clear distinctions between causes, flows, and accumulations.

Flowcharts are also rigid, making it difficult to perceive any dynamics. What can you do with a flowchart? Maybe you can learn the steps in the process as a description of what happens. But what about variation? Surely not every situation is equal. Each stock and flow diagram presents many possibilities – you just have to ask, "What if?" For example, in the model on eutrophication, we simultaneously get a vision of the different dynamics between oligotrophic and eutrophic conditions. To show this in a flowchart, you'd need two separate ones, with different terms. The problem is that flowcharts don't speak the language of *dynamical* systems, whereas stock and flow diagrams do.

Stocks cause accumulations, which cause dynamics

Key idea:
The distinction between stocks and flows makes the models a powerful tool – stocks are accumulations, whereas flows happen over time.

The power of the diagrams lies principally in the distinction between stocks and flows. This is different from Sankey diagrams. These never show any stocks – any accumulations – and just depict flows. This is the key because Sankey diagrams don't show how flows can change – they don't show variation in system performance – and so, they don't show dynamics. Sankey diagrams are often used to depict energy flow through food chains and were important in portraying this idea to the public in the early days of ecosystem ecology (e.g. Woodwell 1970). They are intuitive, but their fixed nature doesn't allow us to generate variation in the classroom.

In fact, it was the systems ecologist Howard Odum who revolutionised his field by bringing energy flows – and Sankey diagrams – to the centre of ecology. Yet, those initial studies of energy flows were carried out in habitats chosen precisely due to their "steady state" unchanging behaviour (Kemp & Boyton 2004). It's the distinction between stocks and flows that brings forth variation and dynamics. But why? Here's some ideas (translated from Sterman 2000).

Stocks characterise the state of the system and provide the basis for actions.
The homeostatic processes we teach in biology all depend on information of accumulations. For example, in blood glucose regulation, the quantity of blood glucose serves as information about the state of the system, not the rate of its absorption. The same for breathing rate, which is regulated based on accumulations of oxygen and carbon dioxide.

Stocks provide systems with inertia and memory.
As stocks can only change via inflows and outflows, their accumulations can tell us about past events. Mammals that go through a bountiful period of nutrition may accumulate fat stores that persist for weeks and months through winter. It's similar for greenhouse gases emitted into the atmosphere. The CFCs that were internationally phased out long ago, persist in the atmosphere because the rate at which chlorine exits the stratosphere is slow.

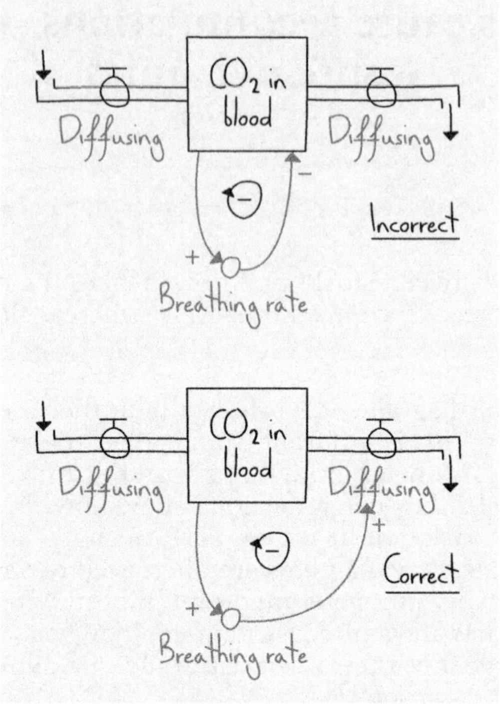

Figure 19: A comparison to show the correct way of connecting variables to flows.

Stocks are the source of delays.
Delays are the result of an output occurring much after the original input. There is a lag. For example, when there is a good growth season for plants a large accumulation of herbivores may appear. But their predators will take time to hunt and reproduce. Therefore, the predator population won't increase until after a delay.

The reason for the examples above is that stocks act as buffers that allow inflow rates and outflow rates to be different. It's generally an exception for inflow and outflow rates to remain equal. It's important to remember that stocks only change via their flows. See Figure 19 for an example of correct and incorrect notation.

Another important point is that stocks are accumulations. If a rate is placed as a stock, the model becomes confusing. In the example shown in Figure 20, you can see the difference. Using the snapshot test, we can't observe transpiration, but we can observe the quantity of water in a plant. That makes "water in a plant" a candidate for the stock, with transpiration being the outflow.

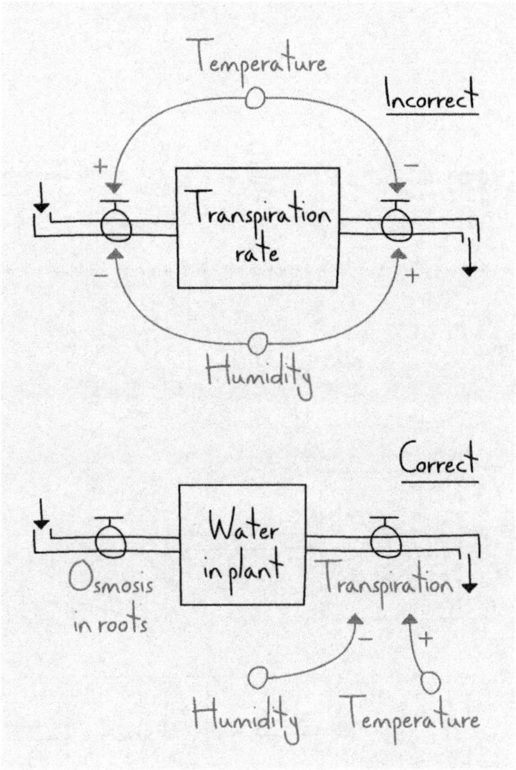

Figure 20: A comparison to show the correct designation of a stock (as an accumulation) and a flow (as a rate).

Finally, it's crucial to remember that whatever accumulates in a stock has to be the same thing that flows through its conjoining inflows and outflows. For example (Figure 21), thyroid stimulating hormone doesn't convert into thyroxine (another hormone). Thyroid stimulating hormone triggers the production of thyroxine. Therefore, the two stocks of the different hormones mustn't be connected via a flow, but a connector.

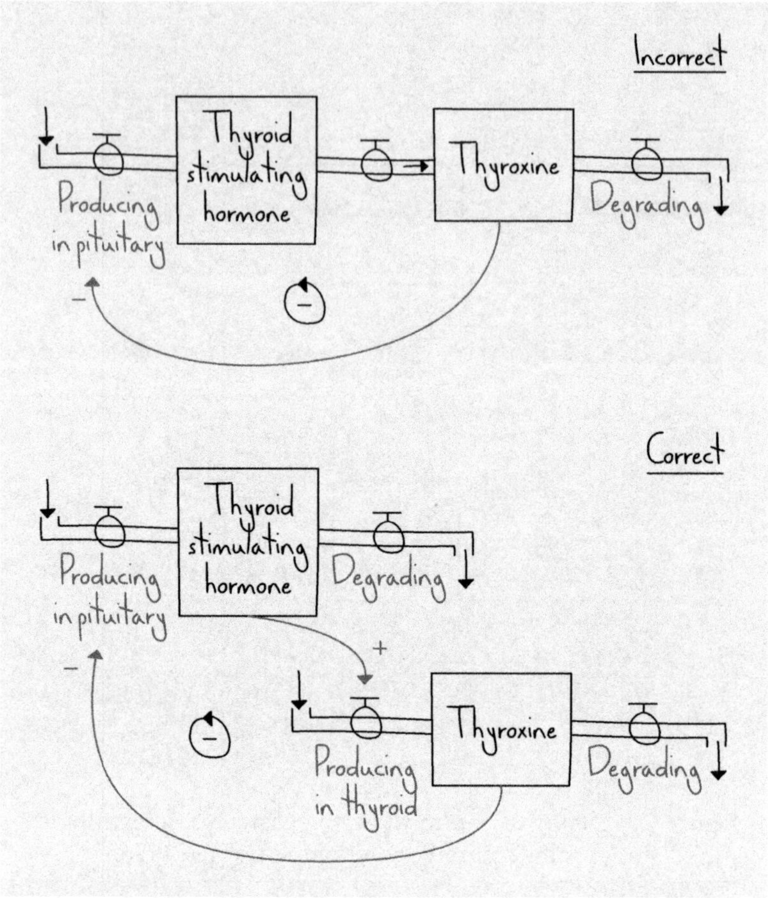

Figure 21: A comparison to show the correct separation into two different systems (of stocks) because thyroid stimulating hormone does not convert into thyroxine (another hormone).

Draw stock and flow diagrams to show system dynamics and draw iconic diagrams to show shape, structure, or movements.

Key idea:
Stock and flow diagrams can be complemented with other forms of diagram to help share meanings.

There are times when stock and flow diagrams don't fit, and more conventional diagrams convey our understanding better. A great example is the chromosomes during mitosis, it's their movement and structure that matters. In such cases, it's better to draw "icons". Charles Sanders Peirce categorised signs, that we may use in diagrams, into three types: the icon, the index, and the symbol (Misak 2004). An icon resembles the thing it stands for, such as drawing a lake as part of a diagram on eutrophication. An index "signifies its object because it is connected with it – a symptom is an index of a disease and smoke is an index of fire" (Misak 2004, 8). Finally, symbols don't resemble what they stand for, nor are they connected with them. You just have to learn symbols, the best example being the word. Another example is the symbols in stock and flow diagrams.

An argument against using stock and flow diagrams in the classroom is the necessity of learning a set of symbols in addition to the extra vocabulary of a course. Some teachers I've spoken to have said, for this reason, that they prefer iconic diagrams. And, if students aren't acquainted with the symbols of stock and flow diagrams, they too, often say they prefer more iconic diagrams. The key is to embed stock and flow diagrams as students get used to them quickly. Nevertheless, most of the time it's not a forced choice. It's possible to complement stock and flow models with icons and indices. On other occasions, like with the nephron or the leaf (Figure 6), a simple stock and flow model can complement a more complex iconic diagram. To show you how I've mixed models with iconic diagrams, I've left an example in Figure 22.

In the appendix, you can find a large collection of these models. If you don't like some of them, or think they could be better, brilliant. It means you understand how the models work and could fit into your context. In the next section I'll explain how I build the models during my lessons.

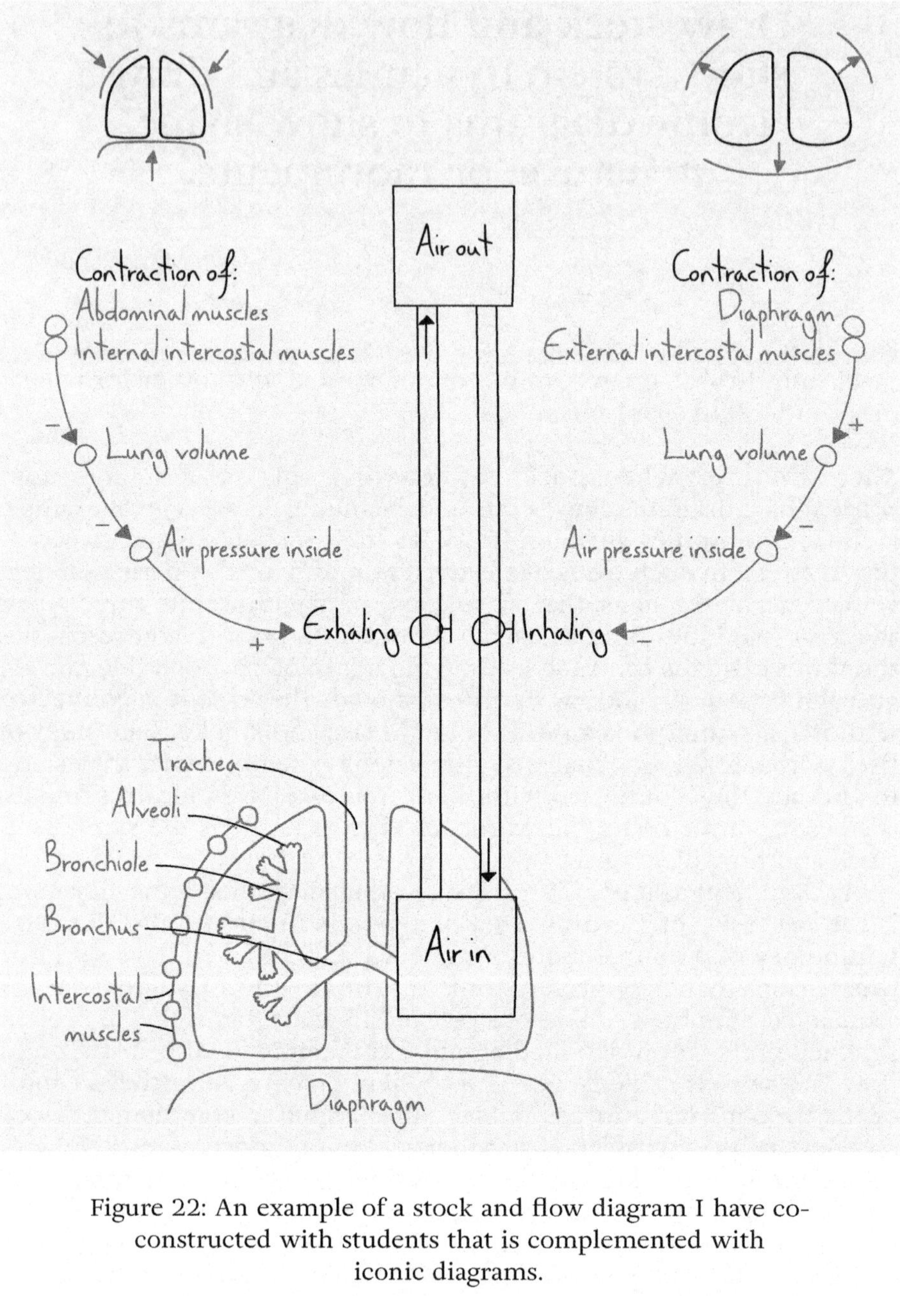

Figure 22: An example of a stock and flow diagram I have co-constructed with students that is complemented with iconic diagrams.

How to construct stock and flow diagrams through conversation

There is a way of building models with my students that has evolved from my teaching. In this section, I'll explain how I do it, but the framework I'll share is a simplification. It linearises and categorises something that has overlaps and circularity. Use it as a rough heuristic for you to begin exploring model building with your students. Don't worry if you're not able to include every step. Sometimes the goal is just to share the structure of a system, rather than its dynamics. In this case, you may show stocks and flows without other variables. For an example, see the digestive system model in the appendix.

You'll see that the process is similar to the steps of learning proposed by variation theory. If you remember, it begins with discerning aspects and ends with simultaneously considering the aspects together: from separation to fusion. However, there is an additional step called delimitation, which is also discussed in variation theory (Marton 2015). Here I'm using the term to mean the contextualisation of the system so that the students see the system in its usual setting. But, as the term suggests, it also involves allowing students to see the system as a distinguishable entity within that context. For example, in a lesson on the heart, you would contextualise the heart within the vascular system and the whole body. But you'd also point to where the heart begins and ends.

From here, the process involves discerning the key aspects of the systems and making sense of them through the use of variation. This is the separation phase. The final phases encourage students to bring to mind these aspects simultaneously and think about the whole model. This is the fusion phase. Therefore, the whole process involves seeing the whole in its context, before discerning the parts, and then simultaneously seeing the parts together within the whole system.

Several actions typically remain constant throughout the process. Conversation and participatory sense-making always occur for example. As does having students draw with me and tracing ideas with fingertips to develop a sensorimotor connection with the model (Varela et al. 2016). The framework I give in Table 2 is a good example of all the assumptions in action. Here are the assumptions as a reminder. We'll be returning to them again in the next chapters.

- **Assumption 1:** Understanding a system involves knowing an explanation of its parts and whole, plus their potential variation.
- **Assumption 2:** An explanation of a system arises in tandem with – not separate from – variation of its critical aspects.

	Phase	Example questions & actions for provoking sense-making	Typical student actions in my classes
Delimitation	**Delimit** the system within a context	• Showing images or videos of the system in a context • Drawing an iconic diagram of the system • Discussing the purpose of the system (the purpose of the system is what it does in a context)	Class discussion Peer discussion Hands-up voting
Separation	**Identify** the stocks & flows	• What processes do these flows represent? • What stock is this?	Class discussion Peer discussion Hands-up voting
	Select the variables	• Does this variable connect to the inflow or outflow? • Is this connection "same" or "opposite"? • If this variable increases does this section of the model still make sense? • If we then decrease the same variable, does it still make sense?	Class discussion Peer discussion Hands-up voting
Fusion	**Simulate** the whole model to perceive its usual dynamics	Explain the model thinking about variations: • What If the stock was lower, or higher? • What if the inflow increased? • What if the outflow decreased? • What if variable X increased?	Following links with fingertips Class discussion Self explanation Peer explanation
	Explore the whole model to by inferring new explanations of unusual dynamics	Example contexts for biology put the system within an organism and/or environment. Context examples: • A mutation in a desert plant caused... • Deforesting an ecosystem caused... • An infection in a human caused... Variation examples: • Variable W decreased by 70%? • Variable X increased by 50%? • Variable Y stopped functioning? • Variable Z couldn't vary from 100% capacity?	Following links with fingertips Class discussion Peer discussion Written answers: Inferring an explanation about parts and whole, as per the taxonomy of understanding biological systems

- **Assumption 3**: Vary one aspect of a system at a time – a key structure, or key process.
- **Assumption 4:** Meaning can't be transmitted, so respond to how students infer their own explanations from variation – not just how they restate a given explanation.
- **Assumption 5**: Regulate the number of aspects that you expect students to explore simultaneously according to their understanding – from discerning a single aspect of a system to deliberating the interconnected effects of variation on a whole system.

Contextualise

Before drawing the symbols it's important to have a shared understanding of what they represent. This can involve showing a real specimen, such as a plant in a potometer before developing a model of transpiration. In my classes, it often involves viewing photographs and illustrations of the system, before drawing an iconic diagram next to where the model will be drawn. In other cases, it might be a video. Once you feel the students have an adequate conception of what constitutes the system you're talking about, and what the system does, then it's time to model it.

Identifying stocks & flows

Once we've delimited the system, it's time to separate its parts so we can discern them individually. There are two steps to this process when using stock and flow diagrams. Firstly, students need to discern the principal structure of the system – the stocks and flows – and then the other variables. Always begin with the stocks and flows. Then either label all the stocks or label some and ask students to identify others (depending on their understanding). If the model is large, consider adding stocks over time. For example, with the eutrophication model (Figure 18d), I've tended to start just with the algae stocks and flows, adding the rest later.

Have students identify and name the inflows and outflows. This bit is crucial to making sense of the whole model, so don't rush it. Students are likely to mix up the actual flows with factors affecting those flows. If there are some they're unlikely to know, label them yourself and explain the name.

Table 2: A framework for co-constructing stock and flow diagrams with students, explained further in the main text.

Selecting variables and connections

Have students deliberate variables that affect the flows and discern their relationships – same (+) or opposite (-). There are many ways this can be done, here's some examples:

- If students are likely to be able to offer variables, you could ask them to discuss in pairs what those variables are, and then again as a whole class discussion.
- If you think they could offer some variables with guidance, you can draw the circles and connectors without any labels. This indicates to students the number and location of variables they must discuss in pairs.
- For variables that students are unlikely to know, label them yourself and explain them.

The above examples suggest attending to all variables at once. This can work for small models, and when students have strong prior knowledge. Another option is adding variables to a model bit by bit.

With any addition to the model, must come new dynamics. Ask students about them, "So if this variable and connection are added, what if the variable were larger, does it still make sense?" This should be an iterative process while building the model. Remember that systems occur through time, so students must think about them that way. If they don't, they may protest that they don't know how to answer. Having students follow dynamics with their fingers on the diagram can help.

Simulating usual dynamics

This step reflects the step of fusion in variation theory. It's a case of seeing all these aspects acting together simultaneously as a whole model. More often than not, I'll have students carry out either self-explanation of the model, or peer explanation during which students in pairs explain the model to each other. This gives them the chance to think, and talk about, the whole model and what the system does. Students can then identify parts that don't make sense to them and ask you to clarify the distinctions they've missed.

Exploring unusual dynamics to infer new explanations

In this final step, we're continuing with the phase of fusion. But here we need to push students to think more deeply about the relations between the system's parts. In other words, provoke students to think with the model so they have to infer their own explanations. Do this by introducing *unusual* variations by using "What if?" questions (see examples in Example Box 11 of Chapter 4). This requires more time during lessons.

It's best to avoid variations that utterly break the system so that it inhibits thinking about much at all. Effective variations could involve a new mutation that causes a component to fundamentally change its mode of action – decreasing or increasing its efficiency by 50%, for example. These questions force the students to think about the relationships within the model. To answer, have students compose their answers in terms of the taxonomy of understanding: explaining both parts and wholes (explained in Chapter 4). Depending on time and context it's a good idea to have students write their answers. I read all my students' answers, make notes of misunderstandings, and give feedback to the class later on. When time is short I discuss the answers during the same lesson or the next.

Let's see these ideas in action in Example Box 7 and 8, and don't forget the other examples in the appendix. Stock and flow models are also included in Example Box 12 (Chapter 4) and 13 (Chapter 5), with the latter being the most detailed and encompassing of the ideas of the book.

Example Box 7

Building a model with students: population controls

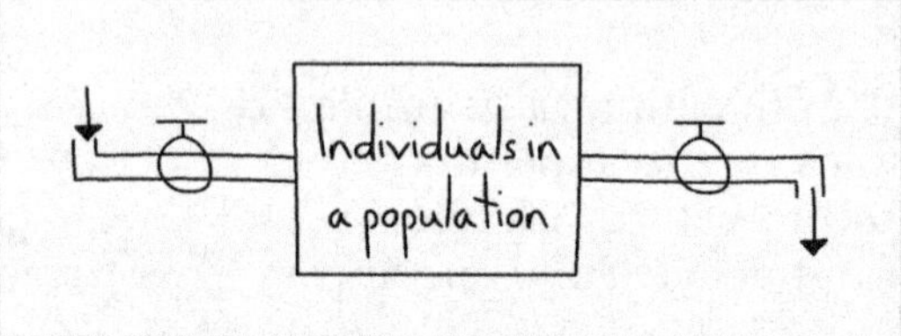

Figure 23a: The stock and flow structure I began with for teaching about population constraints.

If this is the first time developing a model with students, a nice place to begin is with a simple model of population size. Students generally have prior knowledge to build upon, and the concept is not abstract for them. Therefore, more focus can be placed on understanding the model itself. Here's how I've done it recently with 14-year-old students.

Start with a stock and distinguish between the inflows and outflows. I started with a single stock and its flows (Figure 23a). It's important to remind students that what flows through a tube also accumulates in its stock. If water accumulates in a bathtub, water must flow through its tubes. So, I asked the students, "What must be flowing through the tubes if individuals accumulate in a population?"

After some discussion, they agreed that it must be individuals entering and leaving the population. I then asked them to identify what the flows could be called, "If individuals are coming into the population, what can we call this process? And what can we call the outflow? What causes fewer people in a population?"

In my simplified model (not including migration), the inflow is "births", and the outflow is "deaths" (Figure 23b). You may think this appears simple, but often students have to think hard to clarify their thinking. This is something desirable that stock and flow modelling provokes.

When I asked students what affected a population size, they suggested food availability. This is a factor to be included in the model, but I needed students to distinguish between what directly increased & decreased a stock – in this case, the rate of births & deaths – and what affected the rate of the flows.

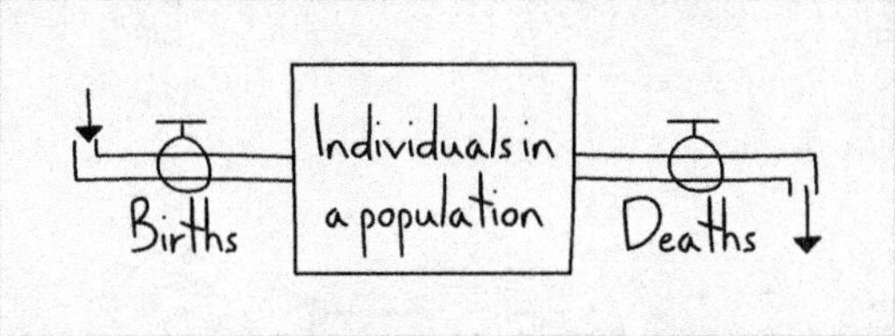

Figure 23b: The partial stock and flow diagram I co-constructed with students to teach about population constraints.

Students fall into this trap even after taking the steps to make explicit the idea that whatever flows through the tubes is also what accumulates. And this is just a normal step towards understanding these models. They have to make these distinctions to think more powerfully, and by making the mistake and receiving feedback on the error, they're more likely to perceive the distinction.

Identify the variables that affect the inflows and outflows

Next, I asked students to identify (in pairs) the variables that could affect birth and death rates. Many of these had already been mentioned when the students had attempted to name the flows. When I collected their ideas the most common answers were food availability, predator populations, and disease. With less frequency, students suggested that the weather and availability of mates were factors. This latter point could be summarised as the population size itself is a factor – the more individuals the higher the birth and death rates. This can be added to the model as connections directly from the stock to the inflow and outflow.

What variables are selected will determine the model. Once I'd accepted a few responses, I asked students how many variables were enough, "Should we include everything we know? At what point will the model become too complicated?"

This was a great opportunity to remind students of the purpose of models – simplifying complex problems to make them mentally tractable. Therefore, I asked the students, "Which variables are the most important? Which cause major changes in the population, instead of minor changes?"

The students chose food availability; and predators, parasites, and pathogens. I wanted to add "weather extremity" to make a distinction between circular and linear causality (Figure 23c). I'll come to that in a moment.

Identify the relationships between the variables

This step is the key to understanding this model, but in general, it shouldn't be too hard for students because they are familiar with living in populations. With my class, I asked them to discuss it in pairs before

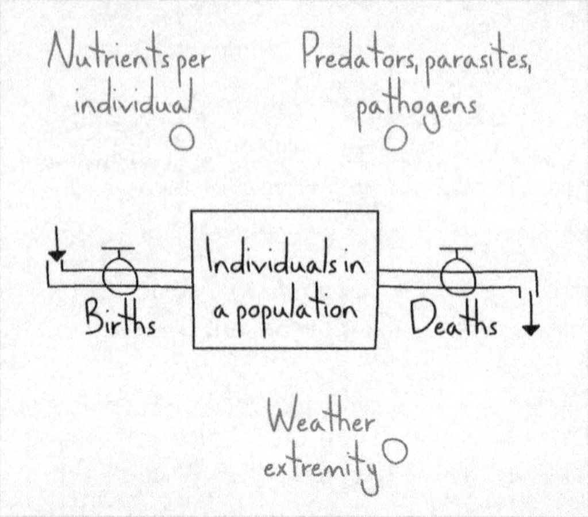

Figure 23c: The partial stock and flow diagram I co-constructed with students to teach about population constraints.

I asked for their ideas. When I did so, I expected a student to say which flow a variable affected, and whether the relationship was "same" or "opposite". To see how the class thought, I asked the class to vote – by raising their hands – if they agreed with an idea or not. I also asked the class to vote on whether relationships were "same" or "opposite". This is something I'll elaborate on in Chapter 5.

"How do the nutrients per individual affect the population?" I asked before listening to some ideas. The students gave many ideas and some were too ambiguous. To these answers, I asked, "OK, but in terms of our model, do they affect the births or deaths?"

At this point, some students mentioned starvation. So I discussed the possibility of connecting it to the outflow but mentioned that starvation could be sporadic. Does nutrient availability affect the birth rate of a population? I explained to students that growth rates would be slower with fewer nutrients, and many organisms would become infertile during periods of low nutrient intakes. Even the human menstrual cycle pauses (Ellison 2001).

I drew the connection between nutrients per individual and births (Figure 23d), and asked students to vote, "Is this connection 'same' or 'opposite'?" The students needed a moment to think about this, and as I felt they needed some help, I followed the question with a partial sentence, "The higher the nutrients per individual the..."

Once the connection between nutrients-per-individual and births had been established, it was time to ask what affected the nutrients per individual. Again, I gave my students some time to share ideas in pairs before I picked people to answer. Many students saw that the number of individuals would affect the share of nutrients they'd have

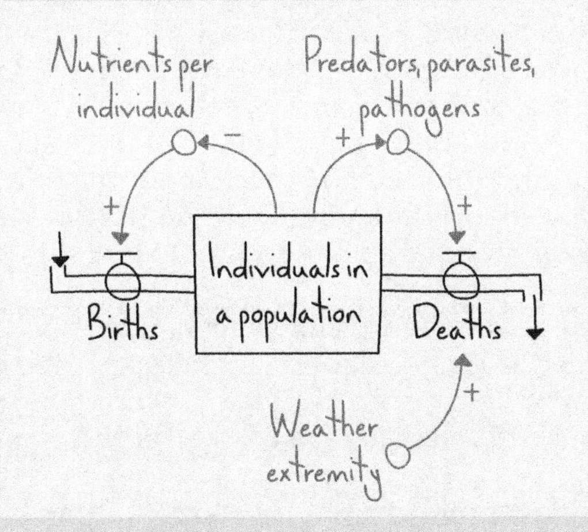

Figure 23d: The completed stock and flow diagram I co-constructed with students to teach about population constraints.

access to. However, for those who didn't immediately see the idea, I gave the example of sharing a cake between a few students in the class and all of them.

I then drew the connection between the stock and nutrients-per-individual, and asked students to vote on the direction of the connection, “Is this connection ‘same’ or ‘opposite’? The more individuals in the population the...?”

Now the feedback loop was complete, I made it explicit. To do this, I followed the causal relationships – through time – while asking the class for their effects. I also asked them to follow the loop by placing their finger on the diagram as I asked questions like the following:

1. What does a rise in the birth rate cause? A rise in population size.
2. What does an increase in population size cause? Fewer nutrients per individual.
3. So, what does a decrease in nutrients per individual cause? A lower birth rate.

A rise in birth rate ultimately comes back round to cause itself to be lowered again. That's a negative feedback loop. I asked these questions while tracing the loop with my finger. Then, I described the loop again but with hand gestures. I raised my hands parallel to each other (flat and with my palm facing downwards). I kept my left hand static but raised my right hand when I said that the birth rate increased. I then lowered it back to the level of the left hand when I mentioned that the birth rate decreased again.

“How about predators, pathogens, and parasites, what do they affect?” I asked. They were quick to reply that they affect the death rate, and were also confident when I asked them to vote if the connection was "same" or "opposite". Again, I asked what affected the number of predators, parasites, and pathogens. Some students suggested that the population size would affect the number – the larger the population, the larger the number of predators, etc. But others didn't perceive this immediately. I gave them the example of the Iberian lynx and its rabbit prey, "In the past, when the rabbit population was higher in Iberia, do you think the lynx population was also higher, the same as now, or lower?" I had them vote by raising their hands. "The lynx population was higher because there were more nutrients per lynx. Then a disease killed most of the rabbits in Iberia, what do you think happened to the lynx population? It decreased, stayed the same, or increased?" I had them vote again.

I drew the connection between the stock and predators-pathogens-parasites and asked whether it should be marked as "same" or "opposite". With the circularity complete, I followed the same procedure – of making explicit the negative feedback loop that emerges – that I did with the previous loop.

Finally, we came to "weather extremity" to see how it differed. I asked students what affected the weather extremity, and they realised that nothing in the model did. To make the point explicit, I asked, "Does a rise in population size cause more, or less, extreme weather?" And they agreed that it didn't, so I asked, "What's the difference between the factors at the top of the model and weather extremity?"

A student suggested, "The weather doesn't depend on the population, but the others do". And here I gave the labels of density-dependent and density-independent.

Have students think with the whole model

At this point, it was time to have students think about the whole model. Typically, I'd ask them to either self-explain the model individually or take turns with peer explanation. Then, I'd ask them "What if?" questions.

The first question I asked was to predict the population size over time on a sketch graph. I had students predict in pencil before adding a permanent version in pen (Figure 23e).

Finally, here are some examples of questions that I've used to have the students think about the whole model:

- What if the only predator in a food chain went extinct?
- What if, on scrubland near a village, the locals left food for feral cats (predators) to consume?
- What if, on private land, predators were excluded and herbivores were given surplus food?

I may have students discuss these questions in pairs, before discussing the answers as a whole class. If time is available, I may also ask them to write an answer for me to read. In both cases, I would expect students to attempt mechanistic answers (how the parts interact), and holistic answers (how the whole system is affected). I'll elaborate on these types of answers in Chapter 4.

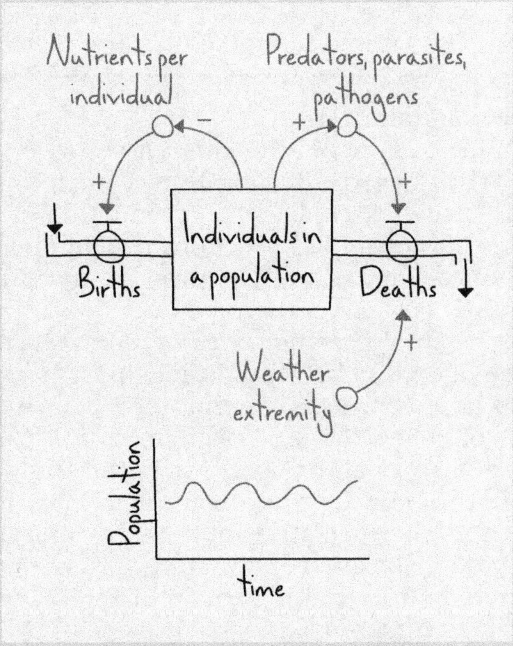

Figure 23e: The completed stock and flow diagram I co-constructed with students plus a sketch graph I asked students to draw.

Example Box 8

Building a model with students: end product enzyme inhibition

The conventional diagram

This lesson, with my 16-year-old students, was about enzyme inhibition and how cells exploit negative feedback to regulate the production of components. The usual example is the production of the amino acid isoleucine from the amino acid threonine. The diagram in Figure 24 shows the typical diagram of the process, in which a metabolic pathway – consisting of several enzymes – modifies precursors in sequence until the final product is made. To prevent the runaway production of isoleucine in bacteria, isoleucine acts as an inhibitor of the first enzyme in this process. Therefore, when its levels are high, it prevents more of its production, when levels are low, the inhibition is low, and production begins again. It is the first enzyme that is inhibited because threonine is a useful amino acid, whereas the others in the sequence (the intermediates) are not. If a different enzyme were inhibited then, you'd see an accumulation of useless intermediates. I wanted my students to see this version of the diagram as it's what they're likely to see in textbooks.

Generalising to a stock and flow model

This example is useful because it shows a diagram teachers are probably used to employing in the classroom. However, the diagram doesn't make clear it's dealing with stocks, flows, and system dynamics. It could

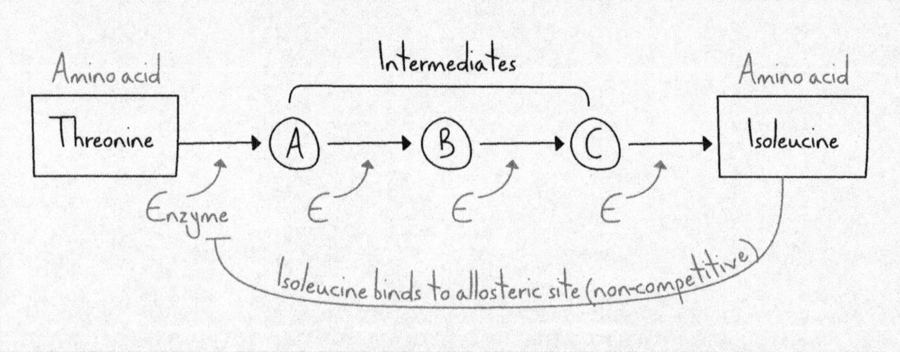

Figure 24: A conventional diagram showing feedback inhibition.

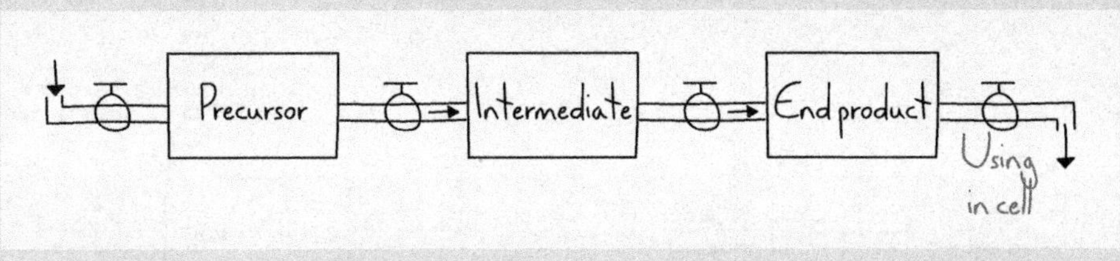

Figure 25: The stock and flow structure that I give to students to co-construct the mechanism of feedback inhibition.

be read as "step one leads to step two, etc". Another problem is that variation is harder to generate in this diagram as the relationships are not clear either. So, after explaining the concept with the conventional diagram (Figure 24), I provided them with a generalisable three-stock model without any variables of connectors (Figure 25).

With a copy of the stocks and flows, I then asked the students to add the variables and connections from what they'd understood from the conventional diagram. After giving the students time to work on this in pairs, we discussed it as a class before settling on the model shown in Figure 26. You may think that the diagram is not so different from the conventional one shown in Figure 24. However, if I'd asked the students to do the same with the conventional diagram, they'd have had to grapple with both the concept and how to represent it with novel symbols. With the stock and flow symbols they already knew, they could focus their thinking on the relationships within the system. Therefore, this example also shows how students can contribute to partial models – by thinking hard about the concept – precisely because they understand the symbols.

With the model completed, I could add variation, using "What if?" questions. I asked, "What if the bacterium had a mutation in the gene for the first enzyme of the pathway, which made the inhibition 50% less efficient?" Again I allowed the students time in pairs to mentally simulate the model, before discussing their answers as a class.

Contrasting concepts via two stock and flow models

Finally, in this lesson, I also contrasted the feedback inhibition model with the use of statins. These are inhibitors of an enzyme in the metabolic pathway that produces cholesterol in the body. The difference is that there is no feedback loop between the enzyme and the medication. For the inhibition to continue you simply need to keep taking statins. This contrast helps highlight the self-regulatory nature of end-product inhibition. My students didn't know this system, so it was an example of me explaining the system to the students, drawing the diagram, and then asking what the difference is between the models (Figure 26).

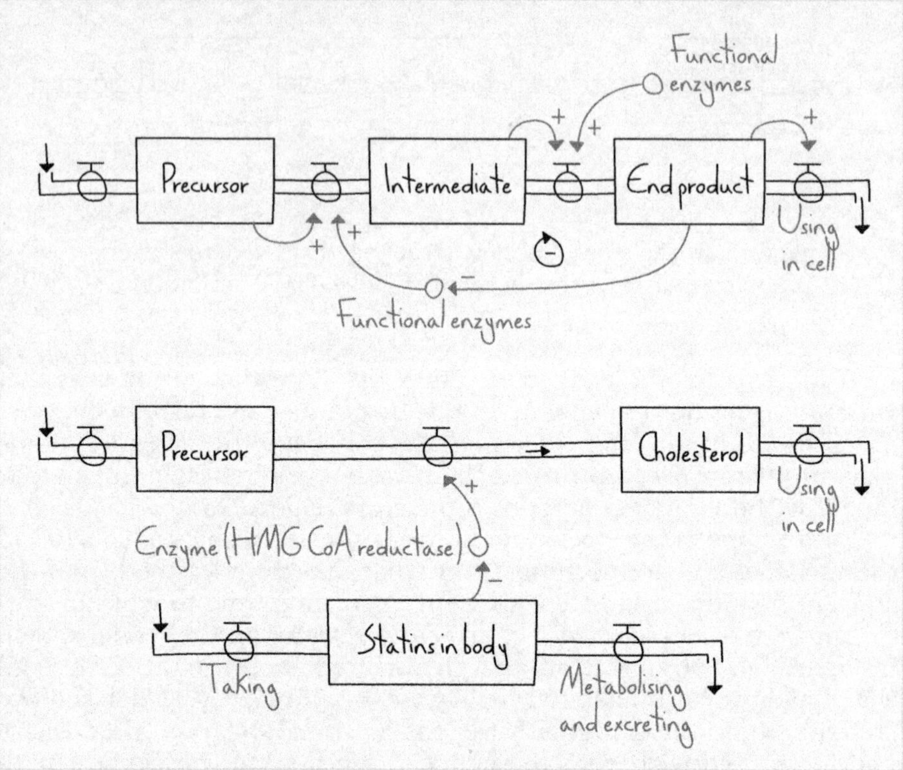

Figure 26: The completed stock and flow model of feedback inhibition, and another model showing inhibition (without feedback) of cholesterol production.

Model design is lesson planning, and the lesson is a conversation exploring the model

Throughout this chapter, I've conveyed that stock and flow diagrams have benefits for biology students. Here's a summary:

- They speak the language of systems, whereas words and other diagrams don't.
- They allow us to clearly share our distinctions with students and colleagues.
- A single diagram offers many explanations. It invites the interpreter to generate variation and follow its ramifications because these are system dynamics models, not static flow diagrams.
- Designing a model forces the teacher to think about the "object of learning". The design will include the key aspects that you want students to perceive, and those aspects should be readily variable.
- By embedding stock and flow models, the diagrammatic format doesn't vary when you teach different topics. This lowers the cognitive load relative to when both format and content vary – allowing students to focus on understanding the content itself.

They bring together, therefore, systems theory and variation theory in a manner that promotes classroom conversation. Models are often supported by images, videos, graphs, and iconic diagrams. But, when I design a model for a lesson, I know that I've got the central structure from which to begin provoking students and responding to their thoughts.

I often ask others for their opinion on a model, but if you do this, be careful. Many people like to dispense their knowledge into models. The suggestions I receive are often to add to the model – to make it more complex – rather than omit or simplify. While some content has to be included, the art of modelling is knowing what to omit. So to provide something coherent, cognitively tractable, and useful for inferring how the world will behave. Models are not so much about their parts but how they emerge as a whole for a person.

Nevertheless, feedback from colleagues often uncovers inconsistencies that I hadn't spotted or not understood well enough myself. This is another benefit of stock and flow models. I can share them with colleagues, and they can immediately see my intentions – the distinctions and relations I want my students to discern. When teachers do this by other means, such as slide decks, this is much harder to determine.

This takes us to the next chapter in which we begin to explore the recursive teaching model with respect to the students' active role. As we're about to move into a new domain of the model, I've added the image again (Figure 27).

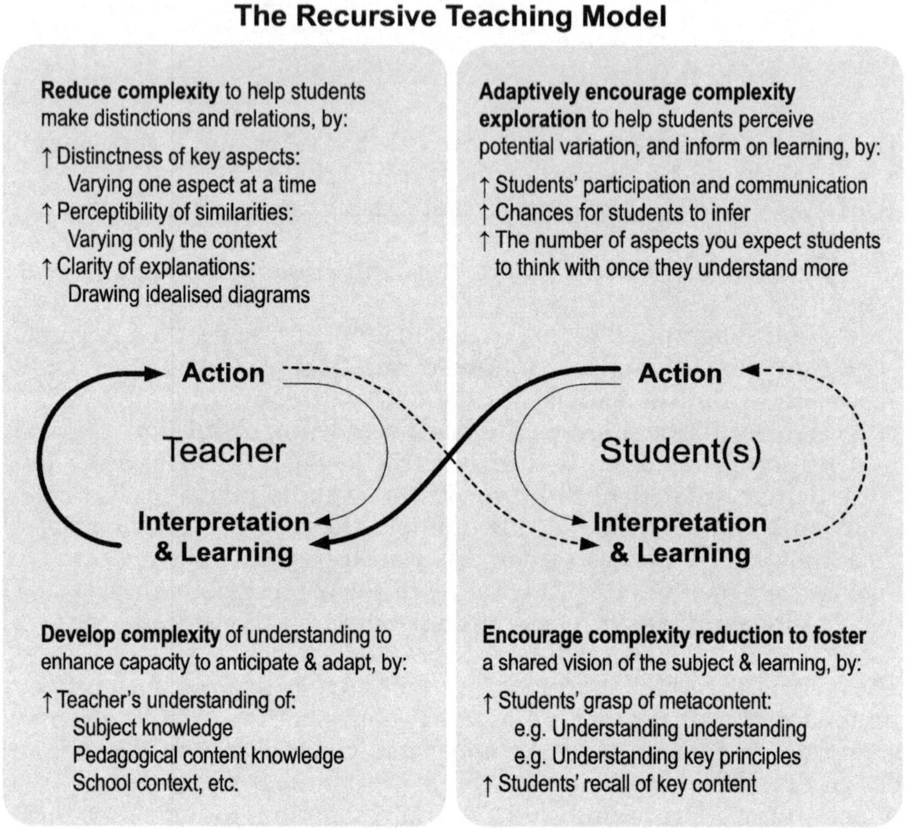

Figure 27 (repeated from Figure 2): The recursive teaching model.

4.
TO SEE CONTENT IN A SIMILAR WAY, TEACHERS CAN SHARE METACONTENT WITH STUDENTS

It's time to shift our focus. The last couple of chapters have focused on how we, as teachers, can reduce the complexity of the concepts we teach. In this chapter, I'll stick to the theme of reducing complexity, but this time the emphasis is on helping students do it for themselves. There are three principal ideas I want to discuss: sharing domain-specific principles with students, helping them gain an understanding of understanding, and finally, helping them remember key content. Before we explore these, however, we need to address what I mean by students reducing complexity by themselves. Let me introduce you to something that I call metacontent.

Metacontent makes the teacher's assumptions clearer

Key idea:
Sharing our fundamental distinctions with students helps them reduce the possible variety of interpretations of our subject.

Sometimes I have experienced – as a student myself – biology courses that felt one-dimensional. There was a path that involved the collecting of facts along the way. I suppose understanding was seen either as a summation of knowledge tokens or implicitly left to the learner to construct alone.

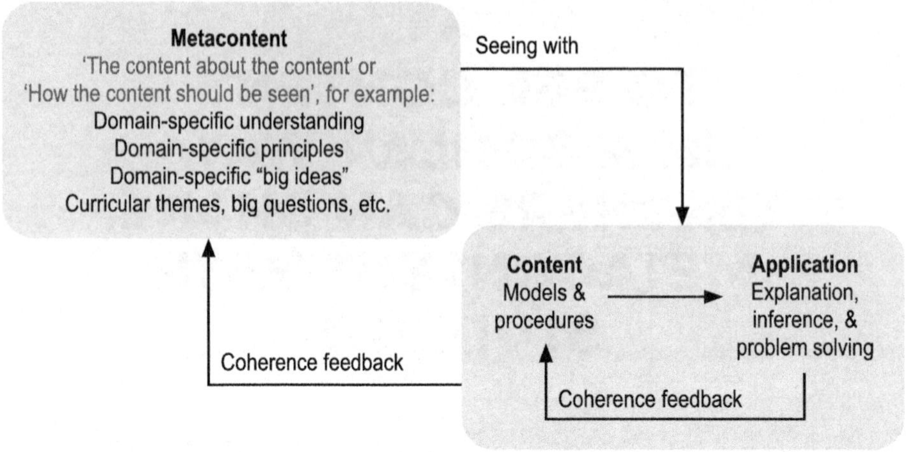

Figure 28: A two-cycle model that shows the distinction and relation between the content and metacontent of a curriculum.

More recently, major institutions of science education have acted to organise curricula to help students see structure among the content. There are, for example, the Big Ideas of Harlen et al. (2010; 2015), and the Royal Society of Biology's Big Questions (RSB 2021). Equally, the International Baccalaureate's 2023 biology syllabus is organised into four themes. In *Biology Made Real*, I also suggested another organising concept called "direction". This represented the ideas students would work on throughout a course, such as evolutionary thinking.

What these have in common is the distinction between two types of content: 1. Content, and 2. Metacontent: a special type of content that informs students about the content (Figure 28). Metacontent is the content about the content or, in other words, the content that makes explicit "how the content of the course should be seen".

But what is metacontent exactly? Think about it this way. Seen from information theory (Shannon 1948) in telecommunications between machines, redundancy was to be avoided. The less repetitive the message was, the better. Gregory Bateson, however, knew that communication between humans was different: "The essence and raison d'etre of communication is the creation of redundancy, meaning, pattern, predictability, information, and/or the reduction of the random by 'restraint'." (1972, 110). For Bateson, it was the redundancy of human communication – its repetitiveness – that allowed people to perceive patterns. By the same pattern appearing in several communicative events, it becomes meaningful, and something to take note of (Harries-Jones 2016).

The trouble with the courses I had experienced as a student was a lack of redundancy. Each lesson appeared to bring new information with scant repetition or redundancy, which would have allowed me to perceive any implicit patterns.

The theme of this chapter is helping students reduce the complexity of what they themselves interpret. So, how does metacontent help? Bateson's use of the word "restraint" (or constraint) is useful here, so let me repeat the quote: "The essence and raison d'etre of communication is the creation of redundancy, meaning, pattern, predictability, information, and/or the reduction of the random by 'restraint'." (1972, 110). Metacontent helps restrain students to fewer ways of interpreting the content of the course. By making metacontent explicit, the teacher shares how the content should be perceived (at least in a way that's compatible with the teacher's perception). Metacontent therefore reduces the variety of ways of seeing the course content.

Bateson saw ways of being and seeing as arising from an ecology of ideas (1972). Bateson would call himself a cyberneticist, but he had studied biology at Cambridge and subsequently revolutionised the field of anthropology with his, then-wife Margaret Mead (Chaney 2017). At the time, perspectives in anthropology were based on seeking an objective truth about a culture from the outside. Bateson shifted perspectives in the opposite direction. He saw that participating in a culture was the only way to acquire viable knowledge about it (Glasersfeld 2007). An ecology of ideas isn't fully understandable from the outside without insight into the interacting system of concepts a person, or a culture, holds.

This is easily perceived when observing another teacher of a different specialism, and who is halfway through a two-year course. As you observe, many things go straight over your head. The content, the questions, yes, but also the actions and reactions of the class. Only the members of the system – those with a shared ecology of ideas – compatibly understand what's happening.

Isn't this, at least, one purpose of teaching our subjects in schools? Inviting students into an ecology of ideas? Helping them see how a biologist sees. Not just as spectators who take peculiar words as memorabilia to be uttered here and there. But to *see with* the ecosystem of concepts in some form or another. While studying biology is seen as learning about living systems, it can also be seen as an anthropology of biologists, with us (teachers) as their hosts. Through recursive interactions we don't simply teach content to our students, but a way of living through our subject. Such that students don't just learn biology, they learn biology teachers (Maturana 2011, 162). And this way of being is something our students may continue beyond our time together in the classroom.

This is where I see metacontent playing a role in curricular design and enactment. Metacontent acts as a frame for an ecology of ideas to develop. As discussed in the second chapter, all thought must stem from assumptions, or distinctions. Our students arrive with their own assumptions, distinctions, and ways of seeing. Metacontent invites students to see the course content through domain-specific assumptions shared by members of the subject guild.

I believe that bigger ideas are unlikely to be perceived by students experiencing a course taught from a content-only view. In *Biology Made Real* (Moore-Anderson 2023) I made the case for making biology meaningful from the student's perspective. Metacontent is the concept that I have come to perceive as the curricular means for explicitly helping students discern those bigger ideas and patterns.

It would be wrong, however, to say that metacontent is purely a holistic concept. Instead, I see metacontent and content as mutually dependent – mutually forming and mutually shaping. Like how the Earth shapes how life evolves, and life itself shapes how the Earth system evolves (Margulis 1998). And Winston Churchill's (1943) vision that, "We shape our buildings and afterwards our buildings shape us." Both content and metacontent feed into each other recursively. Therefore, I see content and metacontent comprising a two-cycle model (Figure 28).

The first cycle is that of content. The details of a course – the models and procedures we teach. This cycle involves the learning and application of content in the questions and tasks we give students. Upon application of the content, errors and incoherence generate feedback so that the student reconsiders their original understanding of the content.

However, this cycle sits within a second cycle: the metacontent. Metacontent informs students on how the content should be seen. It encourages students to search for the same patterns they've seen before. This recursive process encourages students to perform complexity reduction for themselves. And, in circularity, the perception of many examples of metacontent – over many contexts and topics – feeds back to inform their understanding of metacontent itself. Therefore, the two cycles feed into each other positively. The more they grasp the metacontent the more students will see the patterns in the content, which allows them to access the content better. This, in turn, gives them more practice thinking with the metacontent, by generalising it over new contexts and examples.

In this sense, metacontent doesn't just help students reduce complexity, it can become a major goal of the course itself. Ultimately, when students have finished formal education in our subject, we must ask what will persist. We all intuitively know that forgetting occurs. As time passes the details begin to fade. What remains of all our mutual efforts as students embark on life outside the classroom? I propose that well-planned metacontent can form part of a web of an ecology of ideas that persists.

For the classroom biology teacher, I believe it could help solve another problem. The two loops proceed at a different pace. The content cycle is fast, involving many cycles per lesson before we move on to the next topic. Yet, the metacontent loop cycles more slowly and always revisits what came before.

When faced with the inevitable variation in our students' outcomes in our classroom, a content-only model can seem unjust. As some students speed ahead in the content loop, others advance more slowly. Lower attainers may access the content at a more superficial level. As we pass from topic to topic, not all students appear to learn a topic to the depth we'd like. The gap widens as the system demands we keep moving through the curriculum. The school system – by its very structure of timed courses and age-grouping – inevitably produces disparities (Allen et al. 2021). But we can choose the emphasis on the content so that all students can find the meaning of deeper ideas. When explicitly adding metacontent all students could advance towards a deeper understanding of the metacontent itself. All students get the opportunity to revisit fundamental ideas that they can take with them beyond the classroom.

In the following sections, I'll explore two types of metacontent. The first is a set of principles – a teacher's fundamental distinctions – to be seen and applied throughout the topics of a course. The second is understanding what understanding is in biology.

Domain-specific principles are examples of metacontent

Key idea:
Sharing domain-specific principles with students helps them to interpret content in a similar way to us.

Firstly, let me distinguish between domain-specific principles and the big ideas concept (Harlen et al. 2010; 2015). I interpret big ideas to be like an ecology of ideas. For biology Harlen et al. posit four:

- Organisms are organised on a cellular basis and have a finite life span.
- Organisms require a supply of energy and materials for which they often depend.
- Genetic information is passed down from one generation of organisms to another.
- The diversity of organisms, living and extinct, is the result of evolution.

These were chosen because they "have explanatory power in relation to a large number of objects ..., provide a basis for understanding issues ..., lead to enjoyment and satisfaction ..., [and] have cultural significance" (2015, 14). These are worthy goals, chosen by a large group of experts in biology and education. They make explicit to teachers and curriculum designers the important ideas shared among biologists. And yet, they aren't single concepts or ideas – they're complexes of many aspects. Understanding these big ideas will take time and students will need to discern and relate many concepts into a larger system of interconnected ideas. The big ideas concept is a type of final purpose – teleological – metacontent. It marks end goals for teachers to link to and talk about.

My vision of principles is that they're a type of metacontent that is a generalisable rule that can be used to interpret curricular content. This contrasts with big ideas because principles are accessible and utilisable throughout a course. Principles make explicit, at the beginning of a course, some of the important assumptions with which the teacher is discussing the content they teach. In this sense, they are a set of distinctions the teacher considers fundamental. They become metacontent by being continually, and explicitly, shared with students.

Before I discuss the idea any more, let me show you the principles I have recently been using in my biology courses for students aged 14–18:

Second Law of Thermodynamics

- Things in the universe tend towards disorder – *to disintegrate, dissipate, diffuse, etc.*

Homeostasis Principle
- Stable systems maintain key variables within limits.

Law of Requisite Variety
- Systems can maintain stability if: The variety of their responses (or options) matches the variety of situations they encounter.

Variation & Selection Principle
- Systems adapt by having a variety of options and discarding unstable ones.

Circular Causality Principles
- Negative feedback loops counteract changes – *and drive stability.*
- Positive feedback loops intensify changes – *and drive state change.*

For this idea, I was influenced by Heylighen (1992) who had curated a list of cybernetic principles. He describes his selection as following three main criteria:
1. They must be primitive, so to be the beginning of a system of thought.
2. They must be simple, enough to be almost semi, or even self-evident.
3. They must have universal applicability within a domain.

Heylighen's first criterion is key to discerning the difference between big ideas and principles as metacontent. While big ideas are an end goal, principles act as "the beginning of a system of thought". They are a direct invitation to see the biological content through the principles, and therefore with the teacher's assumptions. And yet, as with Heylighen's third criterion, they are universally applicable. They can be discussed recursively during a biology course, no matter the topic, which enables students to see common patterns. They increase Bateson's redundancy, and so help students take part in complexity reduction.

When I chose my list of principles, I thought about the ideas I discussed most often in my courses, and which were most useful for students to know. If a principle isn't discussed much, it may be nice to know but not worth making a listed principle. In the process, I quickly learnt two things: don't have too many principles and invest time writing the descriptions in concise and accessible language.

What do I recommend in general? Introducing principles into a course is not easy. Deep subject knowledge, plus strong pedagogical content knowledge are both required. Metacontent is at its most powerful when consistently used by all teachers of a department. Therefore, I recommend that people consider my principles part of a whole-department conversation about their curricular vision. I recommend implementing metacontent as part of something larger than a single course. I encourage curricular designers to think about what principles fit their courses.

Why did I choose the five principles I did? Because I want my students to see my biology courses through the lens of adaptation – biological systems pursuing stability in a world of possibilities and constraints. What is an adaptation? Bateson defines it this way (1979, 227): "A feature of an organism whereby it seemingly fits better into its environment and way of life." And what does it mean to adapt? "The process of achieving that fit."

> "One system is within the individual and is called learning; the other is immanent in heredity and is populations and is called evolution. One is a matter of the single life-time; the other is a matter of multiple generations of many individuals." (1979, 149).

This is a distinction between genetic adaptation and somatic adaptation. For the individual, "flexibility and survival will be favoured by any change tending to keep variables floating in the middle of their range." (156). This reflects the homeostasis principle, yet the fact that living is a continuous act of adapting is often left implicit in biology courses. An organism must continually compensate for disturbances to ensure it persists – to ensure its identity as a living system is maintained.

Instead, biology courses tend to group explicitly circular phenomena, such as blood sugar regulation and other hormonal systems into a single topic called "homeostasis". When I say explicitly circular, it's because the circularity is specified as content that students should learn. Other circularities are left implicit suggesting that circularity and homeostasis are phenomena of just a few specific examples. This is an unviable distinction, in my mind.

Bateson (1979) gave the example of acclimation to high altitude and low oxygen concentration. "If a man goes up from sea level to 12,000 feet in the mountains, he will, unless he is in very good condition, begin to pant, and his heart will start to race." (155). This is somatic adaptation via feedback loops. The level of oxygen in the blood decreases, which causes the breathing rate and heart rate to increase so that the oxygen level returns to acceptable levels. Yet,

> "It would be an extravagant waste of flexibility to use panting and tachycardia as the ongoing adjustment to mountain atmosphere. What is required is somatic change which should be less reversible because we are now considering, not temporary emergency, but ongoing and lasting conditions." (155).

What Bateson means by "flexibility" is that while panting and elevated heart rates do the job of homeostasis, they also reduce the person's ability to adapt. If, for example, they had to run from a charging herd, they'd struggle. So, the organism doesn't just adapt to maintain key variables, such as oxygen in the blood, but also adapts to maintain adaptability – to maintain a variety of options – or as Bateson said, to maintain flexibility.

Therefore, there are shorter and longer feedback loops in somatic adaptation that help to maintain the stability of the organism.

> "The man's heart will undergo changes, his blood will come to contain more hemoglobin, his rib cage and respiratory habits will shift, and so on." (155).

Ultimately, organisms aren't simply adapted or not. Adaptation is an invariant process of being alive. "If adaptation were not an invariant, it would stop, and the organism would disintegrate, die." (Maturana 1987, 77).

To study biology then, is to study homeostasis and adaptation. It's to study systems persisting and maintaining an identity. As such, body temperature regulation is as much an example of homeostasis as the behaviour of the immune system – a homeostatic system for maintaining the identity of the organism (Varela 1991). The respiratory and vascular systems act to maintain optimum oxygen and carbon dioxide levels. Eyes focus and the pupils dilate in acclimation to changing visuals. Plants open and close their stomata as they conform to water availability. They invest in larger roots when minerals are in short supply and in vertical growth when shaded by others. They develop and adapt according to how they experience their environment. Ultimately, individuals that act in ways that don't maintain their stability, don't fit their environment and are eliminated by natural selection (Bateson 1972).

The principles I have chosen are to share this view of biology with my students. To share that there is more to biology than a list of content about "how your body works", or "the parts of plants". But, I imagine, you're probably wondering how I refer to principles in my lessons – how I discuss them, and with what content. I'll elaborate more on this in Example Box 9 and 10. However, to give a brief answer. During most lessons, amid a discussion, I'll project the list of principles and ask students which apply to what we're deliberating. The key isn't for students to answer correctly all the time, but to discuss them often. Understanding of the principles comes with time. The ideas begin as abstractions and only gain concreteness with every new example.

Example Box 9

Introducing systems principles to students

Figure 29: A diagram I have drawn for students to make the distinction between living and nonliving systems.

I like to introduce the principles early in my courses. Students must first discern them before I can embed the principles as examples seen over different topics. Here I'll show you an example of how I recently introduced the second law of thermodynamics, the homeostasis principle, and the law of requisite variety to 14-year-old students.

I began by drawing an image of a living and dead tree (Figure 29). "All things being equal" I told the students, "except that one is living and the other dead. What difference would it make over a hundred years?"

Intuitively they knew that the dead tree would decompose while the living tree would remain identifiable. This is my introduction to the homeostasis principle – system stability. What was it, in this case, that would remain stable if its structure is continually changing? The *organisation* of the tree (Maturana 1987).

Now we had the context of the lesson in focus, and it was time to dig deeper. "What causes the difference? Why do dead organisms degrade, diffuse, and disintegrate?"

Instead of taking answers, I gave my example – a plate. Plates break over time, but they don't fix themselves. If you watched a video of a plate breaking in reverse, with all its shards returning to form a perfect plate, you'd know something was amiss. The universe doesn't function that way, this is the "arrow of time" of the second law of thermodynamics, "one of the all-time great laws of science, for it illuminates why anything ... happens at all" (Atkins 2007, vi).

To show this, I drew a plate (Figure 30) and asked the students, "What will happen to the plate over time?"

I like this question. It's a question of whether it'll stay the same or change. Some students said that it would stay the same, others argued that we continually fix them. "But," I said, "what if no one ever fixes the plate, what is its eventual fate, allowing for as long as it takes?"

It'd break, of course. I drew the next plate. This was now the crucial point in discerning the concept. I provoked them again, "So, what's the fate of this broken plate? You've got two choices, either it'll mend itself or break even more."

Now they thought I was mad. They'd experienced the world long enough to know that plates don't fix themselves. But I wanted them to see a reason for it. "It's actually possible for a plate to reform itself. If the parts came together in just the right way, with the perfect orientation, temperature, and pressure. If all the conditions came together, it could come back together. It could... but what's the probability of it happening?"

Negligible, so much so, you may as well say that it'd never happen. But we needed a difference that made a difference, "So what are the probabilities of it breaking even more? The broken plate can change in many ways, how many result in it reforming a whole plate and how many ways could the plate break even more?"

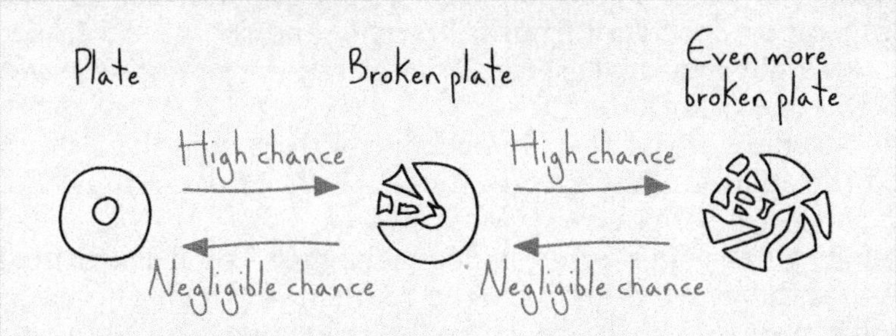

Figure 30: A diagram I have drawn for students to teach the second law of thermodynamics (copied from Moore-Anderson 2023).

There are almost endless ways for it to break even more, and so the odds are overwhelmingly in favour of it breaking. This was the aspect I wanted students to discern – a probability view of the second law of thermodynamics. After the students and I seemed to have come to a similar understanding of the plate's fate, I generalised the concept to the school buildings. "What would happen if everyone abandoned the school buildings and never returned?"

They all agreed that it would slide into disrepair, like a car, or their clothes, which, over time, disintegrate. "Right then, how is it that the school building persists?"

The students agreed that it was due to maintenance. As the building degrades, the energy and materials are mustered to repair it – tables and chairs are replaced, and rusting fences are repainted. I told the students that this was similar to how biological systems managed to maintain stability. Organisms are a continual process of maintenance – a continual process of resisting the second law of thermodynamics.

It was time to move on to the final principle – the law of requisite variety. I drew the circle (Figure 31) and said that it represented an organism attempting to maintain stability. I then drew the first arrow extending from the environment representing a change. I mentioned that the organism adjusted to the change and therefore remained stable. But what if the change was large, and the organism couldn't adjust? Death, the students agreed.

I drew the next arrow and labelled it: "can't adjust". Here I was provoking the students to discern the concept of the capacity of an organism to maintain homeostasis, which is not infinite. There are limits to the flexibility of an organism. Next, I told them the name of the law of requisite variety. This needed attention because students don't often know the term "requisite", and "variety" in this context is rather abstract. I gave some synonyms for variety, "responses", or "options" and a synonym for requisite, "having enough". Having enough responses to match the different situations that you encounter. The capacity to counter a change in the environment and remain stable.

Next, I gave them a concrete example of thermoregulation. I drew the temperature spectrum from cold to hot and showed an inner range where we could survive. I asked, "What variety of responses do we have when we get too hot or cold?"

This was drawing on their knowledge of their own lived experience. I added the answers they gave to the diagram. Easy enough. "So, what would happen if we got even hotter?"

"Death," an easy answer for biology students – their favourite. In this case, I told them, we don't have the requisite variety. The interesting question came next, "If that's right, why haven't we evolved the requisite variety (of responses) to live in incredibly hot or cold environments?"

The students found this somewhat intuitive but couldn't express it well. They said things like "we don't need it". I helped them by suggesting that "we don't need it" means that it was unlikely that we'd ever be in a situation like that. They were right, but I kept pushing by asking why we didn't evolve it anyway, just in case. The students found this more difficult. So I switched to a better-known example: cars.

I asked students about the variety of responses that cars had to keep them alive in the event of a crash. Seat belts, airbags, and crumple zones were examples they gave. Why didn't a car have the requisite variety to keep someone alive in a high-speed crash? I made clear that this example was analogous to the previous one, which exemplified that humans didn't have the requisite variety to remain stable in extreme environments. The answer was, of course, that it was too expensive. To equip a car with extra variety for such an event would come at an

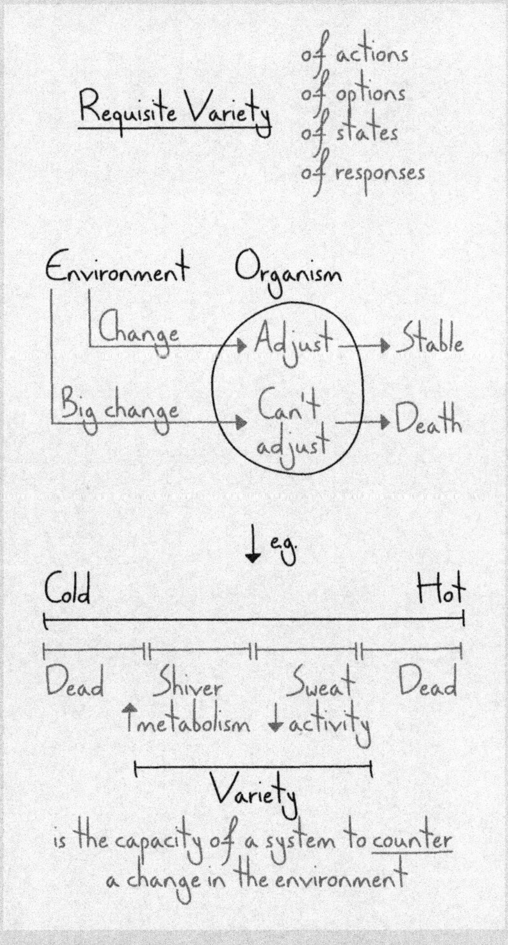

Figure 31: A diagram I have drawn to teach students about the law of requisite variety.

expense, and people would feel like it's not worth it. They considered it highly unlikely that they'd ever be in such a situation. The same is true in organisms then. "Variety is expensive," I told them, "but, in evolution, it's expensive in terms of energy". If an organism invested in something that wasn't likely to help it during its life, it had a disadvantage compared to other organisms that invested that extra energy in growth and reproduction.

For the rest of the lesson, I discussed other examples of requisite variety. My students related well to the example of a variety of responses we had as a school to maintain learning levels, such as house points, prizes, commendations, verbal warnings, sanctions, detentions, and the like.

Example Box 10

The principles of systems in the curriculum

Second law of thermodynamics

This is a ubiquitous concept in biology but is often left implicit. I like to remind students of it whenever I can, as it gives meaning to the other principles. It appears whenever I discuss diffusion because nature abhors a gradient. This is especially true for gas exchange in the lungs, where equilibrium signals death. Organisms must act to maintain their gradients despite the second law diffusing them away. The natural degradation of molecules and cells – due to the second law – is the context I use for teaching need for regeneration via stem cells. I also discuss photosynthesis as the process that temporarily captures energy on its journey to dissipation into space. Equally, I discuss why the heat generated during cell respiration isn't "reusable" as an energy source. While the first law states that the quantity of energy remains the same, the second law states that its quality reduces over time.

Homeostasis principle

I like to have students identify the variable(s) that are being maintained in the systems we're studying. My goal is to have them think in terms of the whole organism and what variables are essential to maintaining its stability. This is something they often find difficult, in my experience. For example, when it comes to ventilation of the lungs, students often say that the essential variable is air in the lungs, rather than oxygen in the blood. Or, with thermoregulation, some suggest that the essential variable is the ambient temperature. In other words, they seem to suggest that homeostasis is an attempt to control aspects external to the organism, rather than internal ones. Challenging these assumptions helps students understand the autonomy of the organism. For many topics in high school biology, referring to the maintenance of cell respiration rates is common, and conceptually easy for students. The glucagon system can be seen this way, while the insulin system can be seen as maintaining the integrity of the organism (preventing oxidative damage). The immune system can be seen as maintaining the identity of the organism by only permitting certain antigens. Plants, for example, act to maintain the water levels (or water potential) of their tissues by opening and closing stomata. Ecosystems also have essential variables – the flow of energy and matter – that must be maintained lest the system shift into an alternative state.

The circular causality principle
Understanding homeostasis is dependent on understanding circular causality. Therefore, I discuss this often when producing stock and flow models. When a loop arises (see the examples in the appendix), I ask students if it is an example of positive, or negative feedback. Students take a while to understand circular causality. One way I help them is by gesturing a variable as I narrate the loop. Let's say we're discussing thermoregulation and the sweating system. I'll hold out my left hand (palm facing downwards) and say that this represents the heat in the body. I then put my right hand next to it and begin raising it while keeping my left hand in its original position. As I raise it, I say that the body is warming up due to carrying out exercise. Then I stop raising my right hand and say that the body sweats. I begin lowering my right hand back to the original position with my left hand and narrate that the body temperature drops back to normal. And I say, "So, the increase in body temperature, eventually caused a decrease in the body temperature. Is this a negative or positive feedback loop?"

Variation and selection principle
This principle arises whenever I ask students why something evolved as it is today. Specifically, I ask about the traits we study, for example, intestinal microvilli or capillary thickness. Organisms and populations offer variety, selection discards unviable forms that aren't compatible with survival and reproduction (Varela et al. 2016, 195). So, it's not ideal to ask students why something has evolved to be as it is. Instead, we have to ask why the alternatives didn't make it. This is a negative explanation (Bateson 1972), and I'll discuss exactly how I formulate these questions in the next chapter.

There are two types of variation (Stoltzfus 2021). One is standing variation, like a buffet, in which the variety of meals is there at the same time for you to select from. This is the common way of discussing variation and selection in biology courses. I may ask, for example, "If there is a population with variation in the quantity of microvilli, why don't we see those with fewer microvilli?" We can also discuss the idea within organisms. For example, between sperm cells during copulation or somatic selection of plasma cells within the adaptive immune system.

Another type is the variation that appears sequentially, like those buffets in sushi restaurants with conveyor belts that bring one plate at a time. This is seen, for example, with the sequential selection of egg cells, and embryos. Typically only one enters the menstrual cycle at a time, but many aren't viable and die. You can see it with ecosystems also. These can evolve to a stable state in a particular place and persist until disturbed and tipped into an alternative state (Lenton et al. 2021). I also talk to students about how a protein will sequentially go through a variety of configurations during its folding process until it hits upon a stable form. Just like your seating plans – unviable configurations are discarded until you find one that works.

Law of requisite variety

Finally, as the law of requisite variety may be less familiar to teachers, I've written more examples of where it can be discussed. Ashby (1956) thought of it in terms of the ability to maintain the stability of essential variables despite changes and disturbances coming from the environment. It's the ability to regulate, or block, this "flow of variety" of changes and perturbations. He suggested that if the people in a room noticed that it was getting hotter outside then the air conditioner had failed in blocking the flow of variety (changes) from the environment. A good conditioner would maintain the temperature of the room no matter the changes outside. Ashby saw this as analogous to the human body's attempts at shielding the vital organs from the variety of temperatures experienced by the skin.

Ashby also distinguished between two ways of blocking the flow of variety. One is active and consists of "skilled counter-action" by obtaining information and acting on it. Like "the fencer, in some deadly duel, who wears no armour and who trusts to his skill in parrying." (201). At the other extreme of the spectrum is the passive. For this example, Ashby suggested the "tortoise's shell, which reduces a variety of impacts, blows, bites, etc. to a negligible disturbance of the sensitive tissues within. In the same class are the tree's bark, the seal's coat of blubber, and the human skull." (201). Here's some example contexts where I've discussed it with students:

- Immune system. The adaptive system of vertebrates vastly increases the organisms' variety by producing a huge variety of unique B lymphocytes. Each produces its own unique antibodies. This gives vertebrates the flexibility to confront any pathogen that may come their way during their lifetime.
- Kidney. If a species selectively removed substances, they would need a protein for each one. In such a scenario, if a species dispersed into a new ecosystem and consumed something new, they may not be able to excrete any new toxins from their bodies. Instead, ultrafiltration filters all small molecules and reabsorbs what the species requires back. Therefore, ultrafiltration gives an almost infinite variety of options for excreting small molecules – affording the organism vast ecological flexibility.
- Respiratory system. Other species manage to climb to higher altitudes than us, such as bar-headed geese who can fly over the Himalayas. Birds have a circular respiratory system that allows them to avoid mixing older air with fresh air. By better maintaining concentration gradients in their alveoli, they can assume a larger variety of states than mammals with regard to obtaining oxygen for fuelling activity. On the other hand, students have often asked me why we can't

breathe 100% oxygen. To survive among oxygen in normal conditions we have to fill the body with antioxidants, such as vitamin C and glutathione. We can't breathe 100% oxygen because we don't have the requisite variety (of antioxidant types and concentrations).

- Vascular system. The vascular system is highly plastic. In training for a marathon, for example, haemoglobin levels increase, capillary density increases in muscles, and the heart grows larger. Each of these increases the person's variety of possible states. On the other hand, people suffering from a congenital disorder – such as sickle cell disease or beta thalassemia – have a reduced ability to supply oxygen due to abnormalities in their red blood cells. This reduces their variety of possible states, and therefore, flexibility when it comes to intense activity.
- Biodiversity. Biodiversity can be categorised into three types: ecosystem variety (different ecosystem types), community variety (different species), and genetic variety (different alleles in a population). The planet requires a variety of ecosystem types to maintain energy and matter flows. The ecosystem as a whole depends on a variety of functions (species) to maintain the same. Species depend on genetic variety to evade extinction.
- Genome size. The number of genes (or genome size) could be used as a rough proxy of variety – the variety of possible states an organism can assume. For example, parasites tend to have smaller genomes. As they often live within the homeostatically controlled environments inside organisms, there is less need for them to be able to control certain variables. There is, therefore, a lower requisite variety and parasites can evolve to have fewer genes. Due to the complexity of multicellular organisms – requiring a variety of cell types – their genomes are larger than unicellular organisms.

Understanding understanding is an example of metacontent

Key idea:
Sharing with students what we see as a good understanding is key to helping them achieve just that.

The motive for this idea came from noticing that students were rarely informed about what we expected of them or what type of understanding we valued. The purpose of the taxonomy of understanding (Figure 32) is precisely to bring forth a mutual understanding of what is expected. Therefore, when facing new content and questions, students can reduce the complexity – the variety – of possible ways of interpreting what they should understand and how they should answer.

Helping students understand understanding, contrasts with a trend I sometimes see in schools – the use of "success criteria". These are often recipes for carrying out a task (e.g. Clarke 2021). In such cases the criteria are designed to help students know what is expected of them, but only with the content of a single concept. Therefore, the process must be repeated for each new topic. It represents a *recurrent* teaching activity. In contrast, understanding understanding – as metacontent – indicates what understanding is to the teacher across all concepts and topics. As such, it becomes a central part of ongoing *recursive* conversations with students.

To be useful, I needed to define a spectrum of understanding specific to the biology classroom. Something practical enough that students could use it. This was the endeavour that culminated in the taxonomy of understanding biological systems that I published in *Biology Made Real* (Moore-Anderson 2023). I won't retrace my steps here but will move forward with a fresh perspective on the taxonomy.

At the heart of the taxonomy are two distinctions. The first is between describing and explaining. The second is between parts and whole. Let's begin with the first distinction by looking at the following sentences.

Stating a description includes sentences that look like this:
- X is Y.
- X has Y.
- X does Y.

Stating an explanation includes sentences that look like this:
- X causes Y to increase due to Z.
- When X increases, it pushes Y so that Z occurs.
- X contracts, which reduces Y, leading to Z.

It's often the case that we teach students mechanistic explanations – in lessons we answer questions such as "How does X work in this system?" or "How does *this* behaviour come about?" For example, we may teach how the heart works, or how breathing occurs. Generally, it's agreed that mechanisms involve explaining how the parts of a system interact in a process (Krickel 2024). They indicate how one step causatively leads to another, following this format: "If this and this happens, then the result is such and such" (Maturana & Verden-Zöller 2008, 14).

Looking back, you'll notice how the descriptive statements have a dyadic structure, whereas the explanatory sentences are triadic. There's a reason for this. Imagine if I told you: "Releasing sewage into rivers causes algal blooms." This has the dyadic form: Input → output. It feels like a descriptive overview that provides an outcome. It urges me to ask why as I wish for causes that link the input and output. Consider this alternative: "Releasing sewage increases the nutrient concentration in a river, which causes an algal bloom."

The mediating cause gives the triadic form: Input → cause → output (Foerster 2002), which feels more explanatory. There can be more than one mediator if we wish. Let's add another: "Releasing sewage increases the nutrient concentration in a river, which increases the growth rate of algae, resulting in an algal bloom."

While the statement has two mediators, we can still summarise it in the triadic form: Input → cause(s) → output. We now have two causal mechanisms, whether we accept one or the other will depend on the expectations of the curriculum. Here's an example of stating an explanation of inhalation that we'd expect in the classroom: "The diaphragm and internal intercostal muscles contract, which causes the thorax to increase in volume. This creates a lower air pressure in the lungs (compared to outside) and so causes air to move in."

Notice how I called it "stating" an explanation. This is because the student isn't so much *explaining*, as *repeating* a known explanation. There is a variety of one – it's restating *the* explanation. Students do need to learn canonical explanations, this is true. A higher level of explanation involves inferring how it could be different. This is *inferring an explanation* when asked, for example, "What if?".

Inferring an explanation of variation includes sentences that look like this:

- If the rate of X increases, Y will also increase so that Z.
- If X decreases, it will prevent Y, because of Z.
- Reducing X would raise Y, leading to a decrease in the capacity of Z.

By asking students to infer we can get a real view of how they think with a concept. This is because students alone have to select which critical aspects to hold in their focal awareness and infer how they interact. With the stating of explanations alone, we can never really know the extent of their understanding – it could simply be verbatim memorisation. Students aren't expected to select aspects from a variety of possibilities or think about how they interact as they vary. Here's a summary:

- **Description** – stating a system's components and their functions.
- **Stating an explanation** – stating how the system's usual causative steps bring about its usual performance.
- **Inferring an explanation** – inferring how a variation in a system changes the causative steps and performance.

This relates to the assumptions that I discussed in Chapter 2, especially assumptions 1 and 4. Here's a reminder (we'll return to all the assumptions again in the next chapter):

- **Assumption 1:** Understanding a system involves knowing an explanation of its parts and whole, plus their potential variation.
- **Assumption 4:** Meaning can't be transmitted, so respond to how students infer their own explanations from variation – not just how they restate a given explanation.

Before I discuss the distinction between the parts and the whole, let's have a look at the whole taxonomy in graphical format – an image I regularly share with students (Figure 32). Notice that there are two axes,

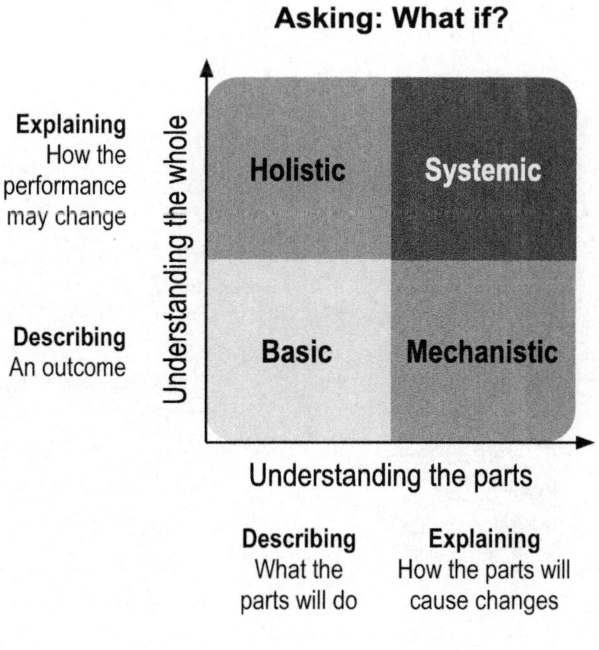

Figure 32: The taxonomy of understanding biological systems, explained in the text (adapted from Moore-Anderson 2023).

which represent the distinction between parts and whole. And on each axis, you can see the distinction between describing and explaining. The distinction between stating and inferring an explanation isn't seen on the axis because the taxonomy is designed to work with the "What if?" question.

It therefore encourages students to infer, rather than just restate. The axes are not intended to be an objective spectrum but as a pragmatic tool for judging our students' answers. In other words, we can listen to, or read, our students' answers and we'll find that there'll be sections that feel more descriptive and others that feel more explanatory. Where we place the answer as a whole depends on the difference between two things: 1, the overall expectations of the students, and 2, the overall qualitative feel of the answer.

To support students with writing – about the distinctions between description and explanation, and between parts and wholes – I provide them with these example sentences (Figure 33).

Now for the second distinction, a major theme of *Biology Made Real*. Explaining the observed phenomena for the whole organism (or whole landscape) is not the same as explaining the mechanism of the parts that brought it about. Learning, for example, the mechanism of

	Describing *an outcome*	**Explaining** *the change*
Parts	• Part **X** will be **Y** • Part **X** will do **Y** • Part **X** will have **Y**	• Reducing **X** will cause an increase in **Y**, resulting in **Z** • If **X** grows larger, it will prevent **Y**, so that **Z** • If rate **X** increases, it will cause Y because **Z**
Whole	• If **X** happens the organism will **Y** • If **X** happens the population will **Y** • If **X** happens the ecosystem will **Y**	• Reducing **X** causes **Y**, so the person will **Z** • The change in **X** causes **Y**, therefore the ecosystem will **Z** • If **X** changes, then **Y** may decrease, so the organism will **Z**

Figure 33: A set of example sentences that I provide to students to help them make the distinction between description and explanation.

ultrafiltration in the nephron, is not the same as knowing what that means for a whole organism's way of living. As our students live in a world of whole organisms (or whole landscapes) we must motivate students to integrate this dual view of parts and whole. Otherwise, the mechanisms they learn may never be connected – in their mind – to the world they experience. In this case, the knowledge becomes trapped in the abstract.

This distinction is approachable from the perspective of levels of organisation, something familiar to biology teachers. Let's say we're studying the digestive system and how organic molecules are broken down in the intestine. Namely, the role of the gallbladder and bile in the digestion of fatty acids. The parts are the components of the system that are central to understanding how it works at the level of organisation at which you explain it. Bile, fatty acids, and the enzyme lipase, would all be parts of the system. Consider anything below this level of organisation to be a part. Consider anything above this level to be a whole. The most important wholes are those that our students live in – the whole organism and the whole landscape (Moore-Anderson 2023). These are the ones I encourage my students to think about.

To reveal understanding then, we must test the extent a student can think with a concept and follow its ramifications. What could this look like in the biology classroom? Let's say I ask the students (14–16

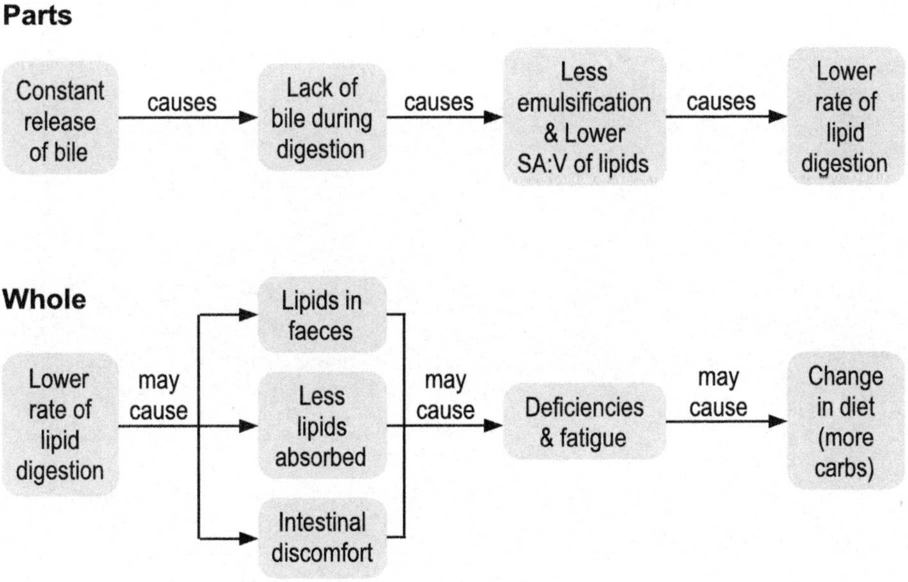

Figure 34: A flow chart showing the possible answer – split into a focus on the parts and whole – to the question "What if a person's gallbladder were removed?"

years old) this question: What if a person's gallbladder were removed and bile was secreted constantly? In this question, I've changed a part, which has changed the secretion rate. This acts as a hypothetical contrast between what we think would normally happen and this new situation. The starting conditions are the same – it's the same person – but by changing a part, the system will begin to behave in a new manner. The flow diagrams in Figure 34 show an example of the type of (systemic) thinking I could expect from my students in terms of parts and whole.

I would categorise an answer of this type as systemic according to the taxonomy. The answer (inferentially) explains both the parts and the effect on the whole's performance. As answers can contain a mix of description and explanation, how I classify them depends on whether they feel (coherently) explanatory or not.

How do I use the taxonomy, exactly? I use the same vocabulary during class discussions and often prompt students to give mechanistic answers. But, the most important use, I believe, is having students test their understanding according to the taxonomy. At the end of a learning sequence – where possible – I'll ask students to write answers to "What if?" questions. I prefer written answers because I want students to make the details of their thoughts explicit, not just to me, but to themselves. As their answers to these questions tend to be long, having a written copy keeps them available for later perusal. In the next chapter, we'll return to this idea of students acting on ideas and making them available for everyone to evaluate.

I project the example sentences while they write, and their work is marked according to the taxonomy. How I do this is explained in Example Box 11 and 12.

Example Box 11

Some "What if?" questions used in my classes that students have given written answers to

These types of "What if?" questions come at the end of a sequence of learning. Let's look at some examples that I have used in my classroom.

Students aged 11–12

- **Object of learning:** The structure and function of the vascular system.
- **Question:** What if a person suddenly had 50% fewer red blood cells?
- **Expected mechanism:** They could absorb less oxygen; therefore the person could deliver less oxygen to cells. The cell respiration rate would be lower.
- **Expected holistic significance:** The person would feel fatigued and probably couldn't do much exercise.

- **Object of learning:** Food chain feedback relations between trophic levels.
- **Question:** What if a new parasite infected the herbivores of a food chain?
- **Expected mechanism:** The herbivore population would decrease. It may give more food to the predators as they are weakened. The predator population may have less prey in the future. Producer populations would benefit.
- **Expected holistic significance:** There may be an increase in the diversity of plants in the area. If the parasite is strong, it may permanently decrease the herbivore population leading to fewer animals in general.

Students aged 14–16

- **Object of learning:** How water is absorbed by plants and controlled via osmosis.
- **Question:** What would happen if you watered a plant (in a pot) with seawater?
- **Expected mechanism:** Discussion of a change in water potential in the soil, causing water to move out of the roots.

- **Expected holistic significance:** Discussion of how the plant as a whole would lose water, causing a drop in turgor pressure within cells, and wilting.

- **Object of learning:** Mammalian thermoregulation.
- **Question:** What if a person had a condition in which they could hardly sweat to cool down?
- **Expected mechanism:** An increase in vasodilation in times of heat, and a possible reduction in metabolic rate.
- **Expected holistic significance:** The person would seem "redder" than others as they attempt to control their temperature via vasodilation in the skin. They will have to avoid hot climates, and intense exercise, to remain stable.

- **Object of learning:** The interplay between the innate and adaptive immune systems.
- **Question:** What if a person got infected and had 50% fewer phagocytes than normal?
- **Expected mechanism:** An initial fast spread of infection while phagocyte production rate increases. After some time antibody production would commence, but as the infection is larger, and the phagocytosis rate lower, antibody production will be larger and prolonged.
- **Expected holistic significance:** The person will feel ill for longer and more vulnerable to other infections. If they survive, they should have long-term immunity due to a robust lymphocyte response.

- **Object of learning:** The function of the reflex arc.
- **Question:** What if the distance between synapses in a reflex arc were twice as wide?
- **Expected mechanism:** The impulse will take longer to pass the synapse as the diffusion distance is longer. It will reach the central nervous system at the same rate but will take longer to pass through the CNS where the synapses are located.
- **Expected holistic significance:** The reflex action will take longer to complete, therefore exposing the organism to danger for longer. Which may lead to less success in survival and reproduction compared to others.

- **Object of learning:** Gas exchange in the alveoli.
- **Question:** What would happen if a person had a whole lung removed?
- **Expected mechanism:** There would be a reduction of 50% of the surface area for gas exchange, but mainly the same volume of cells to support as before. Oxygen concentrations in the blood may be lower than before, and harder to maintain. They may grow more capillaries around the remaining lung.

- **Expected holistic significance:** The person may have to breathe deeper and faster than before. Their variety of responses has decreased, but they may be fine in resting conditions. When attempting exercise, they'd have to breathe faster than with two lungs, and they probably couldn't carry out intense exercise.

- **Object of learning:** The structure and function of the leaf
- **Question:** What if a plant in a population developed leaves that were twice as thick as normal?
- **Expected mechanism:** The diffusion rate would decrease and the distance between stomata and cells would increase. The rate of carbon dioxide to cells decreases, and therefore the rate of photosynthesis.
- **Expected holistic significance:** The plant will grow slower than those around it and may be outcompeted. If it's a genetic cause, those alleles are less likely to be passed on.

Students aged 16–18

- **Object of learning:** The behaviour of water.
- **Question:** With relation to seals what would happen if the hydrogen bonds between water molecules were weaker?
- **Expected mechanism:** The molecules would be held together with less attraction, this would cause water to be less dense, with less viscosity, and would have less conductance of heat. But also it would provide less buoyancy.
- **Expected holistic significance:** Seals, for example, would find it easier to move laterally through water, but would struggle more to remain buoyant. They would possibly evolve organs of lower density. They would lose less heat to water and therefore may evolve less blubber and thermal insulation.

- **Object of learning:** Blood glucose regulation.
- **Question:** What would happen if a diabetic person self-injected glucagon after eating a meal instead of insulin?
- **Expected mechanism:** The glucagon would cause the release of glucose from the liver. Added to the input of glucose from the intestine, the person would suffer sudden hyperglycemia.
- **Expected holistic significance:** The person may feel sudden thirst due to the lower water potential of the blood and may feel hungry as the liver empties of glucose. They could suffer some damage to blood vessels as glucose reacts to them, but not much as long as they remember to inject insulin.

- **Object of learning:** How species perform under varying selection.
- **Question:** What if a fast-growing triploid plant appeared after an extensive forest fire, which was generally adapted in this current environment?
- **Expected mechanism:** The plant will be sexually infertile but may propagate asexually. With low competition and high fitness, the plant will spread. However, as succession continues, more competitive plants will grow, which changes the environment. Now the triploid may not fit so well, and as it doesn't carry out sexual reproduction can't adapt to changing environments. Slowly it may be driven to local extinction.
- **Expected holistic significance:** The quick-spreading plant may initially reduce biodiversity by taking over free ground, and quickly outcompeting other plant species.

- **Object of learning:** The mechanism of mitosis.
- **Question:** What would happen if, during G2 of the cell cycle, one of the centrosomes duplicated, leaving three centrosomes (centrioles) in the cell for mitosis?
- **Expected mechanism:** The three centrioles would produce spindle fibres and attach to chromosomes. The chromosomes would subsequently separate and be pulled towards the centrioles. If the third centriole were positioned next to another (at a pole), the chromosomes would probably separate normally. If the third centriole were not found at a pole, then it would pull sister chromatids away from a pole and may be excluded from any nuclear envelope that forms.
- **Expected holistic significance:** If the third centriole continues to separate chromatids correctly so they end up at the poles, then the cell will remain stable. If not, the cells may become aneuploids, which may or may not be stable. If the cells remain viable, they may not function normally.

Example Box 12

How I've supported students with writing "What if?" questions, and used the taxonomy to evaluate and feedback to students

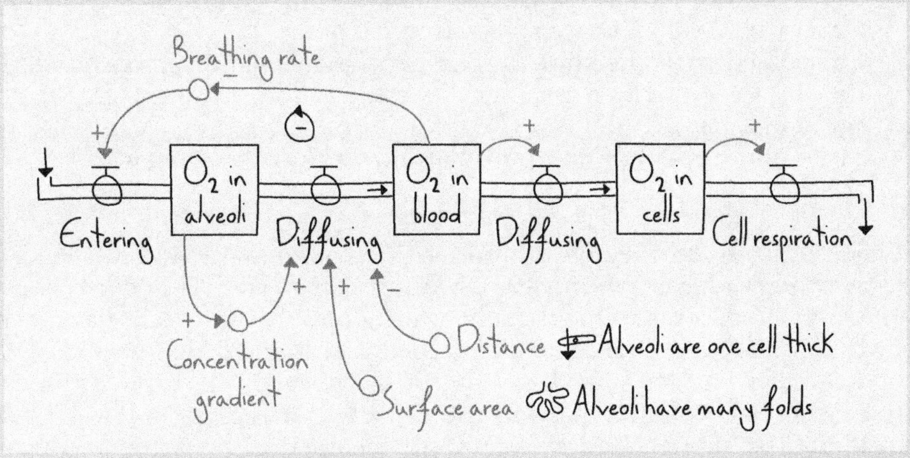

Figure 35: A stock and flow model that I co-constructed with students before asking them to write an answer to a "What if?" question (explained in the main text).

During several lessons, my class (of 14-year-olds) and I studied the alveoli and how their parts fit into the organism and its endeavour to remain stable. We created the model shown in Figure 35.

By the end of building and making sense of the model, it was time to have my students reason deeply. And at the same time, test my students' thinking and reveal their ideas to themselves and myself. Therefore, I asked them, "What if a person had surgery and a lung was removed?" To support the students I went through this process:

- I first wrote the question on the board and let the students think about it.
- I projected the systems principles (discussed in the previous section), and asked students to discuss how they applied to this question. This gets them thinking about what is relevant and what isn't. In this case, we discussed these ideas:

  Homeostasis principle: The key variable for the organism is oxygen concentration in the blood.

Law of requisite variety: If their variety had reduced, were there now situations in which they couldn't remain stable? Suggestions included not being able to carry out intense exercise or climb mountains.
Circular causality principles: In this case, negative feedback drives the stability of oxygen concentrations in the blood.

Next, I wanted to remind students how I expected them to explain their ideas. To do this:

- I projected the sentence examples of description and explanation of parts and wholes (Figure 33) and reminded them of the triadic structure: Input → cause(s) → output.
- I discussed with the students the parts (e.g. alveoli, capillaries) and the wholes (e.g. whole respiratory system, whole organism) that they could discuss.
- I gave the students time to discuss how they would answer the question.

I had them answer the question in writing, individually, and in silence. I gave the students around 10–15 minutes to write. This constraint encourages students to focus their writing on what they felt was most important. It also reduces the time needed to read them all. I have classes of around twenty-five students, and it might take me thirty minutes to read them. When I marked them, I categorised the answer in a quadrant. If I thought the answer was mechanistic, I drew the two axes of the graph and wrote an M in the corresponding space. My intention with this way of marking is to encourage students to engage with the taxonomy, and other example answers, to see what they were missing.

I've transcribed two examples showing systemic thinking as they explained, at least to some extent, the mechanism of the parts and the effect on the whole. See more examples of each category in *Biology Made Real* (Moore-Anderson 2023).

Example 1

> "By losing a lung, the person would also lose some of the surface area of the lung. This would cause less alveoli and less space to do gas exchange. Without alveoli, the gas exchange would decrease considerably. This would also cause the diffusion rate to decrease. Then there would be less oxygen in the blood, meaning the breathing rate would have to increase more than before. While doing sport to be able to get oxygen for the cells, if cells don't have oxygen there would be less respiration, and much more fatigue. Unfortunately, it would be easier to get equilibrium. By having less respiration the body can no longer respond to all physical activities. More demanding situations wouldn't be able to be done. Overall, the person would get fatigued quicker and their breathing rate would increase."

Example 2

> "If a person had half a lung removed, this would mean this person would have less alveoli to do gas exchange. This would mean that there would be less oxygen in the blood, therefore, less oxygen in cells, meaning less cell respiration. If there is less cell respiration, this would be a problem as there would be less energy. To be able to remain stable, the person would have to respond by breathing in deeper to allow more gases to enter the system, therefore allowing more oxygen in the cells. This person would also be more unable to do a certain amount of physical activity. As there wouldn't be enough oxygen getting to cells quick enough to do cell respiration and obtain sufficient energy for the muscles."

Nevertheless, there were a variety of answer types from the class, which revealed all types of thinking. For example, several students suggested that the person would adapt by producing more alveoli in the existing lung. Others suggested that they would adapt by reducing the diffusion distance in the alveoli.

What did I do with this information? Firstly, I made a note on my lesson plans (the photos of my diagrams). This was a reminder for a future lesson to preempt any students thinking the same way. Secondly, I took photos of the answers transcribed above, as examples to share with the class. There's a reason I do this, which stems from some interesting work on the effectiveness of feedback. Siegler (1995; 2002) concluded that explaining why an answer is correct is more useful for learning than explaining one's own answer. Siegler found that it was even more effective to juxtapose correct and incorrect answers and have students explain why.

Therefore, I gave the students their answers and projected the taxonomy to remind them. I then projected the (systemic) examples and gave the students a moment to compare their answers to the ones on the board. I asked them to think about how they could improve theirs and after this, I discussed the patterns I had noted when reading the work. For example, in this case, I discussed the answers that suggested the diffusion distance could be decreased and asked the class why this couldn't be right.

In other instances, I have given students time to edit their answers. When possible, I've given them time to discuss and compare their answers with peers before rewriting. This option has been the most powerful at improving understanding in my experience. But, as all biology teachers know, our overloaded curricula don't give many (if any) opportunities for this.

CHAPTER 4

Basic knowledge questions should be short, unambiguous, and enable thinking

Key idea:
To serve as a revision tool, basic knowledge questions should be clear enough to allow all students to come to the same answer.

In this final section of the chapter, I want to explore the idea of helping students remember the content they learn. This inevitably helps students access new content. Much work has been done to promote the concept of retrieval practice, which has been shown to aid in remembering. It's not my intention to repeat that here. Retrieval practice involves re-presenting an idea to yourself so that it is re-cognised. However, as von Foerster (1969) pointed out, we don't retrieve memories like unchanged items from a box. Instead, we re-enact and re-construct them in the mind. If learning is an act of adaptation to the environment, then the repeated re-cognition of something signals its importance.

Retrieval practice – as a learning activity – involves the straight re-call of content. The content load in biology can be so high that I help my students by giving them a list of short questions to practise, which cover the content of the entire course. I call these basic knowledge questions, lest students think that memorising is all they have to do. Before I go on, I'll leave you an example of a question: Name the two muscles that cause inhalation when contracting – Diaphragm & External intercostal muscles. Here are my assumptions about basic knowledge questions:

- **Revision tools** – they should provoke students to "re-call", not to learn in the first place.
- **Unambiguous** – students are expected to come to the same answer, so questions shouldn't permit varied answers that can lead to confusion.
- **Short but not fragmented** – the answers should be short enough to be memorable, but not so short they break up relationships.
- **Enable thinking** – there should be variation in question type to avoid developing an ability to re-call alone.

Before I tell you how to design these questions, let me explain the latter point. To help let me quote Heinz von Foerster who wrote briefly about memory (1969). "In the stream of cognitive processes" you can "conceptually isolate certain components" (1969, 105). He gave these examples: The capacity to perceive, remember, and infer. Yet, isolating one or the other is "doomed to fail". Because, if you omit just one of these three capacities, "the system is devoid of cognition [for example]:

- (i) Omit perception: the system is incapable of representing internally environmental regularities.
- (ii) Omit memory: the system has only throughput.
- (iii) Omit prediction, i.e., the faculty of drawing inferences: perception degenerates to sensation, and memory to recording." (105)

What can we make of this? As mentioned, inferring in biology depends on knowing a description of a system. But we must avoid producing a list of questions that fragment knowledge and give the feel of a list of facts. This can happen when they focus too much on structures and functions. Instead, we should create a mix of question types that provide a coherent unit for thinking. Accordingly, here are the categories I have in mind when writing my basic knowledge questions:

Description
- Structural relations (e.g. a drawing of the alveolus).
- Functional relations (e.g. the function of xylem is to transport water and minerals).

Explanation
- Causal relations (e.g. the relationship between volume and pressure, or mechanism).
- Semantic relations (e.g. differences between active transport and facilitated diffusion).

Let's look at how I design my questions with these ideas.

Structural relations are better drawn than written
For structural relations, a student should remember a drawing of a system. This is because the meaning of a structure is in its organisation, something that isn't captured in fragmented questions. Compare the following set of questions, to the question asking a student to draw the system.

1. Name the principal windpipe through which air enters the respiratory system – trachea.
2. Name the two tubes that deviate from the principal windpipe – bronchi.
3. Name the smaller tubes that branch off from the bronchi – bronchioles.
4. Name the bones that surround the respiratory system – ribs.
5. Name the muscles involved in regulating breathing – diaphragm, intercostal muscles.

Alternatively, you could ask a student to draw and label the main components of the respiratory system. For my students aged 14 years

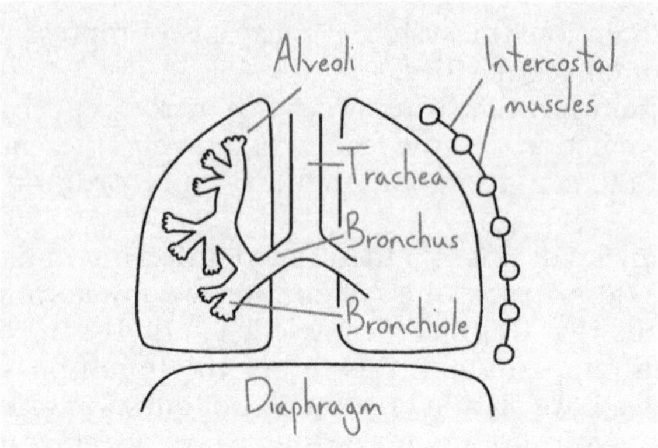

Figure 36: A simple diagram of the respiratory system that I ask my students to learn so they can draw it.

old, the following diagram (Figure 36) is included in my basic knowledge questions. It is, in fact, the drawing that we produce together during the lesson. The prompt could simply be to draw the system as it was taught in the lesson, or it could include a list of the components expected in the drawing.

Avoid ambiguity by stating the context and the aspect
Consider this question for students aged 11–14:

- What is the function of the mouth?

What would you answer? Clarity is lacking, even if I were to tell you that this was part of a group of questions about the digestive system. We could talk about saliva, digestion by enzymes, lubrication for peristalsis, the chewing of food, and even amplifying the voice. It's easy to fall into this trap of ambiguity. When designing the questions, we have an idea of what will be taught during the lesson and expect students to remember it that way. But the purpose of basic knowledge questions is not to have students remember how it was said during a lesson but to remember the answer in relation to the concept. To have students do both can increase the cognitive load enough that confusion gets in the way of the purpose of revision.

Now consider this:

- State two activities the mouth carries out to digest food.

The context is given: digestive system, and the aspect is given: activity leading to digestion. The possible variety of answers is now restricted to just two that are directly involved in digestion: Mechanically breaks up food by chewing and secretes saliva to digest food.

Consider this question for students aged 14–16:
- What happens to the lungs when you inhale?

The context in this question is given (inhaling) but not any aspect of it. The variety of possible answers is too large and leads to ambiguity. Consider, instead, these questions which give the context and expected aspect:
- What happens to the volume of the lungs as you inhale?
- What happens to the air pressure in the lungs as you inhale?

These questions are about causal relations, so we could also write them like this:
- What is the relationship between the volume of the lungs and the air pressure in the lungs?
- In what direction does air move when there is a pressure difference?

These questions are more generalisable than the previous two. I hypothesise that this will help students generalise their knowledge because instead of dealing with one concrete situation, they point to potential variation – how things could be different. Let's look at another example.

Consider this question for students aged 11–14:
- What is the waxy cuticle?

We see the same problem of ambiguity. The student should only be able to get the answer right if they remember what was said during a lesson. So, we could ask this question in terms of function and give the context as the leaf. How about this?
- What is the function of the waxy cuticle on a leaf?

However, we could also pose this in terms of causal relations. Consider this:
- What is the relationship between the thickness of the waxy cuticle and the rate of water loss from a leaf?

Here we have the context (leaf) and aspect (waxy cuticle with regard to water loss). There is also a dimension of variation within the answer. If students remember this, it could help them generalise the idea of waxy cuticles from drought-resistant plants to wetland-adapted plants.

One more example, consider this question:
- When does respiration occur in a plant?

The context is the plant, but the aspect of when is vague. While respiration should be continuous (most of the time), the question could send a student double-guessing themselves. Does respiration occur when plants are seeds? By contrasting it with photosynthesis we can get a nice semantic relationship:

- At what point in a day do photosynthesis, and respiration occur in a typical leaf?

This question evokes a contrast and therefore shows a semantic relation. It gives the context (a typical plant), and the aspect (points of the day). The answer I'd expect would be that respiration is continuous whereas photosynthesis occurs during daylight.

So far, we've looked at questions in isolation, let's now look at groups of questions.

Mix questions about dynamic, causal, and semantic relations to avoid fragmentation

A problem I often see with the design of basic knowledge questions is that they become a list of functional relations: "What is the function of X?". This fragments knowledge too much for my taste. It gives biology the sense of a description-only subject based on the memorisation of facts. There will always be a necessity for descriptive questions. But here I want to show how they can be complemented by causal and semantic relations, such that, as a group, they can give students something to think with. Table 3 shows an example of basic knowledge questions for the topic of the digestive system. Note how there is a mix of question types.

Do I always manage to follow this advice well? No, I work within many constraints as do all teachers. Some topics resist it. Other times it's my busy timetable that prevents it. I also work within the constraints of standardised curricula and exams that demand students know certain knowledge. I share my questions on my blog, so you can see the outcomes there. For this reason, if you like these ideas, take them as a heuristic to have in mind when you design your own.

This brings us to the end of this chapter. We've discussed metacontent – sharing our assumptions with students to help them see as we do. The next chapter, however, takes us in the opposite direction.

Question	Answer
Draw a simple diagram of the digestive system with the functions of its organs	Answer at the end of the booklet (in this case, see the appendix)
Give the overall function of the digestive system	Digest larger molecules (polymers) into smaller molecules (monomers), and then absorb them
Name the substrate and product of amylase	Starch digested to glucose
Name the substrate and product of protease	Proteins digested to amino acids
Name the substrate and product of lipase	Lipids digested to fatty acids
What's the relationship between the SA:V of food and how quickly it's digested?	The higher the SA:V the quicker it's digested
Name two physical ways that the SA:V of food is increased in the digestive system	Chewing in the mouth Churning in the stomach
Name two chemical ways that the SA:V of food is increased in the digestive system	Hydrochloric acid unfolds proteins and increases their SA:V in the stomach Bile emulsifies lipids to increase their SA:V in the intestine
Explain the mechanism of bile and emulsification in the intestine	Bile binds lipids to water making them mix Which causes lipids to break into small droplets (with a high SA:V)

Table 3: A set of “basic knowledge questions” about the digestive system that I have created for my students, to aid them in their revision.

5.
TO TEST THE VIABILITY OF IDEAS, STUDENTS MUST EXPLORE THEM IN WRITING OR CONVERSING

Key ideas:
Learning is triggered when we realise our ideas aren't viable and don't fit our experience.
To put the viability of our understanding to the test, we have to act with the knowledge to make it explicit to ourselves and others – in writing, diagrams, or conversation.

In this chapter we'll continue considering the student in the recursive teaching model, but now from a different angle – encouraging exploration. That is, having students mentally grapple with and explore the new distinctions and relations they've perceived. In this chapter, I want to explain how I promote this in my classroom, although much has been said already. For example, we've already seen the use of "What if?" questions, which was a focus of chapters on variation theory and stock and flow models. We've also explored the use of "What if?" questions with the taxonomy of understanding. Alas, a book can only go in a linear sequence of words, and I've needed to discuss the idea of exploration already, lest the book lose its meaning.

What will I talk about here then? I want to discuss classroom dialogue and share exactly how I enact it. To begin with, however, let's return to cybernetics to understand the context of this section of the model.

As a founder of cybernetic thinking, Ross Ashby influenced those that followed. He thought that "the brain is not a thinking machine; it is an acting machine; it gets information and then it does something about it." (1948, 379). Ashby, like Pask, considered humans to be "variety eaters" compelled to explore and adapt (Scott 2021).

Nevertheless, Andrew Pickering (2010), a historian of cybernetics, thinks that many (in the West) see education as an endeavour to transmit to students a true representation of the world – to enframe it in some way. I see this often in biology education. Our young 11-year-olds begin their journey in secondary biology lessons by being introduced to a consortia of vocabulary to learn. Structures, functions, invisible entities with strange names, all to be remembered as facts.

What is, then, the virtue of knowledge? For Pickering (2010, 150), it's not in having a truthful vision of the world. But, in its "usefulness" in our interactions and engagements with the world we live in. It's not like the Newtonian world of forces, which are to be uncovered and documented, "cybernetics was not one of pushes and pulls; it was, instead, of forward-looking search" (18).

This shifted the focus from "how it is" to "how it could be". Because adaptation is ongoing and the causes don't yet exist, "so cybernetics stages us for a vision ... in which reality is always 'in the making'" (18).

Education improves our students' ability to adapt. They are *in-formed* as lessons nudge their mental activity towards new patterns and habits of mind. It's about provoking students to perceive and *see with*, as Marton (2015) would say. And provoking students to *act with* knowledge – as cyberneticians may say. In other words, knowledge *is* adequate action in a context (Maturana 2011).

Learning then acts similarly to the adaptation occurring in the evolution of species. There is variation among individuals, and selection acts – not to select the fittest – but to eliminate those that don't fit (Bateson 1972). In this sense, selection acts like a filter. The form of things that manage to pass through the filter doesn't matter, just those that don't. Bateson suggests that natural selection is a process that functions on constraints as its mechanism, not on (Newtonian-style) "forces". In this regard, natural selection isn't a process of optimisation, instead it only guarantees the persistence of whatever satisfies the two basic constraints of survival and reproduction (Varela et al. 2016, 196).

The same can be said of cognition – our understanding is that which has satisfied the constraints of what we experience (Varela et al. 2016). Our conceptions explain the ins and outs of our lives. They make sense, they are viable. As long as they fit our perceptions, they can persist, even if they are partial understandings.

Here's an example from when I moved to Granada, Spain. Despite the sun and blue skies, the winters there are surprisingly cold due to the cold air and high elevation. In Granada, a friend told me her road was always cold, even during the day when temperatures rose significantly with the incoming sunlight. That didn't add up for me and I thought she was exaggerating. Because how I posed the problem suggested that the sun would heat the air of peripheral areas, and that warm air would move into her road. This meant, in my mind, there shouldn't have been a difference in perceived temperature between different roads – they should've been similar. And yet, one day I went to her road, and she was right. It was freezing, while the road near it – which got full sunlight – was warm even in the shade.

The concept had always been compatible with scenarios I experienced and thought about. But the new experience made it untenable. I realised that the feeling of warmth didn't just come from the air, but also radiating infrared waves from the road and buildings. If these were heated by the sun, they radiated energy more, and the feeling of warmth was additive with the air temperature. This explained the difference in temperature of different roads. I adapted my way of thinking, or in other words, I learnt.

The idea here is that we bump into reality when we realise we're wrong (Glasersfeld 1995). From the perspective of natural selection, it may be fatal for individual organisms to respond inadequately. In terms of cognition, a failed inference triggers learning. Thought experiments – of the "What if?" type – can therefore provide one of the most useful tools for the classroom.

Key idea 1:
Learning is triggered when we realise our ideas aren't viable and don't fit our experience.

Yet, when question posers only ever expect a variety of one – if only one answer is ever possible – students never get this opportunity. Nor are we informed about our students' ideas. Students must be provoked to act on their assumptions to test their viability to us and themselves – spoken or written. Therefore, we need to hear how students think differently, not ask them all to say the same thing. We need conversation to bring us closer to a shared meaning, not a shared utterance.

Key idea 2:
To put the viability of our understanding to the test, we have to act with the knowledge to make it explicit to ourselves and others – in writing, diagrams, or conversation.

We've already seen how we can provoke students to act (in the previous chapter) with written answers to "What if?" questions. But we also need students to do this in conversation. In this chapter, I'll discuss how I encourage participation and exploration without producing so much complexity that the lesson becomes unmanageable.

Exploratory conversation requires a variety of possibilities but also constraints

Key idea:
Dialogue in the classroom often fails due to a mismatch in expectations between teachers and students.

When we try to promote exploration with open questions it doesn't always work as we'd like. For example, students may discuss seemingly unrelated things and generally lose focus. Many students may not answer anything at all. Qualitative research from the classroom (Nuthall 2007; Brophy 2006) suggests that starting with discussions of students' ideas can be highly problematic, as I'm sure many teachers have experienced. For example, they can be time-inefficient, can favour only the most talkative students, and as students have varied prior knowledge, can turn into a handful of unrelated comments offered by students. What can we do about it?

For conversation to work, it requires the interplay of both possibilities and constraints. Possibilities give students choices in their answers and therefore encourage reasoning. The constraints keep everyone on the same page and encourage participation. Let me put this into a model to give more clarity. In this case, a graph (Figure 37).

The graph represents communication between a teacher, who asks a question, and a student, who interprets it. I used the term variety deliberately as an abstraction. It's summarised more concretely on the y-axis (the same categories can be applied to the x-axis). Low on the y-axis are closed questions. These typically accept one possible answer and are short (low complexity). Logically, these questions expect students to give the same answer on the same concept. High on that axis are open questions, leaving students to answer as they see fit.

Somewhere between the two is what I've called conversation. Here there's a variety of possible answers, but also constraints that maintain conversants on the same concept. In other words, the possibility arises of discussing different ways of seeing the same concept.

That diagonal line represents the point where there's a perfect match between what the teacher expects, and what the students think the teacher expects. So, the further you deviate from that diagonal line, the more ambiguous the question is – the less the students understand the teacher's expectation. Indicated by the darker colour is the zone of conversation. This is where teachers and students mutually understand that what is expected is a variety of possible answers about the same

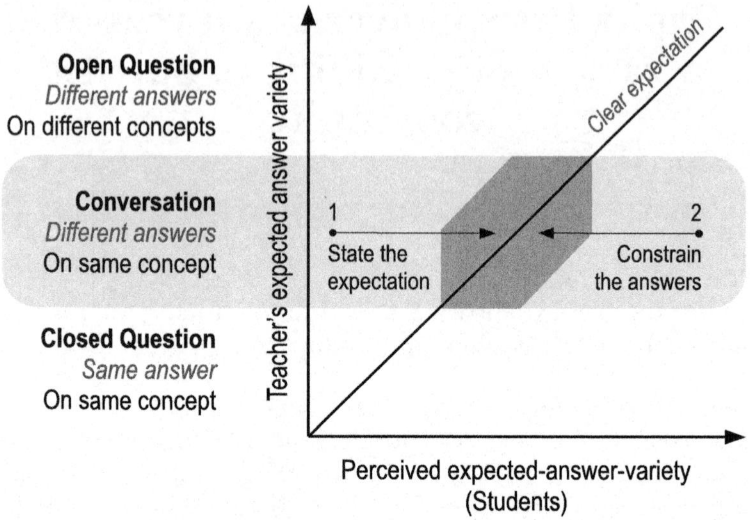

Figure 37: A graph showing the outcome space of expectations when a teacher asks a question to their students. Explained in the main text.

aspect, or concept. Landing in this zone is where good conversation can commence.

What are those numbered dots on the graph? Here I'm highlighting two problems that move classroom dialogue away from that desired zone of conversation, and how to get back in there. Here's how I see it.

Problem one – Teacher expects more, students give less

Dot number one (on the left) shows that the teacher expects conversation, but students perceive that they must give a simple closed answer. They might give one-word answers. It might also lead to students saying words seemingly picked at random (from prior content), or just saying "they'll die". In general, this provoked less thinking than was intended by the teacher and revealed less about the student's learning. Here's a solution:

- State the expectation for the type of answer that is anticipated. For example, request mechanistic responses by gesturing the triadic structure of input → cause(s) → output (discussed in Chapter 4). I convey this by stating the input and the output while I "hold" them in my two hands before asking for the cause(s) that link the two.

Problem two – Teacher expects less, students give more

The dot on the right shows that the teacher expected a variety of answers on a specific point – they expected conversation. Yet, the students perceived that the answer was fully open (I'll give examples in the next section). This may lead to lower participation as students perceive too many possibilities. It may also lead to students giving unrelated answers to the teacher's intended concept. Here are some ideas that can solve the problem.

Constrain the answers by asking questions that relate to at least two things:

- Asking questions about the difference between two things
- Asking questions that require negative explanation – why something doesn't work/occur/exist – relative to something that does
- Asking students to answer a multiple-choice question by hands-up voting before asking them to elaborate on their selection.

The next couple of sections will explore examples of these suggestions. Afterwards, I'll put this together – with everything else we've covered in the book – in a detailed example of how I recently taught about the heart.

CHAPTER 5

To increase clarity avoid asking about a single thing, instead, ask about a difference

Key idea:
A requisite of good conversation is shared attention on the same aspect. To get that, ask questions about differences.

Think about these questions:
- What is selection?
- What is a cell?
- What is adaptation?
- Does anyone know what xylem is?
- Does selection reduce variation?
- Why do plants transport water?
- Why don't bacteria have mitochondria?

The expectation is unclear – are they closed questions or open questions? All these questions are about single concepts, but with little indication to which aspect, and in relation to what. There is confusion and lack of clarity when we ask about single things.

To counter this confusion we need to establish, what Tsui calls, common ground (2004). And there is an elegant method that solves this problem. Previously I discussed variation, and difference, as what catches our attention. In variation theory, they'd say that there are countless aspects that we could potentially perceive, but at any one moment, we can focus on just a few. In variation theory, this would be called our focal awareness (Marton et al. 2004). But there is a distinction here that we can exploit:
1. We can employ variation to have students discern something new.
2. We can also employ variation so that students focus on the same aspect as us – to share our focal awareness, so we're all on the same page.

When a teacher asks open questions about a single concept, there is no variation within the question (like the examples above). The variation – perceived by students – is the scope of possible (but hidden) aspects their teacher expects (Tsui 2004). So this is what the students think about. They puzzle over the possible aspects on their teacher's mind, instead of thinking deeply about the intended concept. What likely occurs to many students in these questions is a sort of mental paralysis at the prospect of so many possible answers. They likely weigh the odds and assume their best bet is not to participate. Others have a go regardless and you get something seemingly random. The teacher only perceives it as random because they have a specific aspect in mind. For the student, it wasn't random.

Yet more trouble lurks when this occurs. Teachers may respond by narrowing their subsequent questions to those that only require recall or simple deductions (Tsui et al. 2004). This is likely because the teacher is eager to help their students come to an answer. But by doing so, the focus is changed from a question that requires conceptual reasoning, to one that doesn't.

This might involve gap-fill questions where the teacher expects students to add keywords to a partially complete sentence. Or a series of closed questions with only one possible answer. The result is for the students to shift their awareness away from variation within the concept itself, to the variation of words that could fit the teacher's question. What can we do instead?

The key is to ask questions about differences, which clarify the aspect we're referring to. This will align expectations in the classroom, as students think, *the teacher expects us to offer a variety of answers about this aspect*. From here you can proceed into a conversation.

Only recently was I abruptly reminded of this. I had slipped into the error of asking students why a farmer might not want to use seeds to populate a field. Just one thing was mentioned – no variation, no difference. I saw their blank faces and realised they had no idea what my expectation was. I then reformulated the question: "What difference would it make if a farmer populated a field using seeds, or cloned cuttings?" Participation increased immediately.

Many times, my questions have this format. I propose a difference and ask what difference it makes. I may point to the left ventricle and right of the heart and ask what the difference is, and then what difference it makes (see Example Box 13 at the end of this chapter). Or I may show different digestive system structures – such as with and without an anus – and ask what difference it makes. The interesting bit comes with the question: what difference does it make? But to get there together, I ensure everyone focuses on the same aspect by first asking: what's the difference?

This was our key idea:
A requisite of good conversation is shared attention on the same aspect. To get that, ask questions about differences.

Nevertheless, the examples above are tied to particular content. Next, I'll show you two question types that can be asked at any point during a lesson and are easily formulated. They can also provide a wide array of feedback from the class about their learning. This is because I have students vote on the possible answers before I have students discuss their choices. This gives me two types of information about learning. Firstly patterns from the whole class, and then elaborated answers from individuals in the subsequent conversation. I'll tell you how I do this in the next section. Before we get there, I want to show you examples of the questions. I've categorised the questions I find most useful – the most easily formulated in the moment – into two types:

1. Stability or change
2. Negative explanation – why something is not, rather than why it is

Questions of the type: stability or change

There are two subtypes here. One is "will it stay the same or change?" while the other is "will it increase, stay the same, or decrease". I use the "stay the same or change" questions when I feel like the students may struggle with specifying whether something will increase or decrease. The question of "increase, stay the same, or decrease" is useful for varying aspects of stock and flow models. Let's look at some examples:

Plant physiology

- If the rate of respiration is faster than the rate of photosynthesis, will the carbon in the plant increase, stay the same, or decrease?
- If stomatal density in a leaf were higher would the rate of transpiration increase, stay the same, or decrease?

Human cardiovascular system

- If a person is running and suddenly stops, would the blood flow rate increase, stay the same, or decrease?
- If the capillaries were wider to fit more blood inside, would the diffusion rate increase, stay the same, or decrease?

Ecology

- If humans abandoned a farm, would the species of plants there stay the same or change over time?
- If predator X were to go extinct, would the diversity of plant species decrease, stay the same, or increase?

Questions of the type: negative explanation – why something is not, rather than why it is

This is a type of question that Bateson called a "cybernetic explanation". He described it in this way (Bateson 1972, 287):

> "Causal explanation is usually positive. We say that billiard ball B moved in such and such a direction because billiard ball A hit it at such and such an angle. In contrast to this, cybernetic explanation is always negative. We consider what alternative possibilities could conceivably have occurred and then ask why many of the alternatives

were not followed, so that the particular event was one of those few which could, in fact, occur."

There are two benefits to using this question type. Firstly, in contrast to positive explanations, it more obviously invokes a comparison between two things, which constrains the question naturally. Secondly, it's not always obvious why something is as it is, which leaves seemingly limitless possibilities.

The quintessential examples are questions about why an organism's adaptations have evolved. In fact, Bateson said (287):

> "The classical example of this type of explanation is the theory of evolution under natural selection. According to this theory, those organisms which were not both physiologically and environmentally viable could not possibly have lived to reproduce. Therefore, evolution always followed the pathways of viability."

I'm sure many teachers have had the experience of trying to get students to think about natural selection by asking, "Why has this trait been selected for?" But natural selection only selects against, not for. And without being able to compare traits and environment, how would anyone know?

This is what I do instead. I tell the students that there is a population showing variety in the trait we're discussing. I hold out my left hand with the palm facing upwards. I explain that this form of the trait represents the output. Let's say it's petalless wind-pollinated flowers. I gesture a spectrum by moving my right hand away from my left hand. My right hand finishes with its palm facing upwards about half a metre away from my left hand. I tell the students that this spectrum represents members of a population with ever larger petals. In my right hand are those with the largest petals; the variety in the spectrum signifies the input. And I ask, "Why don't we see these flowers in modern populations?". Following the triadic structure of input → cause(s) → output, this question prompts students to identify the causes for why the alternatives were discarded via selection. As metacontent, this is something I share explicitly with students. Here are some more examples I've asked students about recently:

- Plant physiology: leaves with more or less stomata.
- Plant reproduction: insect-pollinated flowers with longer or shorter anthers.
- Human cardiovascular system: capillaries with wider or thinner lumens.
- Human cardiovascular system: the right ventricle with thinner, similar, or thicker muscle to the left ventricle.
- Human digestive system: intestines with shorter or longer villi.
- Human urinary system: a longer or shorter loop of Henle.

Another situation – in which these questions are useful – is when comparing one system with another and asking why they are distinct. This often occurs in my classrooms when comparing human systems to those of other species. Many of my comparisons are with other vertebrates. For example, recently I showed students the structure of a frog's heart, which has a single ventricle without the fully formed septum that mammals develop. After a discussion of the structural differences, and what difference they make, I asked students why frogs hadn't evolved a septum after all this time (see Example Box 13). These questions often take us into the organism's ecology and way of life – connecting the parts to the whole (Moore-Anderson 2023). Here are a few other examples:

- Why haven't mammals evolved the more efficient respiratory system of birds?
- Why haven't insects evolved a closed vascular system?
- Why haven't mosses evolved xylem?

Yet, negative explanations can be useful in other contexts. I often ask them after posing a "stability or change" question. For example, "Why wouldn't the community of plants in an abandoned field stay the same?". Another useful place to employ this question type is when adding a section to a stock and flow model, or icon diagram. When wanting to ask students about the new addition, it may be tempting to ask why you have added it the way you have. Instead, it's better to add the section, and ask why you didn't add it in "this other way".

Fine, you may be thinking. But how can we put these questions to use in a classroom of many students? How can they both increase participation and reveal our students' thinking – to us as teachers – from more than a single student? This is what I'll explore in the next section. Before we go there, here's the key idea of this section again.

Key idea:
A requisite of good conversation is shared attention on the same aspect. To get that, ask questions about differences.

To spark conversation have students vote on multiple-choice questions about a difference, and then have them justify their choice

Key ideas:
Get everyone on the same page with a question about a difference, then encourage conversation by having students justify their answers. Get several types of feedback from students by having the whole class vote on multiple-choice questions, before encouraging conversation, and then voting on agreement or disagreement.

I offer multiple-choice answers to most of my questions. Then I ask students to vote by raising their hands. This fulfils two fundamental functions. Firstly, they constrain the possible answers and, secondly, they reveal patterns of thought that help me decide how to proceed. Of course, what I describe here can be done by other means, such as writing on mini-whiteboards and holding up the answers. Here I'll give you one way it could work in practice.

When I ask these questions, I state the question and the possible answers. I pause to let students think and then have them vote sequentially on the options. If they need it (they often do), I'll allow pairs to deliberate, which might last ten to twenty seconds. Keeping an eye on their body language is key to knowing when they've said enough. Then I repeat the options available and have the students vote by raising their hands.

I have them vote sequentially with hands raised to see who, and how many, are voting for what. Simultaneous voting can be cognitively overwhelming for the teacher. Additionally, body language can tell you more than their votes. It's impossible to not communicate, Bateson would say (1979).

Once students have voted, it's time to provoke conversation. Therefore, depending on the question, the students, and how I've perceived their confidence, I choose a student and ask why they've voted the way they have. Students know I expect conversation because I show them the recursive teaching model and discuss the premise that we form a circular system.

If students say that they're not entirely sure, I ask them, "OK, so, what do you know?" They sometimes suggest something pertinent at this point and, when they don't, they nearly always have something to say. If they still have nothing to say, I thank them and remind them that all responses provide information for me to act on.

When an interesting answer emerges, I'll ask the class (with a neutral voice), "Do you agree with that?" and have them vote on whether they do. With this response, I attempt to force students to reveal their hands by keeping my own cards close to my chest. This could, of course, be done through a variety of means. The key is to develop a culture in which their answers aren't subject to judgement but are part of a recursive loop. In other words, students need to sense that their answers can influence the course of the lesson – to sense that there is symmetry in adaptation between teacher and student.

Here's a summary of ideas that can be used for productive class discussion:

- Ask questions about differences between at least two things.
- Let students test ideas in pairs often, especially if students are too shy to speak or vote.
- Have students vote on several possible answers.
- Have students vote sequentially so you can see patterns across the class.
- Ask particular students to elaborate on why they voted the way they did.
- Extend discussions recursively by having students vote if they agree or disagree with a peer's comments and asking students to justify their responses.

There's one last piece in the puzzle that we need to discuss. How much exploration of ideas can we expect from students? My answer to these questions will help summarise my vision of the recursive teaching model.

Regulate the number of aspects that you expect students to explore simultaneously according to their understanding

Key ideas:
Regulate the number of aspects that you expect students to explore simultaneously according to their understanding – from discerning a single aspect of a system to deliberating the interconnected effects of variation on a whole system.

The "What if?" question has been ubiquitous in this book – variation for discerning and variation for exploring ideas. Maybe you've noticed that the examples of variation are all similar. It's a case of varying one thing at a time. How can we organise this when thinking about teaching? It's time to put some order to this idea and give a final detailed example that pulls everything together. This means we must focus on assumption 5: regulate the number of aspects that you expect students to explore simultaneously according to their understanding.

We can begin by assuming that the use of variation is continuous – it always appears in lessons no matter the phase. As we've seen, there is variation for making distinctions, asking questions to encourage dialogue, and testing our ideas in written responses.

It's not just variation theory that discusses variation per se – other models exist that discuss it in terms of practice, task design, and resulting performance. For example, in describing research in cognitive science, Schmidt and Bjork (1992, 207) suggest that "increasing the amount of task variability required during practice ... depresses performance during training, yet facilitates performance on later tests of the ability to generalize training to altered conditions."

This "variability effect" also figures in cognitive load theory: "Increasing variability exposes learners to a greater range of related tasks designed to teach a specific concept or procedure, which yields increased test performance." (Likourezos et al. 2019, 2).

Equally, beyond its role in discernment, Marton also discusses the use of variation in reasoning deeply and putting ideas to the test (2015, 162):

> "You keep asking 'What if?': 'What if this part was different?' 'What if this is not true?' 'What if everything was the other way around?' You have to question what is taken for granted, you have to let ideas come to the fore and you have to put them to the test."

What are the differences between Marton's vision of variation, and, for example, the variability effect described in cognitive load theory? Well, variation theory endeavours to *explain* the relationship between variation and learning.

The variability effect, on the other hand, doesn't explain anything at all. It's what Bateson (1972) would call an "explanatory principle". This is because it's the name given to a consistent observation, but "there's no explanation of an explanatory principle. It's like a black box ... A 'black box' is a conventional agreement between scientists to stop trying to explain things at a certain point." (48). Because, as Maturana thought, "whenever one has an explanatory principle, one invents a mechanism [that] conceal[s] what one wants to explain." (1987, 65).

Therefore, for cognitive load theory, the question isn't *why* variation is key to learning, or *how* to exploit it. Instead, the question being explored is about cognitive performance. Under what circumstances will students have the requisite knowledge (or requisite variety) to cope with exploring variation? (e.g. Likourezos et al. 2019). The assumption here is that students with little knowledge will be cognitively overwhelmed if variation within tasks is introduced too early.

So, how can we consolidate this assumption of cognitive load theory with the fact that I use variation throughout my lessons from start to finish? To answer that, let's return to the fact that variation theory shares a fundamental assumption with cognitive load theory – that our cognitive capacity is limited and can be easily overloaded. For variation theory, there is a limit to the number of aspects that can be held in our focal awareness at any given moment. This is a key reason why variation theory proposes that learning should move from separation to fusion (2015). During the separation phase, you handle a single critical aspect at a time, everything else is kept invariant. Only once students have discerned them individually does variation theory encourage varying several aspects simultaneously – the fusion phase (Kullberg 2024). Therefore, variation theory inherently encourages cognitive load regulation – from varying one aspect to varying several, but only as students are ready.

With systems, varying one part will inevitably cause variation in other parts. Therefore, if we are constantly provoking students with variation, we must regulate the number of aspects, or parts, that we expect students to think with – to explore. From just a couple of aspects (when they know less), to exploration of many aspects in relation and interaction (when they know more). Or, in the terms used in cognitive load theory (Sweller 2011), from low element interactivity to high element interactivity. To clarify this idea, let's contrast three lesson formats.

For my first example, there are learning sequences that involve no variation at all. They consist of just explaining a concept – as it is – and then having students remember this explanation via activities. This may follow a faded support pattern. The teacher explains the concept, then helps students answer questions, and finally, students answer questions with independence. A lesson on the heart may involve a teacher explaining how it contracts to pump blood and where that blood goes. They may ask closed questions that require students to restate what has been said. Then, the students may answer questions in writing with their teacher's help. This may involve gap-fill exercises or some more closed questions that have students practise restating the explanation in smaller chunks. Finally, students may be given questions that require longer answers, but the general goal is for students to restate the original explanation. Maybe the question places it in a different context, but they are still expected to restate the explanation. Where then, is the meaning making? Without variation to explore, it's unlikely to be provoked.

Let's compare this with another format. This one involves two distinct phases: the teacher explaining a concept, and students applying the concept. The assumption here is that students must memorise an explanation before they explore any variation. Therefore, the teacher's explanation is a phase that comes first. Variation is a different phase that comes later. As above, this doesn't mean it begins with a lecture – it may be very interactive. However, the goal in the first phase is to restate the teacher's descriptions and explanations via closed questions. In this format, if the teacher feels like students are not ready to move on, they may retain them in the remembering and restating phase. During a lesson on the heart, this lesson may begin in a similar fashion to the format I discussed above. However, it ends differently as students are expected to answer questions that require them to think with the explanation. For example, they could be asked how a person's heart would be affected after a heart attack that damaged the left ventricle.

This set of assumptions sees variation as a secondary goal – only desirable if an explanation has been remembered. It's considered "high-hanging fruit". There is a problem here. One that was discussed explicitly by Marton (2006), on an occasion when he referred to cybernetics. According to variation theory, students who experience this format won't understand the ideas until they get to the "application of knowledge" questions. Because only here is variation encountered. Do you remember Ashby's story (1956) of the prisoner and his wife's cakes? And that the prisoner needed to know the variety of possible cakes to make any meaning of receiving a cake. In this lesson format, it's as if the prisoner had been receiving the same cake for weeks but only later informed of his wife's communication scheme. The prisoner is then forced to make meaning of the previous cakes retrospectively.

We can't receive meanings like a parcel of contents. When the students come to perceive variation, they create the meaning in their own minds. They draw a distinction that brings forth a new aspect of the world. And then they can think in new ways by bringing into their focal awareness different complexes of aspects. This means that a lesson that only provokes with variation during the "application of knowledge" stage, provokes students to draw distinctions only at the end of a learning sequence. They'll only be able to think in new ways by the end of a sequence of learning, rather than at the beginning.

According to variation theory, learning begins with perceiving something new – a new aspect – and ends with bringing that aspect together with others to think in new ways. You can't bring to mind an aspect that you haven't perceived yet. So, when it comes to a lesson on the heart, students should begin by discerning its parts via the use of variation. This way, they're likely to have those aspects perceptible to them, and therefore available to their cognition.

As students distinguish aspects of the system, bit by bit, we can encourage students to bring them together in their minds. Or, in the words of variation theory, encourage students to think with the aspects simultaneously – to form a complex of aspects in the focal awareness. That could be just a few parts of the heart to begin with. For example, just perceiving the atria and ventricles functioning together. Eventually, the goal is to think with the whole model of the heart – considering its chambers, muscles, valves, and vessels in conjunction. So, rather than giving an explanation and having students learn how to restate it. Here, we're model-building by perceiving aspects in turn, through conversation.

Therefore, explanation and variation are continuously happening throughout my lessons. Unlike in the formats I've just mentioned, they're not separated phases of learning. So, what varies during my lessons? My expectations of students vary – the number of aspects I expect them to think about simultaneously.

Think about it this way. Expect students to explore too many aspects too soon, and they'll be overloaded and unable to see the wood for the trees. But expect too little exploration and meaning-making will suffer. Therefore, my learning sequences follow the same pattern suggested by variation theory, but with a more gradual path from one to the other:

1. Separation – Variation for provoking students to discern aspects of a system.
2. Fusion – Variation for provoking students to explore a system's aspects simultaneously.

This is reflected well in the model I presented in Chapter 3, for how to build stock and flow diagrams through dialogue with students. In each phase of the model building students are provoked with variation. However, in the first phase, the scope of thinking is just the stocks and flows. In the next phase, variation includes the stocks, flows, and some variables. Then, it involves seeing the effect of variation on the whole model, before allowing students to test their ideas by connecting the model to others they have in mind. As the learning proceeds, more aspects are thought of simultaneously.

Let's return to my set of assumptions and see them in a detailed example – a recent lesson of mine on the heart with my 14-year-old students.

- **Assumption 1:** Understanding a system involves knowing an explanation of its parts and whole, plus their potential variation.
- **Assumption 2:** An explanation of a system arises in tandem with – not separate from – variation of its critical aspects.
- **Assumption 3**: Vary one aspect of a system at a time – a key structure, or key process.
- **Assumption 4:** Meaning can't be transmitted, so respond to how students infer their own explanations from variation – not just how they restate a given explanation.
- **Assumption 5**: Regulate the number of aspects that you expect students to explore simultaneously according to their understanding – from discerning a single aspect of a system to deliberating the interconnected effects of variation on a whole system.

Example Box 13

Provoking with variation and regulating exploration in a lesson on the heart

Let's look at a lesson I taught recently to a class of 14–15-year-olds on the structure and function of the heart. The lesson came after studying the vascular system and its blood vessels. Therefore, the students were aware of arteries, capillaries, veins (and their valves), and the general direction of blood through the two circuits (see the model in the appendix). Here, it was the four chambers and their mechanism that needed explaining. In this example, I won't describe the entire lesson but will focus on the use of variation and how I regulated its exploration. In total, this describes two lessons of fifty minutes each.

The lessons started with a video of a beating heart. This was the beginning of contextualising the system so students could relate the diagrammatic description of the heart with something concrete. I then had the students draw a diagram of the heart with me so that we had a description that we could discuss (Figure 38). The stock and flow model was developed later in the lesson. When building the descriptions of the system, new parts – with new vocabulary – were added with whole-class chanting of the names. This helps students get a feel for the pronunciation. It also represents minimal exploration, as students are told names directly to be remembered. Once the diagram was complete, I focused on explanation and variation.

Figure 38: An iconic diagram and a stock and flow diagram of the dynamics of the heart that I have co-constructed with my students.

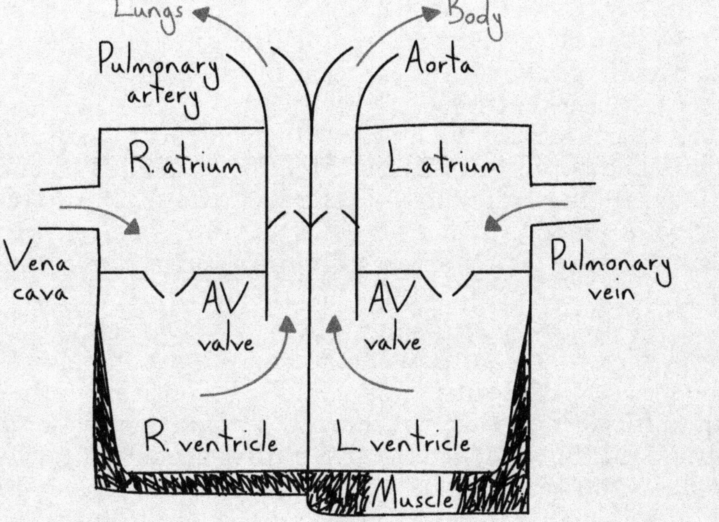
Lungs
Body
Pulmonary artery
Aorta
R. atrium
L. atrium
Vena cava
Pulmonary vein
AV valve
AV valve
R. ventricle
L. ventricle
Muscle

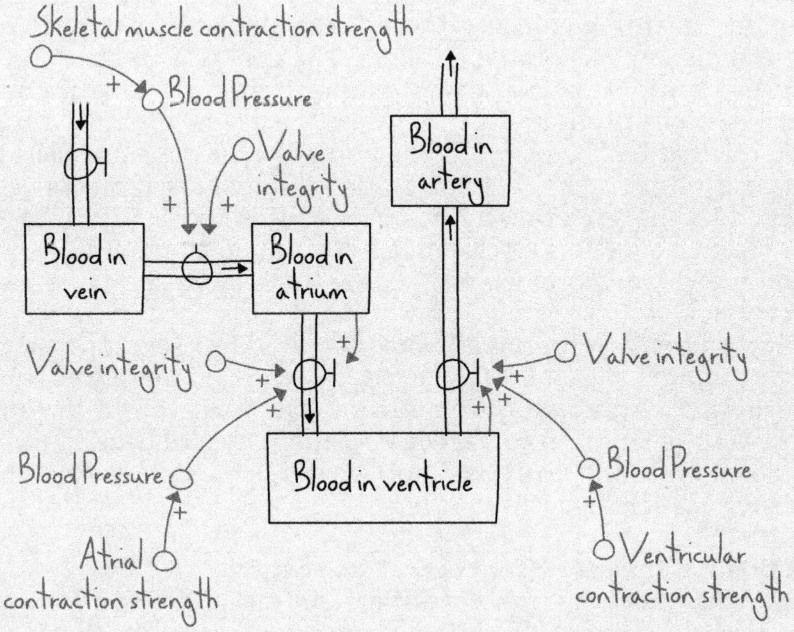
Skeletal muscle contraction strength
Blood Pressure
Valve integrity
Blood in artery
Blood in vein
Blood in atrium
Valve integrity
Valve integrity
Blood in ventricle
Blood Pressure
Blood Pressure
Atrial contraction strength
Ventricular contraction strength

Variation for discerning the parts – the atria

With our diagram and an animation of the heart, I asked the students about the function of the atria. Several suggested that its function was to receive the blood. This set up our first difference. Next, I varied a single part, "Well, what if there were no atria and the blood just went directly into the ventricle?"

At this early stage, I wasn't expecting students to respond. However, students had some prior knowledge that I needed to connect to. I reminded them of the blood pressure in veins, and how the blood would typically pour in at different rates. "No", I told them, "The heart needs something consistent to fill the ventricles." Before giving them my answer, "The atria do receive blood, but their function is to fill the ventricles by pumping blood into them. The ventricles receive enough blood they expand slightly when the atria pump the blood."

The function of the atria was given. This consisted of the aspect of a pump to fill the ventricle but through a crude contrast of atria versus no atria. Had the students discerned it? It needed to vary within the extremes. "You know, some people, especially as they get old, suffer conditions in which their atria don't pump effectively. Atrial fibrillation is an example. The strength of the contraction is lowered... What would happen in that case?"

Again, as this was early in the lesson I wasn't expecting or encouraging any elaborated answers. The goal was to have students discern the function. So, I was attempting to provoke them into *perceiving* potential variation. After giving them time to think, a student suggested that less blood would be pumped into the ventricles. I had been expecting this level of exploration – limited to a direct effect. But I needed them to see one more step. I followed this idea by asking, "And what would happen if less blood were pumped into the ventricle? Would the volume of blood leaving the heart increase, stay the same, or decrease?"

I had students vote, and all voted for the "decrease" option. What had we achieved with this? Tentatively, I interpreted this as the students discerning the function of the atrium. Any variation of the atrium that saw a reduction in its capacity to pump, would cause a decrease in blood leaving the heart. For now, that was enough. It was time to vary the ventricles.

Variation for discerning the parts – the ventricles

The two ventricles bring their own natural variation to explore – they have the same volume but different muscle mass. So continuing with the same theme of pumping blood, I asked students what difference it makes, "If the volume of blood in both ventricles is the same, what difference does the extra muscle make in the left ventricle?"

After giving time to think, a student suggested, "The left ventricle needs to pump to all the body, while the right ventricle only needs to pump to the lungs." *Fantastic*, the student was making connections. But it wasn't the mechanistic answer I was expecting. So, I replied, "Yes, that's the purpose, but what difference does it make mechanistically, what difference does it cause?"

They suggested that it pumped the blood faster, and I asked the class to vote if they agreed. They did, and I thought they'd grasped the idea. I made clear that by having a stronger contraction strength, the left ventricle would pump the blood with higher pressure. We had previously studied the relationship between volume and pressure in lung ventilation, and I reminded them of that model. Then I checked, "What about the right ventricle, then? Why doesn't it have as much muscle?"

After a discussion in pairs, a student suggested that high pressure wasn't needed as it was only sending blood to the lungs. Again the class voted that they agreed. It was time to vary the final parts of the model.

Variation for discerning the parts – the valves

Students think of the valves as a door that is opened and closed with a mechanism that "knows" when to do so. Instead, I showed the students images of the AV valves and the connective tissue that keeps them from turning inside out. I gestured blood pressure pushing on the valves, causing them to close spontaneously. I did this by holding my arms upwards – with both palms facing each other – and then rapidly moving them into a praying position. That's the valve then, but how could it be different?

"What would happen if I cut that connective tissue?" I let the students discuss this in pairs before a student suggested that blood would flow back into the atrium. *Good*, I thought, but... "Would it not flow through the artery anymore?"

They thought it would. Next, I asked the class to vote on what would happen to the volume of blood flowing through the artery: increase, stay the same, or decrease. And they voted that it would decrease. The purpose here wasn't to test knowledge – we weren't there yet – but to discern aspects of the system.

Yet this was one of those part-or-no-part contrasts. I also wanted to vary the aspect within these extremes. So, I told students that valves could become less stable over time (i.e. mitral regurgitation), maybe due to a thickening, or an infection. In this case, the valve does close, but not fully.

"What difference would it make compared to normal, if a person's AV valve suddenly stopped closing fully? Would their blood pressure in their arteries increase, stay the same, or decrease?" They voted that it would decrease. This question focused again on blood leaving the heart, similar to previous answers. So I followed it up with another question, "How do you think it would affect the whole person – how would they feel?"

Note that I encouraged slightly more exploration, from parts to whole, but without expecting full mechanistic answers. And with this, it was time to start adaptively encouraging students to explore more.

Variation for exploring whole system behaviour – connecting valves and flows

Where are we up to? By now, we'd built a description of the system and varied key parts. However, I wanted to build a model that would establish exactly what caused the system to work the way it did. It was time to draw the stocks and flows. I told the students that it was a model for explaining both sides of the heart and that we didn't need two versions. Take a moment to review the model in Figure 38.

To get them thinking, I added the variables of "valve" and "blood pressure" to the flows, but without naming them – just the arrows and the circle. To reduce the complexity, I used two colours – each flow had a green and a red variable connected to it. This way I had signalled to the students that I had in mind two repeating variables that directly affected the flows. And I asked them to discuss in pairs what those variables could be.

When I asked a student and had the class vote on whether they agreed, it was clear that many thought one variable had something to do with valves. I asked a student to justify their answer. They replied that the "AV valve prevents backflow" from the ventricle. *OK*, I thought, *let's see*. So I labelled the variable with "valve" and then provoked the students with some variation. "Does that make sense? If there were no valve would the flow decrease?"

I had them vote if they agreed or disagreed. But at this stage in the lesson, I pushed them further. I pointed to the diagram of the heart and asked, "What would happen to the flow, if there were no valve – just a hole – between the ventricle and atrium? Would the flow through the arteries drop to zero?"

I let them discuss this and then asked a student for their answer. They suggested the blood would flow both ways, through arteries and backwards. The class also voted that they agreed. To follow this, I returned to the example of people with AV valves that don't close fully, due to infections or other causes. I asked, "What would happen to the flow, if the valve weren't functioning at 100% but 80%. Compared to having no valves, would the flow to the arteries be the same, or different?"

Here then, we needed a new word. It wasn't black and white, but a spectrum. I proposed the term "valve integrity". Many students weren't familiar with this, so I pointed to words they did know: "to disintegrate", and "integers" (from maths). I added it to the model.

I asked students to vote if the connection between the variable and the flow should be "same" or "opposite". But few voted – signalling their lack of confidence. Therefore, I let them discuss it in pairs before having them vote again. And, before voting, I helped them by beginning with the partial statement, “The higher the valve's integrity the...” This time, with more confidence, they voted that it should be “same”.

To finish the discussion on valves, I asked if we could add the variable to the other flows, voting if they agreed or disagreed. They generally voted that they agreed. But I wanted to probe further – I asked another question. This time about the atrium, “When the atrium pumps blood to the ventricle, what stops it moving back into the veins?”

This had them exploring further afield, because the valves of veins were not drawn on the heart diagram, and they had to remember a model from a previous lesson. With this, it was time to move on to the next variable.

Variation for exploring whole system behaviour – the causes of blood pressure

To shift my students' focus to the other variable, I asked them, “What causes the blood to move from the ventricle into the arteries?”

One student suggested “the heart”. *A brilliant example*, I thought, *of an idea lacking distinction*. Yet, provoking distinction drawing was precisely my goal. So, I asked again for clarity, “Yes, but what directly causes the blood flow in the heart?”

Another student suggested “the muscles”, and again, I responded with a question, “Yes, but what does that muscle contraction cause?”

As we'd already studied the relationship between volume and pressure in the topic of ventilation of the lungs, and we'd already discussed blood pressure as a cause of blood flow in the vascular system, this wasn't hard for the students. One suggested “blood pressure” and I labelled the variable. I asked if the connection was “same” or “opposite” and had the students vote. I asked the students if blood pressure was a variable for all the flows. As they agreed, I added the variables.

Yet, “blood pressure” across the whole system also lacks distinction. “What causes the blood pressure to increase here?” I asked as I pointed at the flow between the ventricle and artery. To which, the students suggested the ventricular muscle. For the other, they suggested atrial muscle. For the first flow, they suggested “body muscles”, for which I gave them the name “skeletal muscle”. *Fine*, I thought, it was time to check.

“Does this model make sense? If we had a grown man and a little boy, their hearts would be different sizes – they'd have different muscle strength. Would the grown man, therefore, have more blood flowing into the arteries per beat?”

They agreed via vote. But I continued, “If the heart is bigger, there'd be more space for blood. So, if there's more blood in the ventricle, will the flow to the arteries increase?”

Again, they agreed. Therefore, we had to add the connection between the stock of "blood in the ventricle" and its outflow. The more blood in the ventricle, the more will flow out of it. It made sense. I also added the equivalent connection for the stock of the atrium.

Pointing to the atrium in the model, I reminded my students of the people with atrial fibrillation we'd discussed earlier (with weaker contraction strength). They were ready to explore the relations between the aspects they'd been discerning. "Thinking with the model, what would happen in that situation [of atrial fibrillation], compared to normal?"

They now had a description in the form of a diagram, but also a stock and flow model to work with. I expected more from students, but they had the diagrams to aid their thinking. Therefore, I gave them more time to discuss the idea in pairs relative to earlier in the lesson.

Following the model, we could infer that if the contraction strength of the atria were lower, the flow of blood reaching the ventricles would be lower too. Therefore, less blood would be pumped into the arteries. We discussed this as a class, and I asked them how they think a person with this condition may feel. Now I searched for connections between heart function, cell respiration rates, and the whole organism. "Tired," a student suggested, before I prompted them to give a mechanistic answer.

The model was now built, and my students had begun thinking about it as a whole. It'd been varied and explained, and it was time to encourage more exploration. Before moving on to the next phase, I asked my students to explain the model to each other in pairs.

Variation for exploring the interconnections and behaviour of the whole system

To begin with, I wanted students to see the mechanism of the heart within the larger vascular system. This was to help them connect the model of the heart to the vascular system model from a previous lesson.

I provoked students with a simple diagram that contrasted the vascular systems of fish, frogs, and mammals. Fish have a single circuit with just one atrium and one ventricle. Frogs have a double circuit but, unlike mammals, have a single ventricle. Finally, mammals have a double circuit, each circuit being served by its own ventricle. I projected the diagram for them to see and asked them to spot the difference. This was the easy part, which they carried out well. Nevertheless, to make sure, I explicitly mentioned the differences. I then asked the question that mattered – what difference would it make? I let them discuss this in pairs before listening to their responses and having students vote on agreement or disagreement. I encouraged more students to justify their answers mechanistically at this stage, pushing for explicit exploration.

The discussion covered most of the points I wanted them to focus on, but I made the difference makers explicit. Firstly, there is a drop in pressure in the single circuit of fish. The diagram showed the lung capillary bed at the top and the capillaries of the systemic circuit below it. The students had discerned for themselves the problem of blood pressure, but, I asked, "What keeps the blood flowing after the gills?" Interestingly, a student replied with "gravity", and I learnt a lot from that response. After discussing how the diagram was a simplified model – and that fish didn't have all their blood vessels orientated vertically – I returned to images of the branching of arteries all over the body. With this, we established that contractions of skeletal muscle caused an increase in blood pressure.

We moved on to the frog. What difference does that single ventricle make, with its partially formed septum? Many students correctly identified the mixing of oxygenated with deoxygenated blood. So, "What'll happen?" I asked. Again, I was encouraging students to make connections between the heart function, cell respiration rates, and the activity of the whole organism. To provoke them further, I asked why the frog lineage hadn't evolved to have a similar heart to ours. The most common response was "They don't need it" but I wanted to push for more exploration, so asked for justifications. A student said, "You only need lots of oxygen in the blood if you're going to use it, and they don't."

This is the sort of answer I was expecting. This teleological language is legitimate in biology, but as long as the person's underlying model involves blind variation and selective retention in a population (Kampourakis 2020). The key is to embed variation and selection in a course as metacontent and for it to be discussed often. Then, whenever these teleological phrases appear, explore them and see whether students are thinking with the variation and selection principle. Here then, a conversation was needed. I was also interested in exploring the answer because it related to requisite variety.

I asked if humans had the same or a larger variety of responses available to them due to their heart structure. They agreed that we had a larger variety. But why don't frogs evolve the same structure? It might be because they already have the requisite variety to live the way they do. Frogs are not as metabolically or physically active as we are, so if it arose it wouldn't necessarily give an advantage for survival and reproduction. In other words, they can conserve their ongoing adaptation with their environment – their way of being and organisational integrity.

We were coming to the latter part of the second lesson. It was time to provoke students to explore their new distinctions and relations with a good "What if?" question. I set this up by discussing how human fetuses didn't have a fully formed septum between the ventricles while in the uterus. The septum forms completely at birth when the lungs are needed to supply oxygen, rather than the placenta. But in some, the septum had defects – holes that didn't close. Some people call this "a hole in the heart", and I mentioned how the hole could be bigger or smaller, and you could have one or more. A student then asked what would happen to a person with one, and I told them that was exactly what I was about to ask them. Before I gave the students time to discuss in pairs, I reminded them of what mechanistic explanations look like. And we finished the lesson with a whole class discussion of the consequences. In this case, I didn't have the students write their answers, but it was an option that I could have taken.

This brings us to the end of exploring the students' side of the recursive teaching model (Figure 39). To finish, we must briefly return to the teacher to consider how they could handle the complexity explored by their students.

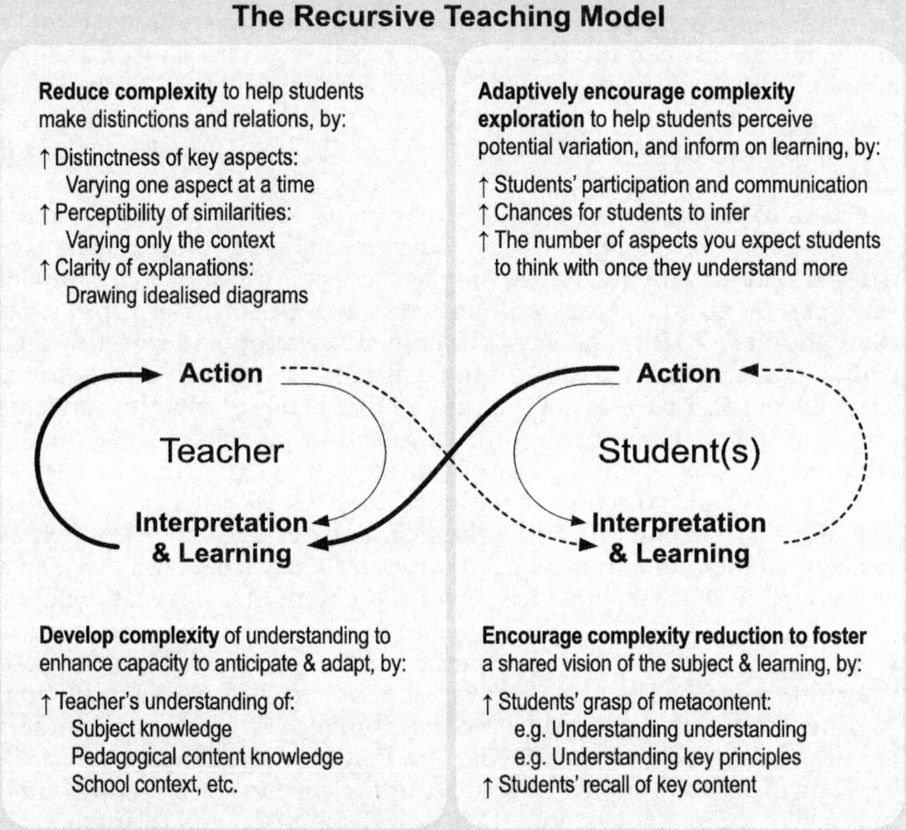

Figure 39 (repeated from Figure 2): The recursive teaching model.

6. TO ADAPT, TEACHERS MUST BE ABLE TO ABSORB THE COMPLEXITY THAT THE CLASSROOM PRODUCES

We're coming to the end of our journey through the recursive teaching model. Here I look at the teacher's capacity to anticipate and adapt in the face of complexity. This short chapter offers a perspective on teaching expertise from the point of view of cybernetics. And serves to complete the loop in the recursive teaching model. Among the many roles the teacher has to play in the classroom, let's look at the teacher as an adaptive regulator.

A teacher's ability to adapt to students rises in tandem with developing a complex understanding of subject, pedagogy, and context

Key Idea:
To anticipate and adapt, a good teacher must know which action to select from the variety of available actions – they must be a good model of the system.

Just over a decade after Ashby's formulation of the law of requisite variety, he and Roger Conant (Conant & Ashby 1970) published a new paper entitled "Every good regulator of a system must be a model of that system." The authors showed that if a regulator of a system is going to be able to do its job well, it must have a good idea of how that system behaves. An alternative name is the law of requisite knowledge (Heylighen 1992). It involves anticipation and adaptation and is intuitive if we take it to the classroom.

From the moment a teacher enters a classroom the variety of possible outcomes is huge. All types of events occur during a lesson that can nudge it off its path. But the teacher has a plan. Let's say they expect the students to have covered certain content. They expect the students to have understood it to a certain extent. They expect the students to be engaged and participate in the lesson. Anything else would be outside their ideal outcomes. The role of the teacher is to steer the lesson effectively to get there. But how would this lesson differ between an expert teacher who knows the school well and a visiting trainee teacher?

In Conant and Ashby's original vision (1970), there was the total variety of all possible outcomes and a smaller subset considered ideal. Feeding into this were the outcomes of the interactions between students and teacher. And feeding into these interactions were any disruptions to the lesson. A disruption could be anything that deviates the lesson from the trajectory the teacher had in mind.

The trainee – with little pedagogical content knowledge, less subjective knowledge, and barely any knowledge of the students and school – may hold the same "ideal" trajectory in mind as the expert teacher. The expert teacher may have provided them with the plan, learning materials, and tasks. Yet, as the lesson unfolds, disturbances occur. Students may ask unexpected questions; their interest may wane. The explanations don't land right, and the students don't understand. No one participates when asking questions. As it ends it's clear that it ended up in the zone of less-than-ideal outcomes.

Yet, the opposite occurred for the expert teacher. With a good understanding of how the classroom system would react, the teacher could anticipate them. And with the requisite knowledge, they were able to adapt to students who were confused or asked unexpected questions. They were able to encourage the students to explore more, as their knowledge allowed them to absorb the questions.

Ultimately, if the teacher doesn't have the requisite knowledge, their capacity to adapt is more limited. Consequently, if the teacher can't absorb the complexity of their students' confusions and explorations, then complexity will be avoided. They're likely only to encourage complexity reduction but not exploration. Superficial learning is more likely to occur in these cases.

How can the complexity of a classroom be measured? Ashby's (1956; 1958) concept of variety (complexity) was quantified by the number of possible states a system could assume. The crucial point here is that the number of states depends on the *observer* counting and how many they can distinguish.

For this reason, trainee teachers are likely to underestimate the complexity of a classroom. They are yet to discern much of the variety of possible events and their unravelling.

At an extreme, a teacher without the requisite knowledge would have to select (almost) blindly from a variety of responses, until they hit across one that would bring the lesson back to equilibrium. Boisot and McKelvey (2011) call this a "behavioural headless chicken" approach. How might this be seen in the classroom? An example is a novice teacher who seems to plan activities randomly to ensure that the lesson time will be filled.

Nevertheless, Boisot and McKelvey (2011) suggest that systems can also do the opposite. When attempting to adapt to complexity – for which they don't have the requisite knowledge – they can overcompensate. This involves oversimplifying the interpreted experiences. The "routiniser" approach lumps many different phenomena into a few categories that allow routine responses. Yet, "if they all 'make sense' and can be taken for granted – human beings lose their sense of the essentially contingent nature of things and either maladapt or fossilize ... losing their capacity to change." (289). How might this look in the classroom? An example is a teacher who oversimplifies learning to memorising and forgetting – answering correctly and saying the right thing at the right time. It allows the teacher to routinise their responses, but they diminish their ability to adapt to complex understandings.

Therefore, providing teachers with an array of pedagogical actions must be matched in equal measure by knowledge of when to put them to use – pedagogical theory. It also requires knowledge of the concept being taught – your subject's theory. In reality, selecting an action will hardly be totally blind, or determined (Heylighen 1992), but an expert teacher is much more likely to act adequately.

So, what does the research on teacher effectiveness suggest? Coe et al. (2020) reviewed the evidence available to them to produce a "Great Teaching Toolkit", which consists of four priorities for teachers (15):

> "Great teachers:
> 1. Understand the content they are teaching and how it is learnt.
> 2. Create a supportive environment for learning.
> 3. Manage the classroom to maximise opportunity to learn.
> 4. Present content, activities and interactions that activate their students' thinking."

Forming relationships and getting to know your students – understanding their expectations and those of their families – are all key to adapting to a specific context and creating a supportive environment for learning. However, let me discuss the first priority in the list: "Understanding the Content". This appears to consist of subject knowledge and pedagogical content knowledge – knowing how to teach what you know. They explain that:

> "Great teachers understand the content they are teaching and how it is learnt. This means teachers should have deep and fluent knowledge and flexible understanding of the content they are teaching and how it is learnt, including its inherent dependencies. They should have an explicit repertoire of well-crafted explanations, examples and tasks for each topic they teach." (17).

This makes teaching a profession of life-long learning and the continual development of expertise. The complexity of the classroom forces a formidable learning curve on new teachers. The burden could be lessened – and the route to expertise made easier – by forming communities interested in enacting systems theory.

This teaching community could learn more rapidly by sharing which aspects seem critical for learning specific concepts. By sharing good examples of differences and variations. And, importantly, by creating, sharing, and deliberating stock and flow models. These would serve both to help novice teachers implement good models and to see what expert teachers see. Something that is clearer than sharing pre-made resources like slide decks or worksheets. Because they explicitly share the distinctions the teacher sees as important and show what they're likely to vary in a lesson.

This is a community I would like to be a member of. In the next and final chapter, I'd like to conclude by pondering what ways of seeing this community could espouse as it lays down a distinct path in biology teaching.

7. CLOSURE: OUR MODELS INDICATE OURSELVES

Throughout this book, I've shared my assumptions explicitly. My motive has been to share a rule set for teachers to explore – rather than a set of activities to follow. Von Foerster (1998; 2014) thought humans were always developing such rule sets. He referred to them as games. Like chess, some rules govern what moves can be played, and which can't. Once you're aware of those rules, you can then go on to explore what's possible – we can build and discover complexity. This is also how scientific theories are constructed.

Variation theory (Marton 2015) for example, begins with the assumption that our cognitive capabilities are limited – hence the need to vary one thing at a time. It also assumes that we act logically according to our understanding – we are autonomous beings who respond according to our own perceptions, not the situation seen by others. An assumption that compels us to converse with students to find out what they know. Maybe its most characteristic assumption is that we can only discern something new when it varies. Another is that perception of particular aspects is *critical* to seeing something in a powerful way – it's not just the accrual of information. Variation theory's assumptions act as a rule set. They set the scene for exploring and developing possible pedagogical moves in the classroom. Some of which are vetoed by the assumptions. For example, beginning learning – of something new to students – with examples of similarity isn't possible within the rules.

The key ideas I've highlighted and the assumptions I've given have put forth a rule set for recursive teaching. It's one that I invite you to play with me – to explore together what's possible.

We can also see the idea of rule sets when building models during a lesson and sharing metacontent. Models are idealisations that omit details to make them understandable and useful. The ideal gas law is a great example. As science works towards the production of *simplified* models, then the goals of science can't be the *whole* truth, but to sufficiently explain (Potochnik 2017). We seek a set of rules that account for what we experience: "Scientific models are distillations of our embodied experience as observers, modelers, and interveners." (Thompson, in Varela et al. 2016, xxvii).

The use of models in biology teaching is similar. We don't dispense all our knowledge into models, lest our students become cognitively overwhelmed. While we want our students to remember key knowledge, we don't design models to be rote-memorised either. Why then, do we produce these models for our lessons? While teachers design and bring the model to the lesson, students and teachers participate as co-players. The students and teacher think with the model's assumptions to see what they can explain about the world. It's like saying, "If we model the vascular system this way, what can we explain?" Information then "comes into being, emerges, grows out of this game" (Foerster 2014, 28). I hope this will be a fruitful concept to have in mind as you browse the models in the appendix and consider how you could teach with them. Remember that these are only examples of what's possible with the set of symbols – feel encouraged to edit or redesign them.

Beyond the assumptions of individual models, metacontent deals with fundamental assumptions. (Of course, other fundamental assumptions don't get shared explicitly, lest there be too many). These distinctions shape a person's way of seeing biology and life. Therefore, I'd like to conclude the book by encouraging the designing and sharing of metacontent with students. Again, I hope this view will be fruitful as you deliberate your curricula with colleagues.

Why is this important? Let me return to von Foerster, who said, "The Laws of Nature are written by man. The laws of biology must write themselves." (1972, 195).

Humans can observe the speed of light as something separate from us but, with life, we must recursively look inward. "In this way we set off on the search for a description that describes itself." (Foerster 2014, 60). Rather than "there is life" – as if we are observers of it – it's a matter of "here I am".

Learning about biology, therefore, represents an interesting example of self-reference. We're not just giving students a bunch of facts about life. We're not just telling students the mechanisms of how organisms and ecosystems function. It's not just, "This is how your body does things". We're encouraging students to develop their self-concepts – how they conceive themselves. Because "through the ways that we talk about life, we create, bring forth, produce life." (58).

Gregory Bateson, for example, believed that the "survival of the fittest" was an assumption that had caused all types of degradation to life on Earth (Chaney 2017). The belief held humankind as the personification – the very embodiment – of that process, as it dominated over all other kinds. Instead, Bateson argued, the unit of survival of biological systems wasn't the species or the individual, but a relation – the organism plus its environment (Harries-Jones 1995).

Species – and organisms – survive by continual adaptation that preserves interrelationships and interdependencies. A lineage isn't just the preservation of genetic material or phenotypes over generations. It's the preservation of a way of being in a co-adaptation between species and environment (Maturana & Verden-Zöller 2008). Therefore, those who destroy their environment will ultimately share the same fate. Bateson thought that our problems stemmed from mistakes in how we perceive the world (Harries-Jones 1995, 169).

Biology then isn't simply a course with lots of content to learn. Concealed below the surface are fundamental distinctions that affect how our students see the world. This makes metacontent the core of biology curricula – not a supplementary extra.

The question, of course, is which assumptions matter. In this book, I've shared a (non-definitive) list of principles that act as metacontent. They aren't based on linearity or controllability. We can never fully control or predict complex systems. Nor can we live with them sustainably while holding these ideas in mind (Meadows 2008). My principles – as much in the recursive teaching model as in my biology courses – are based on variety, circularity, and coadaptation. Could bringing these assumptions to the classroom make a difference to how our students bring forth a relationship with nature? I believe so. For Bateson, at least, (1972, 327) "The most important task today is, perhaps, to learn to think in the new way."

Nevertheless, the first place to begin doing so is not with the curriculum, but with teaching itself. Recursive teaching has worked best when I've shared the model with my classes. Contrasted with linear teaching formats, my students begin to feel their role in the loop as autonomous beings. More than content to learn then, the ideas of circularity and adaptation must be enacted in the classroom. It is, after all, through recursive interactions that students and teachers coadapt. And by doing so, our students learn a way of being through us as their subject teacher.

APPENDIX: STOCK AND FLOW MODELS

The following models were designed for my context. Therefore, you may feel some are too complex for your context, or not complex enough. Feel free to use my models and modify them as you need to. The purpose of this appendix is no more than to give you an idea of the possibilities.

When reading stock and flow diagrams for the first time, always begin with the stocks and flows. This will give you an idea of what the model is about. Then look at the variables that cause changes to the flows. Remember that systems occur over time, so don't think of them statically. You might find it useful to trace your thoughts through the model with your fingers.

Your students will need time to improve their thinking with system dynamics models. But it's not in vain, as students are not just learning the diagrams, they're learning to think about systems. Here's something to watch out for. I've found in my classroom, as did Scott et al. (2022), that students tend to begin thinking only in terms of inflows. There are two ways to fill a bathtub: increase the inflow or decrease the outflow. As students improve, they progress to thinking in terms of inflows and outflows as a sequence of events – first, the inflow happens, then the outflow – before thinking in terms of simultaneous inflows and outflows. Interestingly, the skill appears independent of mathematical ability (Sweeney & Sternman 2000).

Finally, let me give some quick advice on the naming of parts. Give the stock a name of what it is and possibly where it is, for example, glucose in the blood. For the flows, if possible, give them names using a word in its gerund form. For example, "absorbing" instead of absorption. This gives a feel of something that is happening over time.

When naming variables, Sterman (2000, 152) recommends you use words with a clear sense of direction, "Choose names for which the meaning of an increase or decrease is clear, variables that can be larger or smaller." For example, "wind speed" is a better name than wind, because more or less "wind" is ambiguous. Likewise, light "intensity" is better than "light", "chloroplast density" is better than "chloroplasts", and "breathing rate" is better than "breathing".

Sterman also recommends you "choose variables whose normal sense of direction is positive" (153). For example, happiness is a better choice than unhappiness. Increasing happiness, and decreasing happiness, both make intuitive sense. However, decreasing unhappiness takes longer to grasp, which adds to the cognitive load of interpreting a diagram.

Models of Human Physiology

1. Blood clotting

Age of students I have used this model with: 16–18

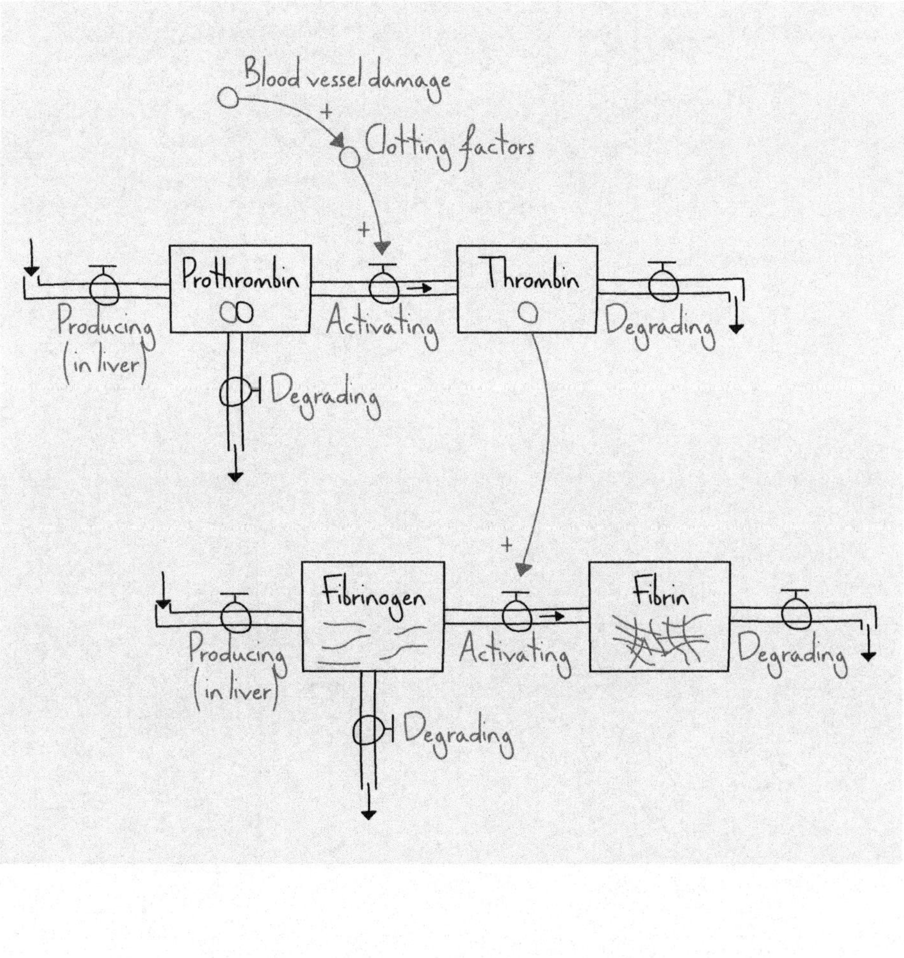

2. Digestive system: overall structure & function

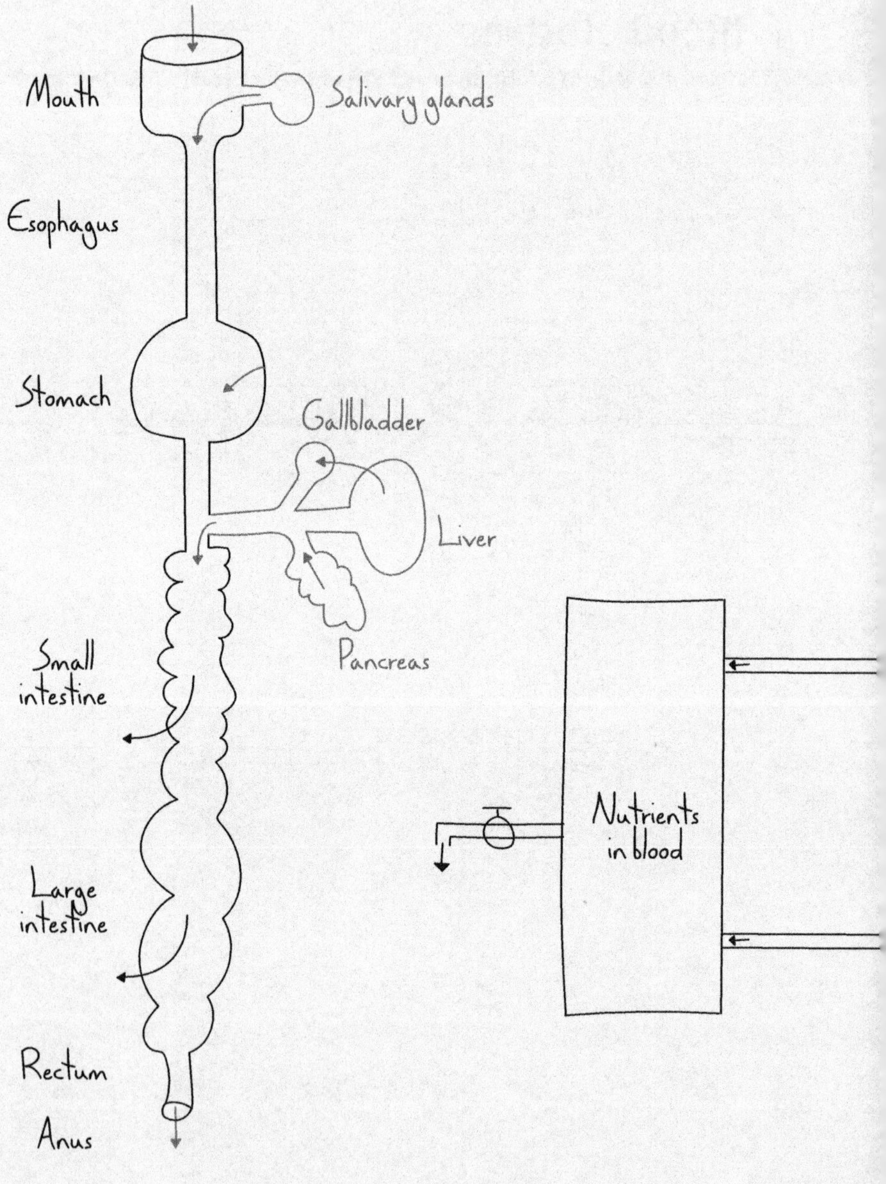

Age of students I have used this model with: 14–16

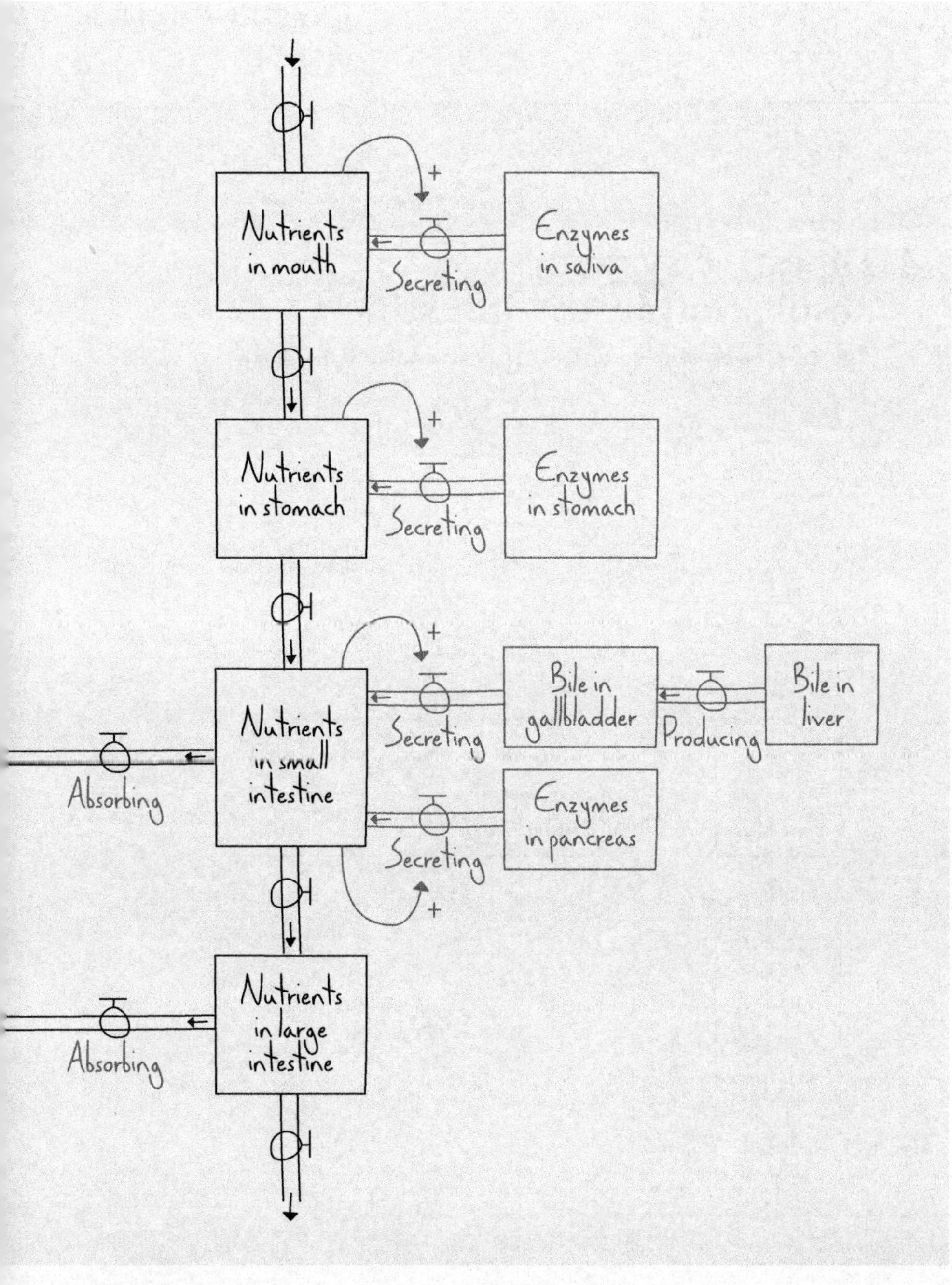

3. Digestive system: enzymes & bile

Age of students I have used this model with: 14–16

4. Digestive system: absorption in the intestine

Age of students I have used this model with: 14–16

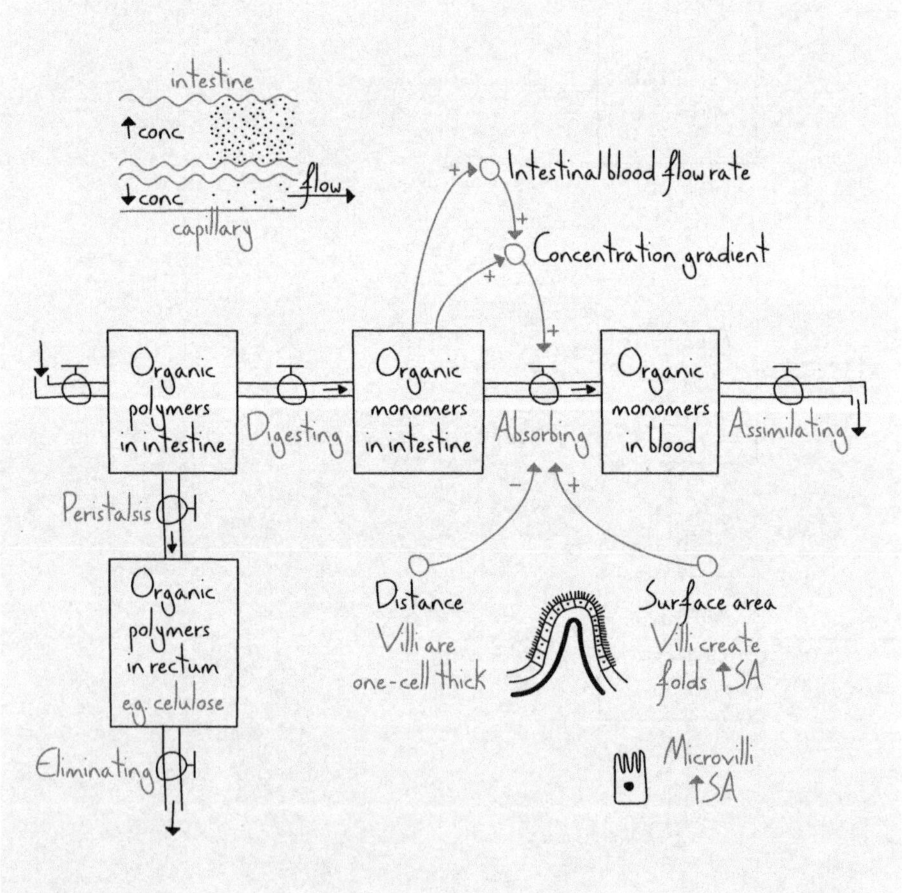

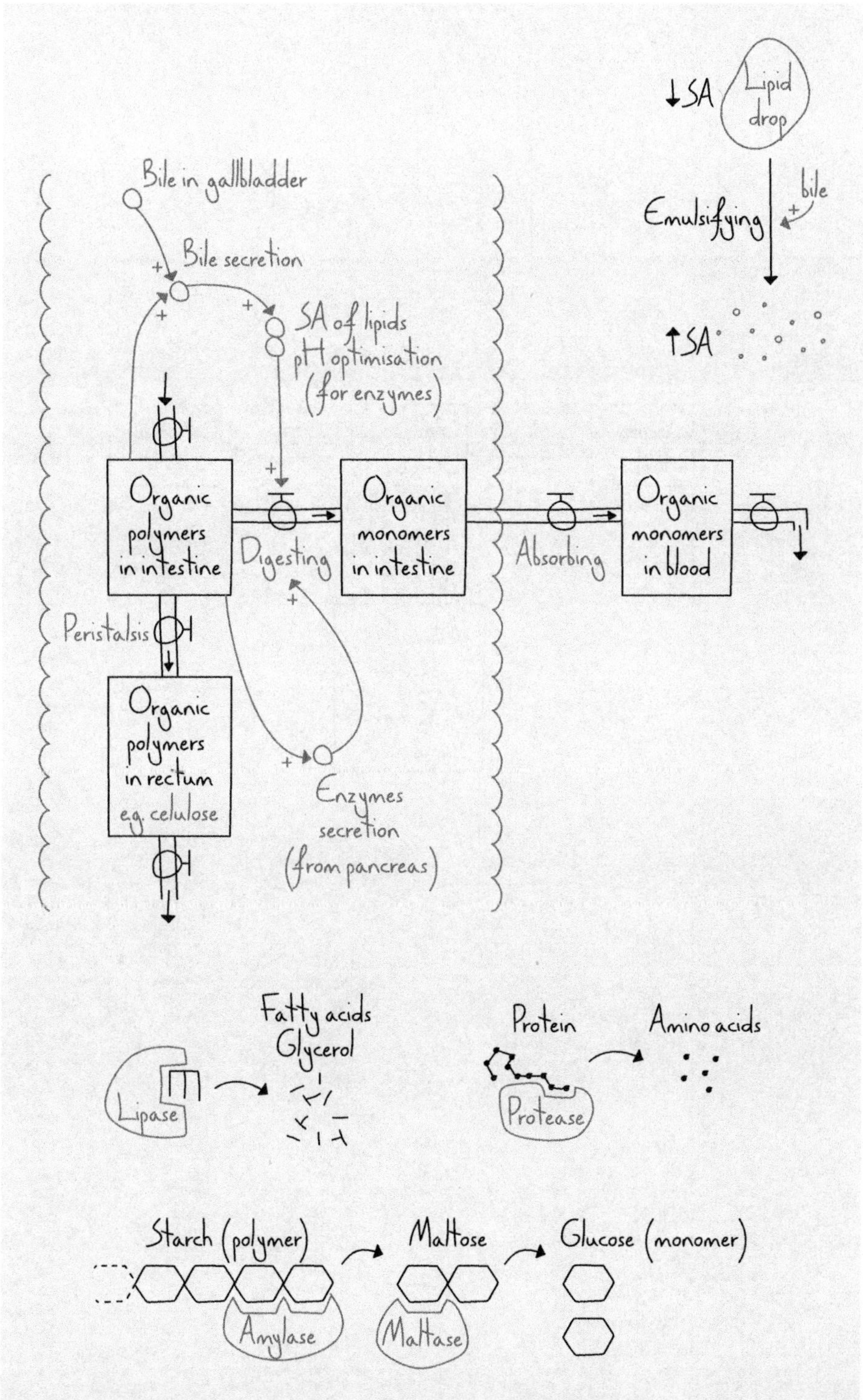
↓SA
Lipid drop
bile
Emulsifying
↑SA
Bile in gallbladder
Bile secretion
SA of lipids
pH optimisation
(for enzymes)
Organic polymers in intestine
Digesting
Organic monomers in intestine
Absorbing
Organic monomers in blood
Peristalsis
Organic polymers in rectum
e.g. celulose
Enzymes secretion
(from pancreas)
Fatty acids
Glycerol
Lipase
Protein
Amino acids
Protease
Starch (polymer)
Maltose
Glucose (monomer)
Amylase
Maltase

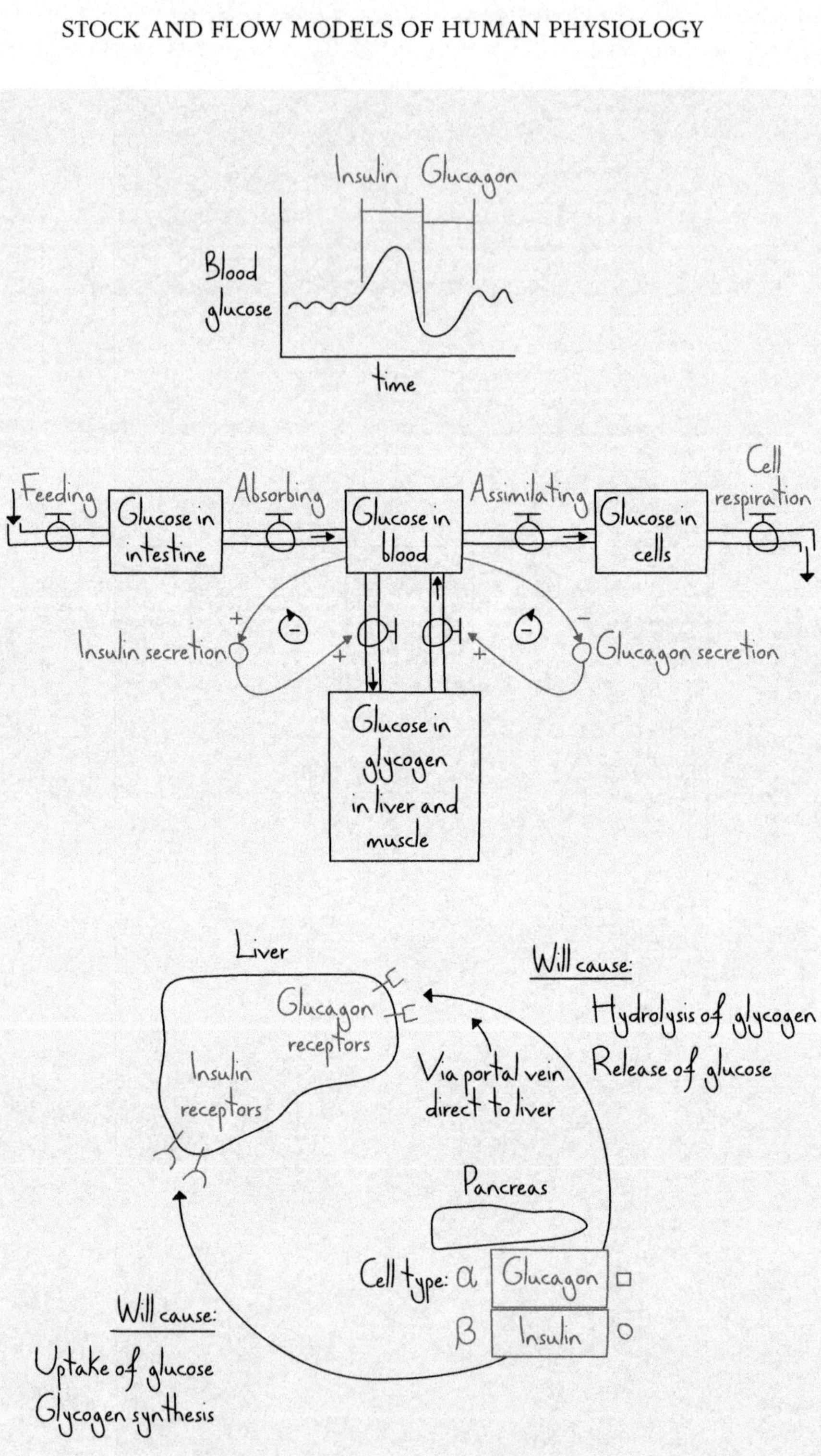
Insulin
Glucagon
Blood glucose
time
Feeding
Glucose in intestine
Absorbing
Glucose in blood
Assimilating
Glucose in cells
Cell respiration
Insulin secretion
Glucagon secretion
Glucose in glycogen in liver and muscle
Liver
Glucagon receptors
Insulin receptors
Will cause:
Hydrolysis of glycogen
Release of glucose
Via portal vein direct to liver
Pancreas
Cell type: α
Glucagon
β
Insulin
Will cause:
Uptake of glucose
Glycogen synthesis

5. Endocrine system: blood glucose regulation

Age of students I have used this model with: 14–18

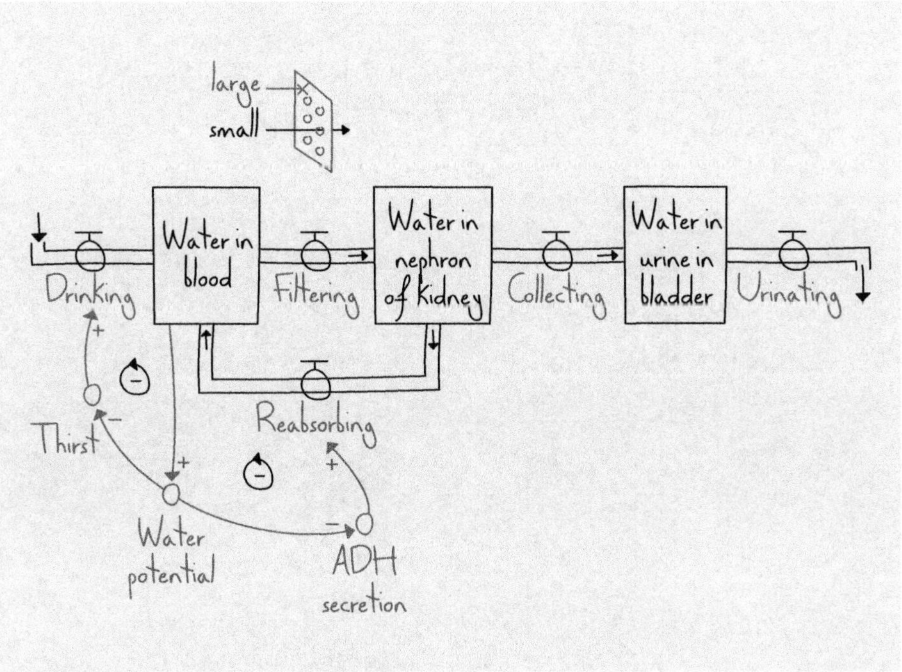

6. Osmotic regulation in nephron

Age of students I have used this model with: 14–16

7. Reproductive system: the placenta

Age of students I have used this model with: 16-18

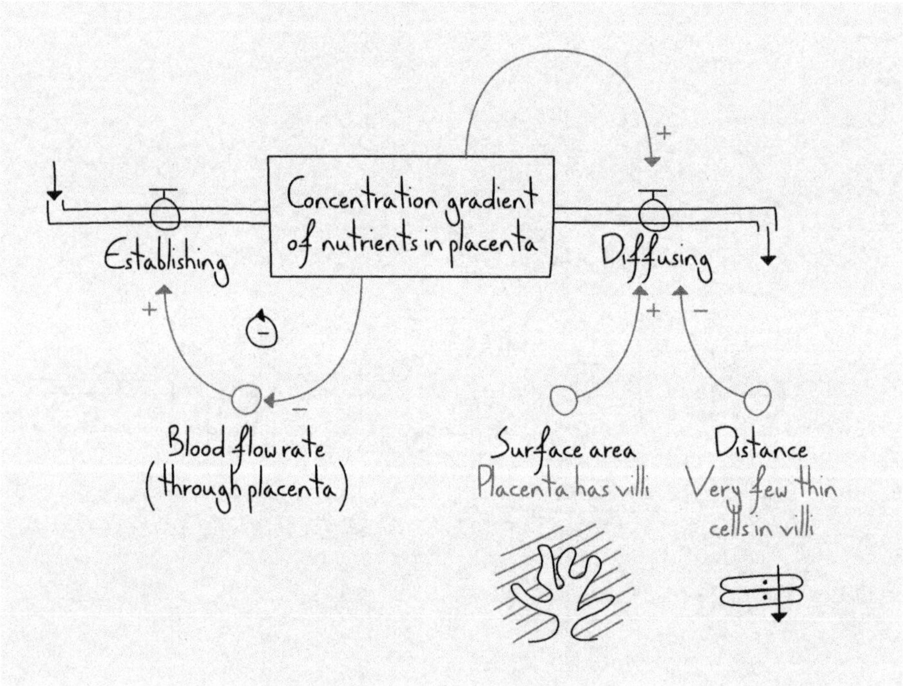

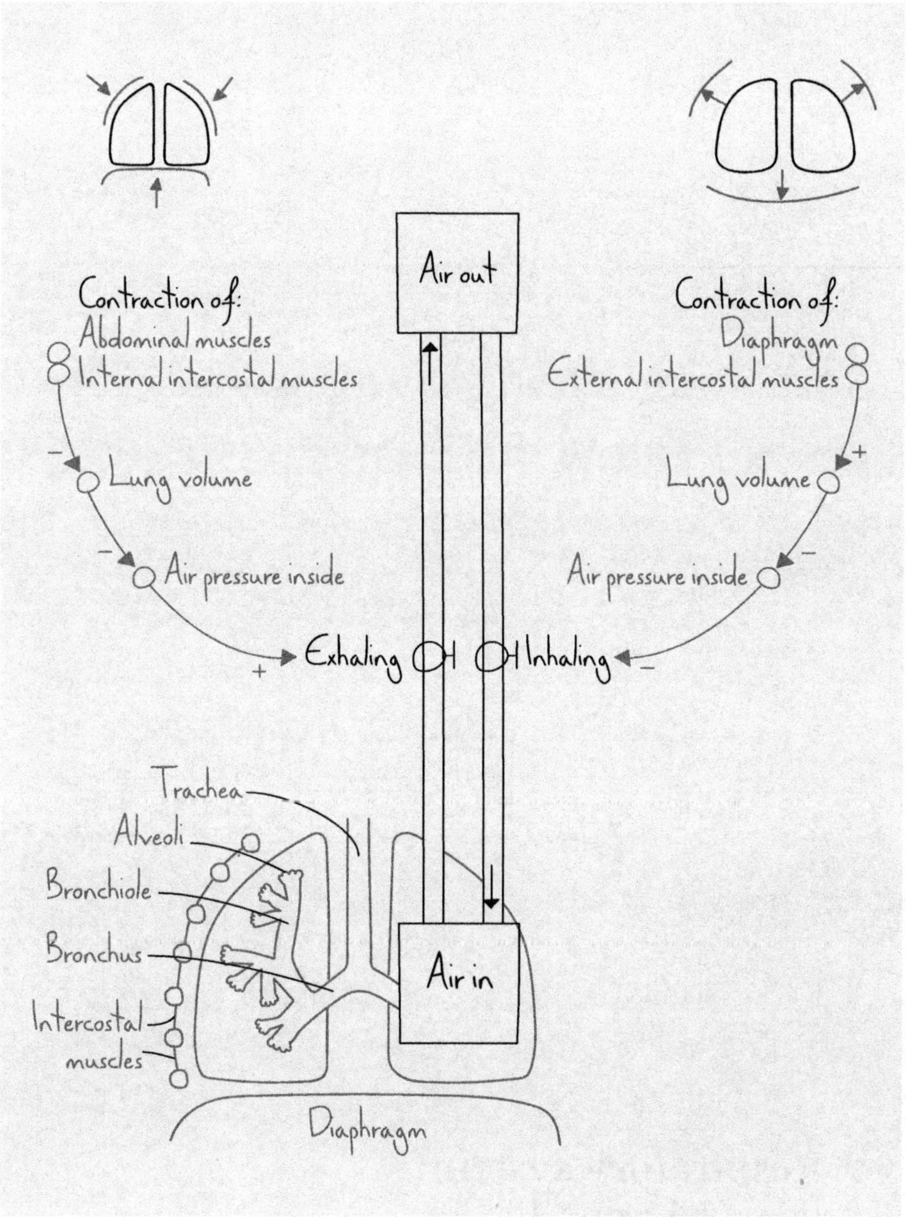

8. Respiratory system: lung ventilation

Age of students I have used this model with: 14–18

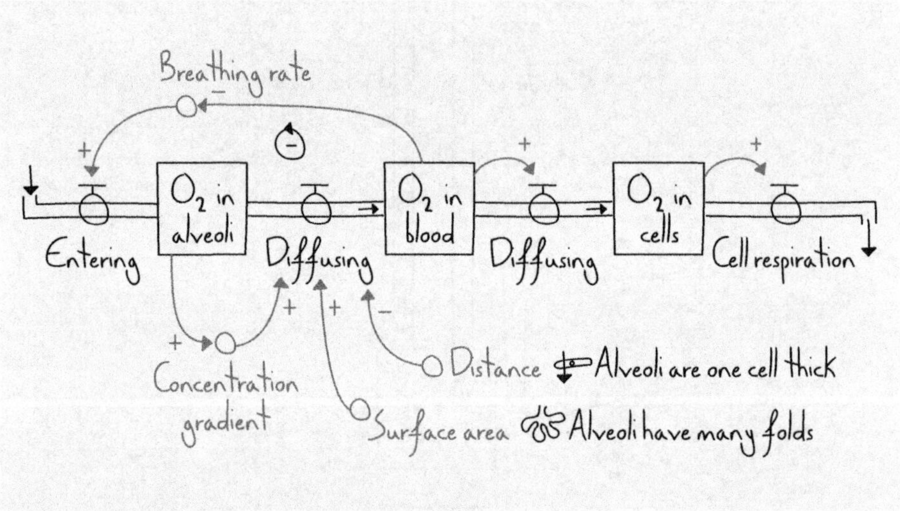

9. Respiratory system: gas exchange 1

Age of students I have used this model with: 14–18

10. Respiratory system: gas exchange 2

Age of students I have used this model with: 14–18

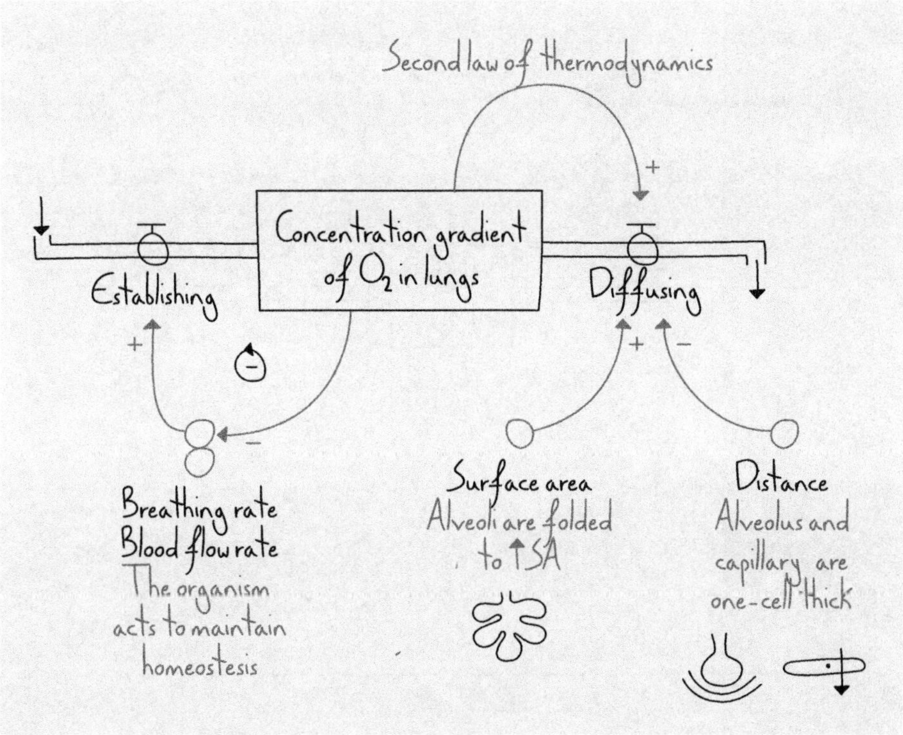

11. Thermoregulation

Age of students I have used this model with: 14–16

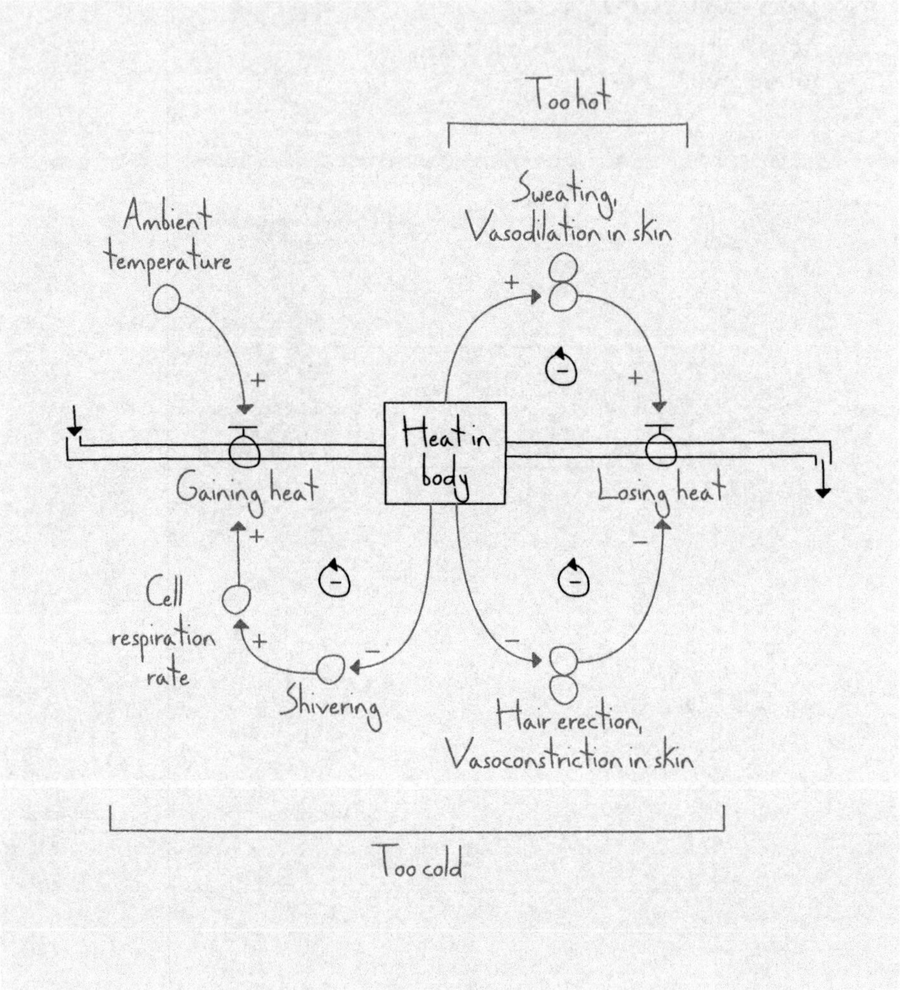

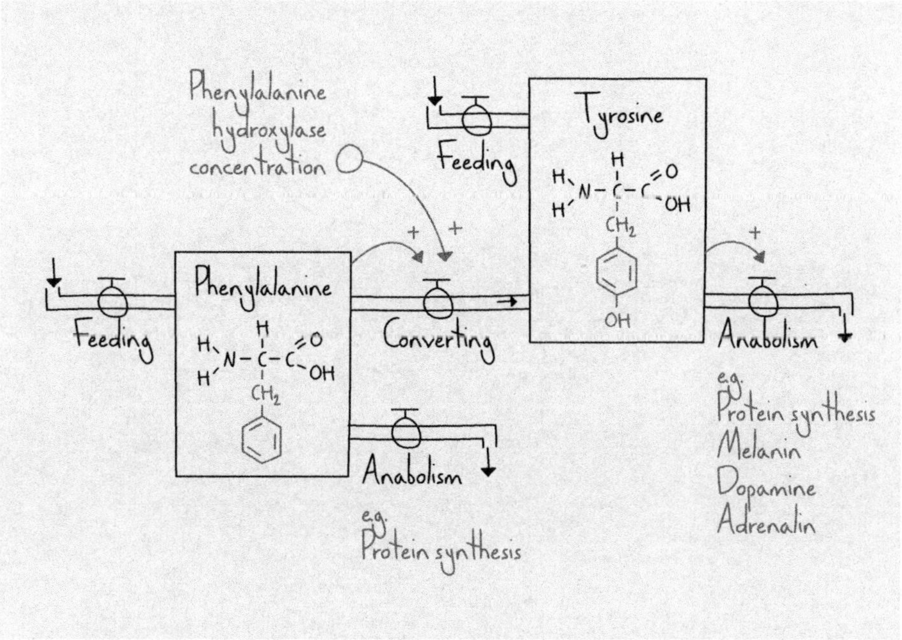

12. Phenylketonuria (PKU)

Age of students I have used this model with: 16–18

13. Vascular system: acclimation to altitude

Age of students I have used this model with: 14–16

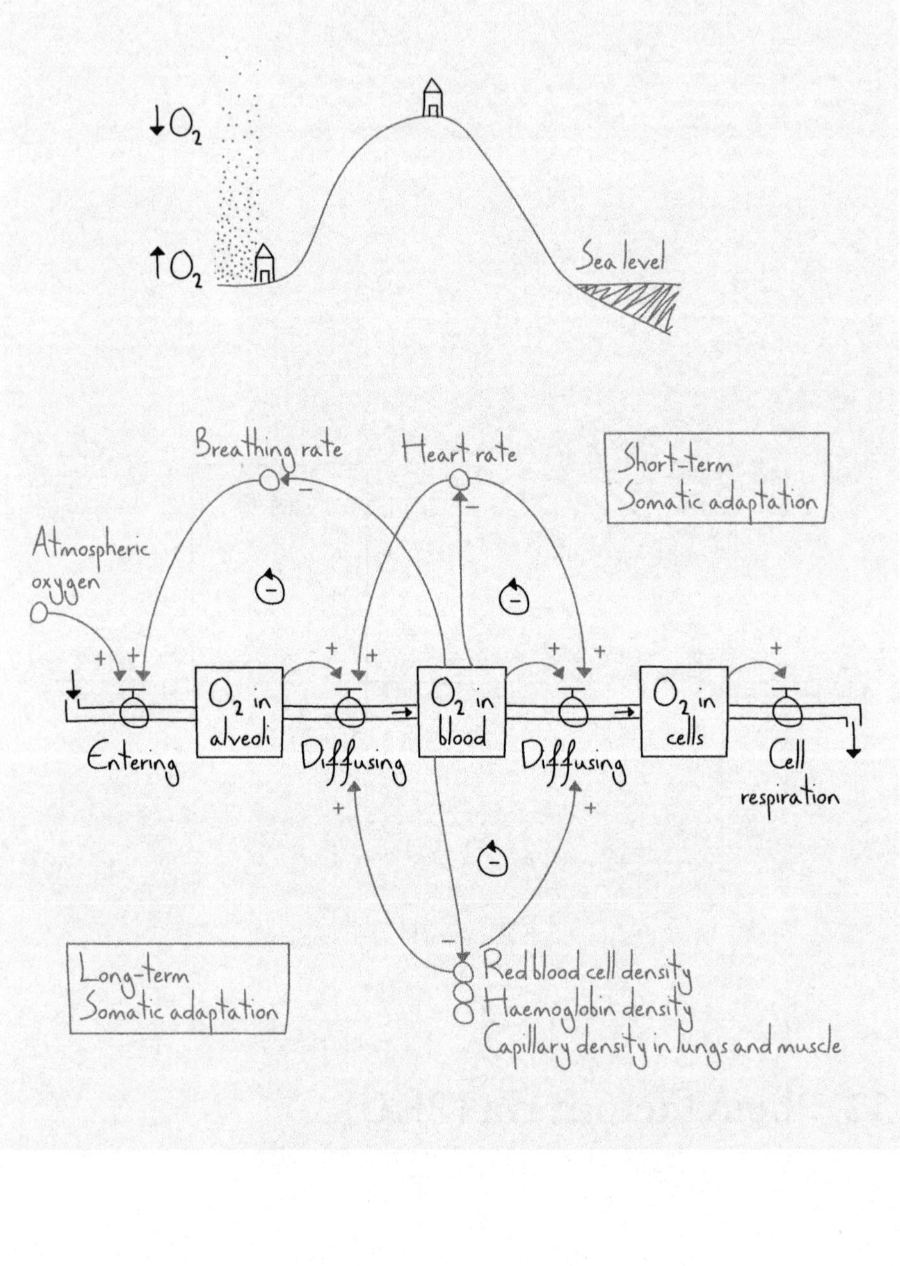

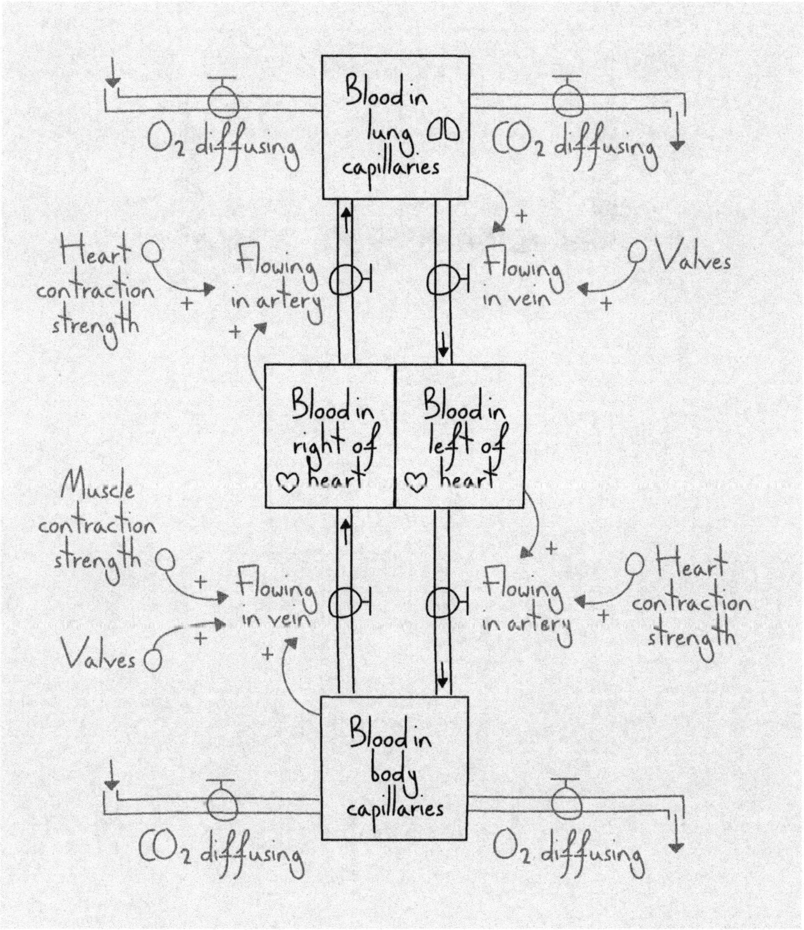

14. Vascular system: blood vessels & circuits

Age of students I have used this model with: 14–16

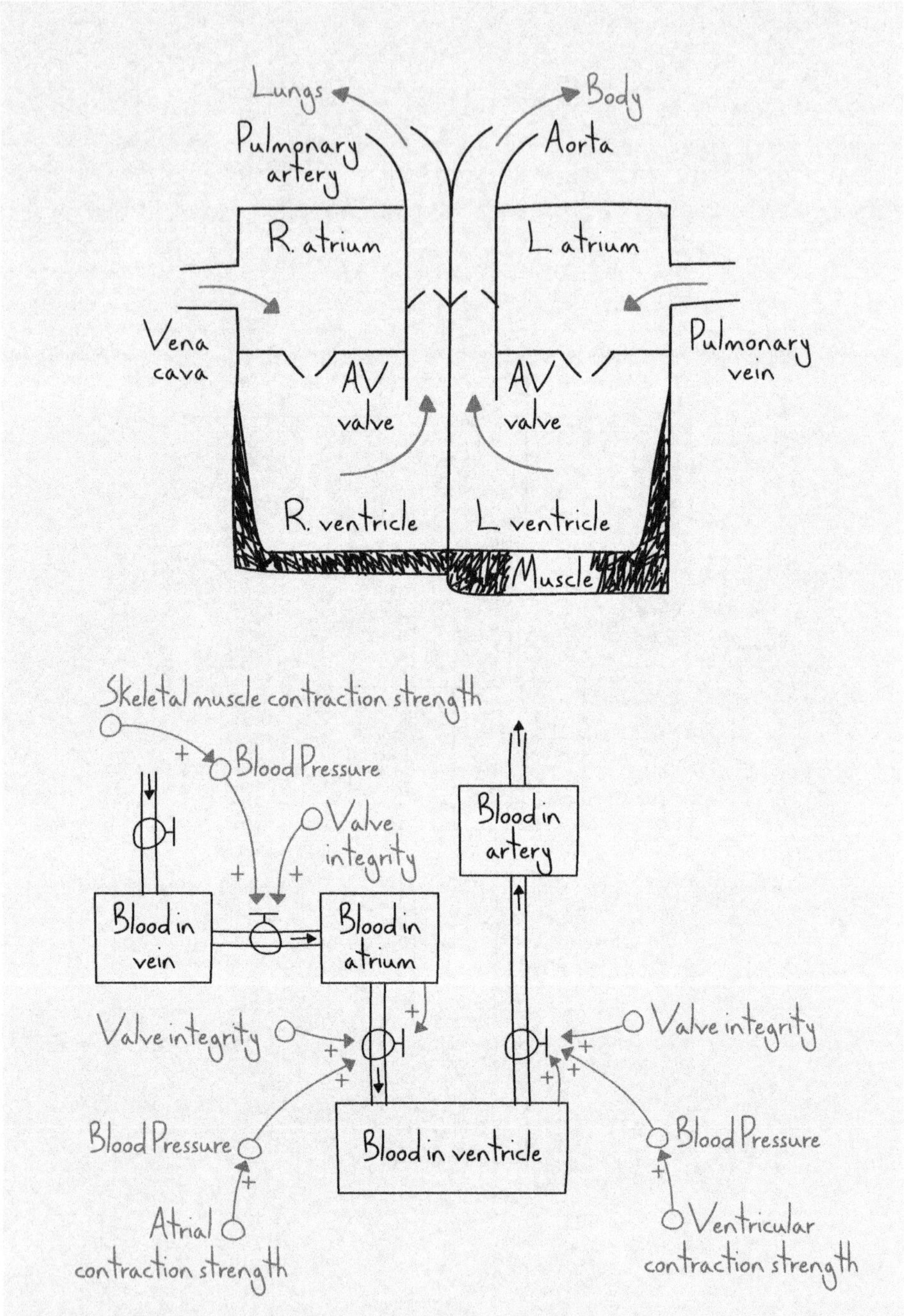

15. Vascular system: the heart

Age of students I have used this model with: 14–16

Models of Plant Physiology

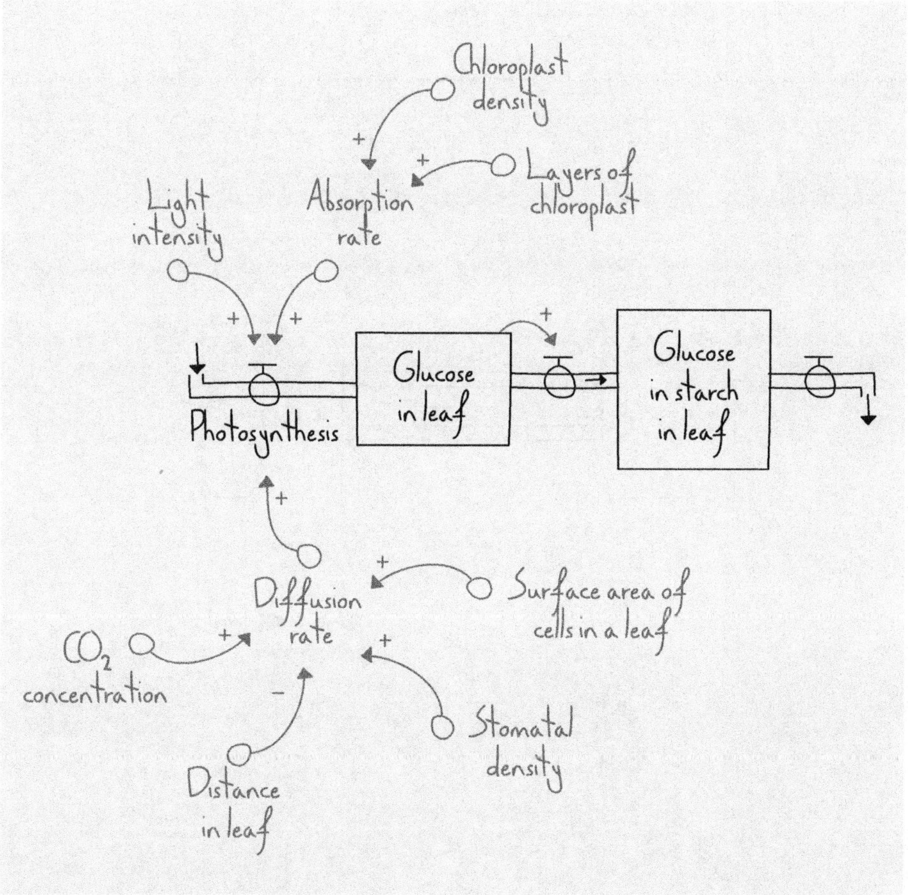

16. Leaf structure and function

Age of students I have used this model with: 14–18

17. Photoperiodism

Age of students I have used this model with: 16–18

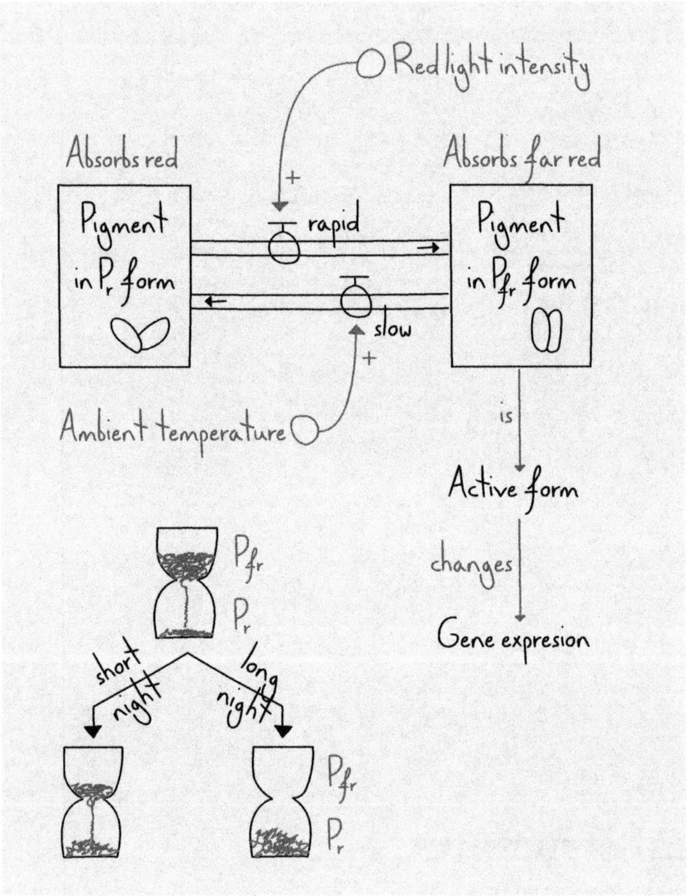

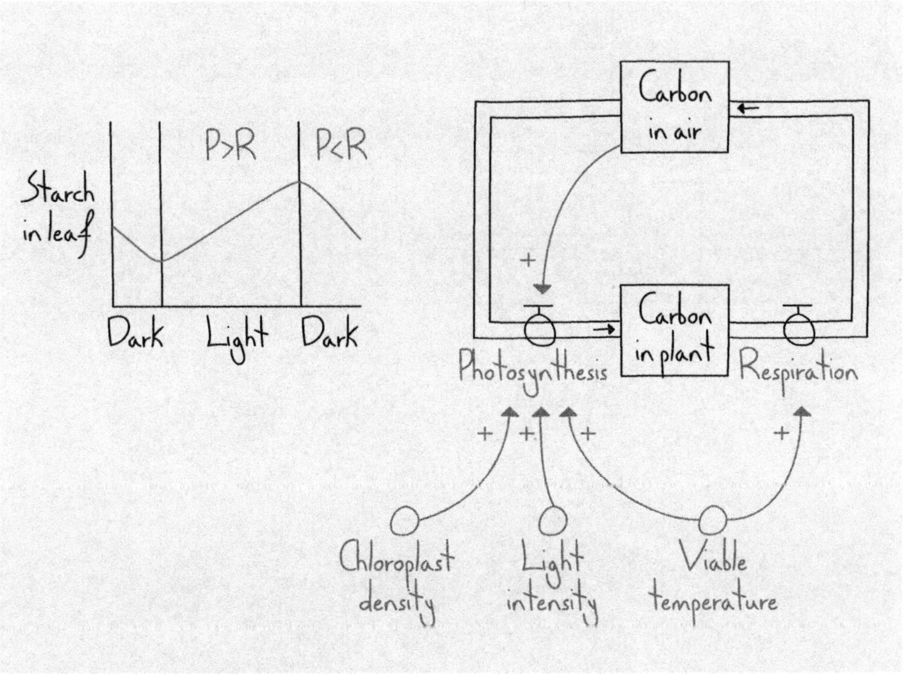

18. Relationship between respiration and photosynthesis

Age of students I have used this model with: 14–18
The idea for this model was shared with me by Jon Darkow.

19. Transpiration overview

Age of students I have used this model with: 14–18

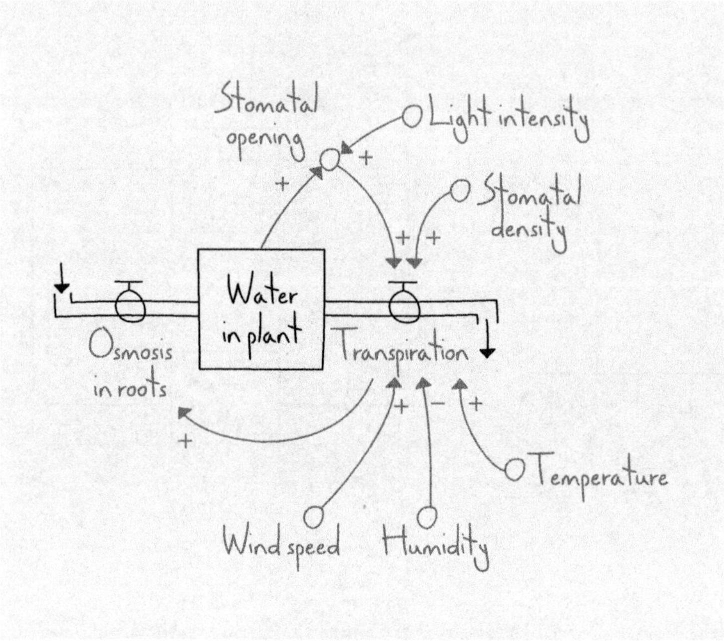

Models of Cell Biology

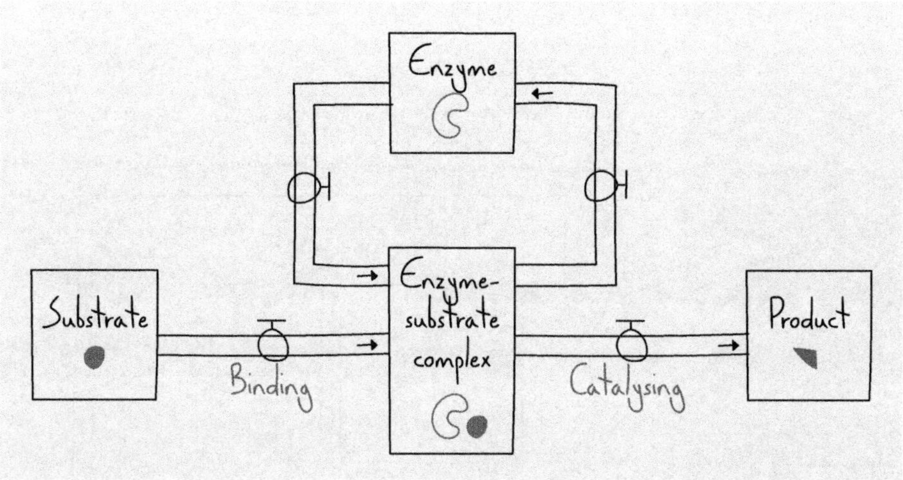

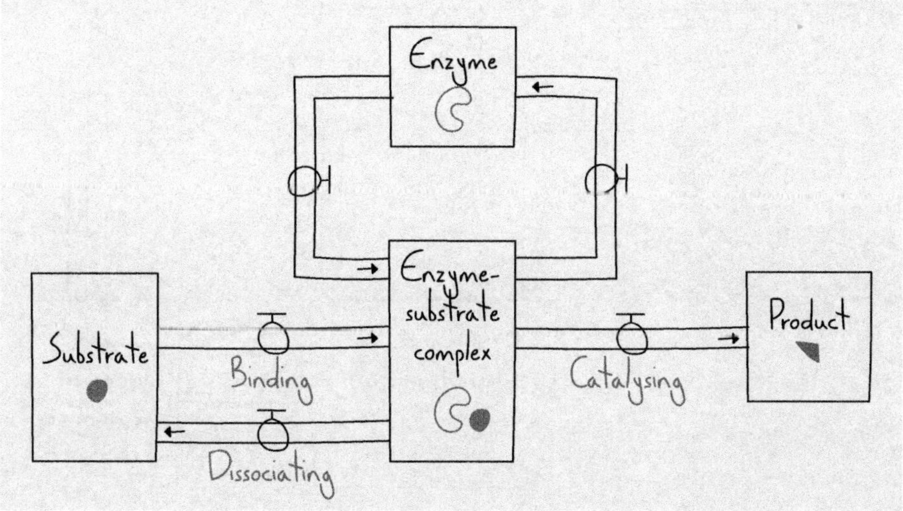

20. Enzyme reactions: simple

Age of students I have used this model with: 14–18
This model was shared with me by Emre Göktepe.

21. Enzyme reactions: advanced

Age of students I have used this model with: 16–18
This is an edited version of Emre Göktepe's model that I made for more advanced biology.

Models of Ecology

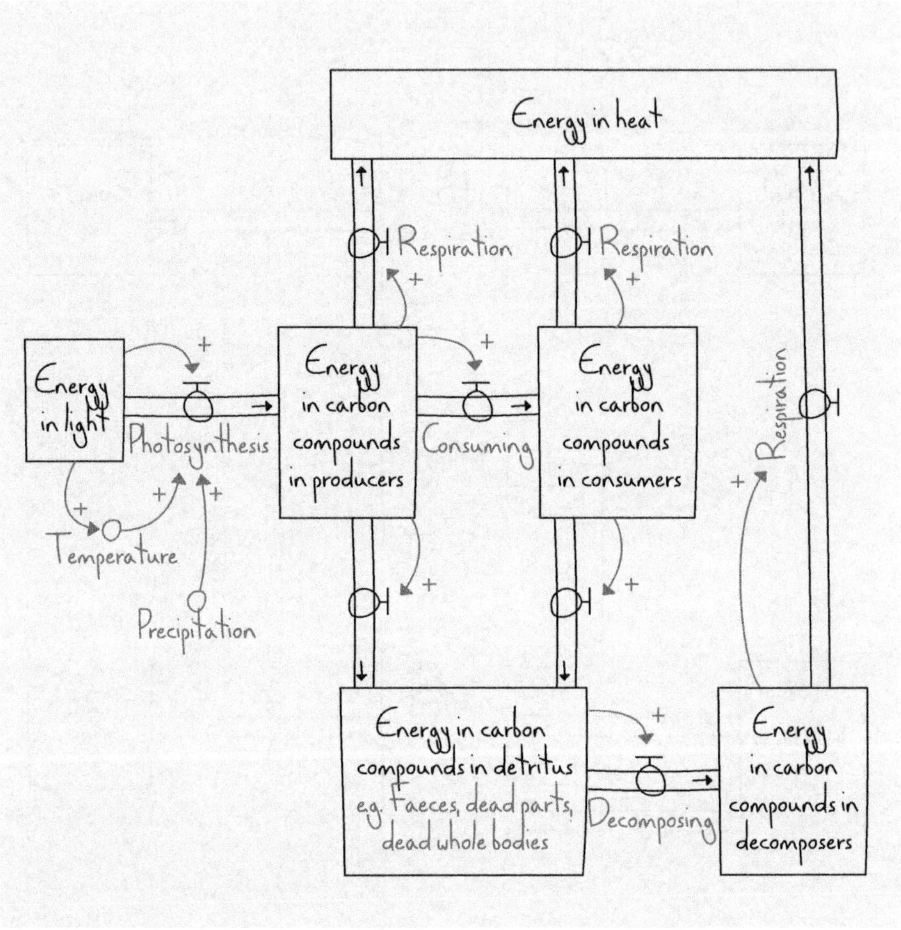

22. Ecosystem energy flow

Age of students I have used this model with: 14–18

23. Eutrophication

Age of students I have used this model with: 14–18

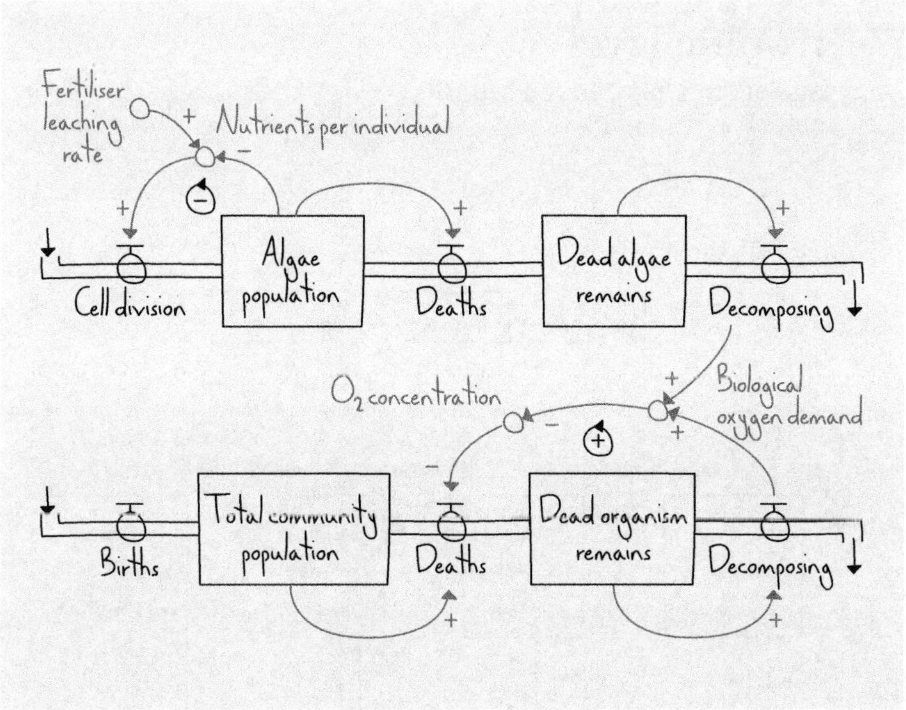

24. Feeding efficiency – energy loss per trophic level

Age of students I have used this model with: 14–18

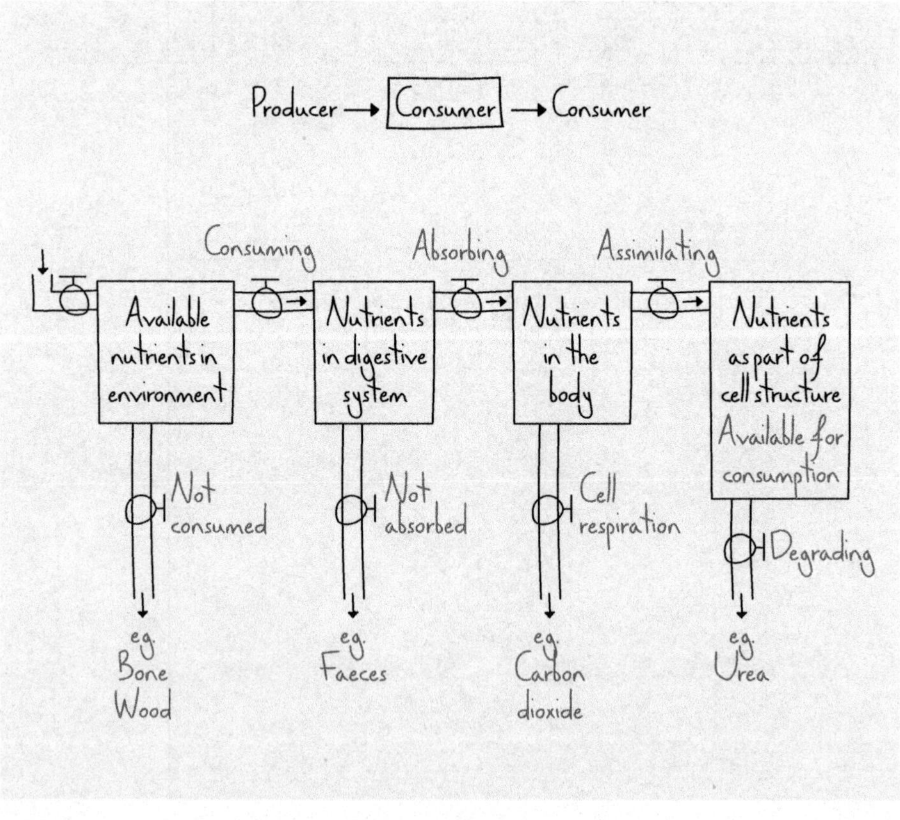

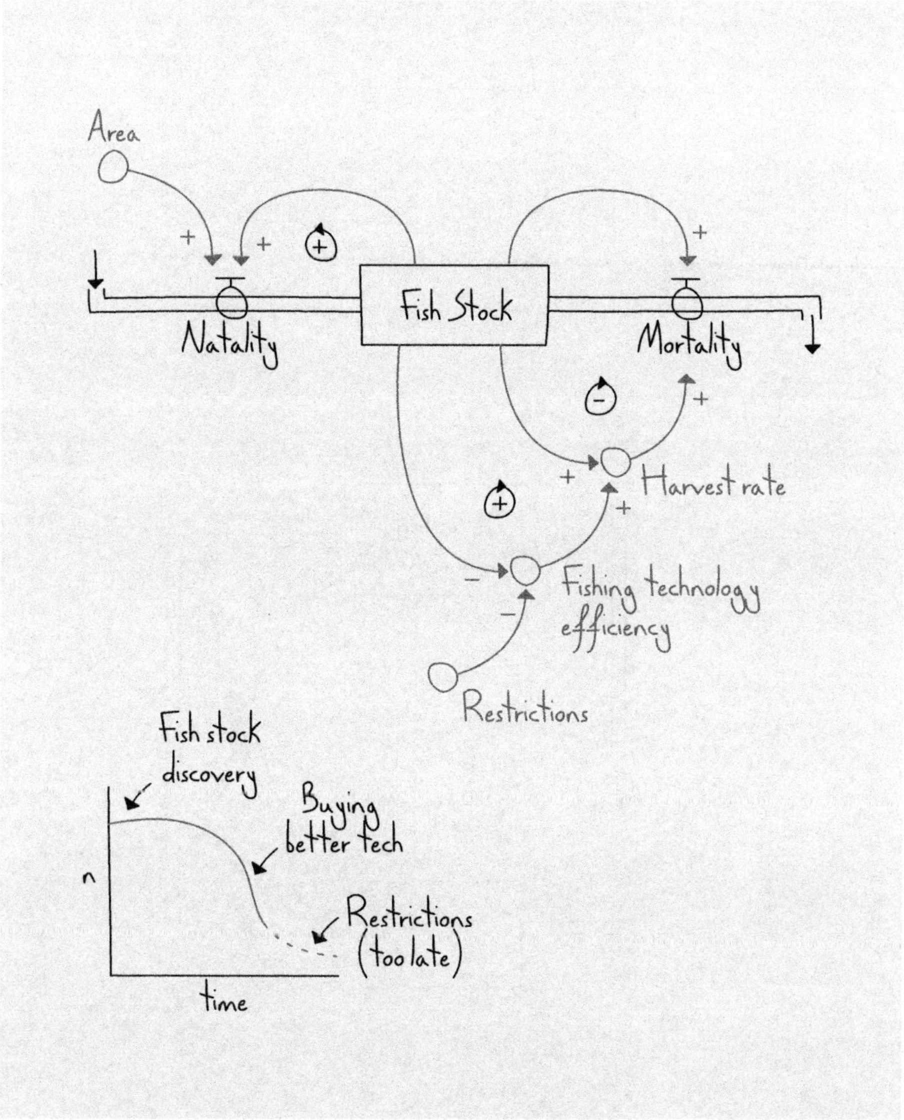

25. Fishing stocks and sustainability

Age of students I have used this model with: 16–18

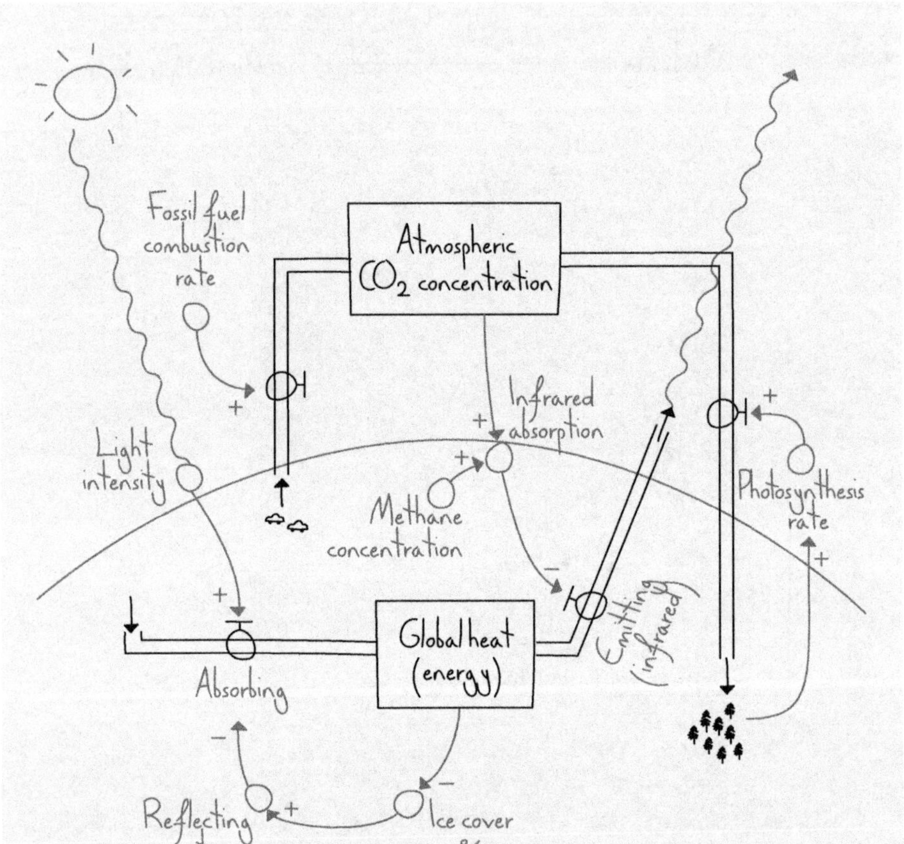

26. Greenhouse effect and climate change

Age of students I have used this model with: 14–16

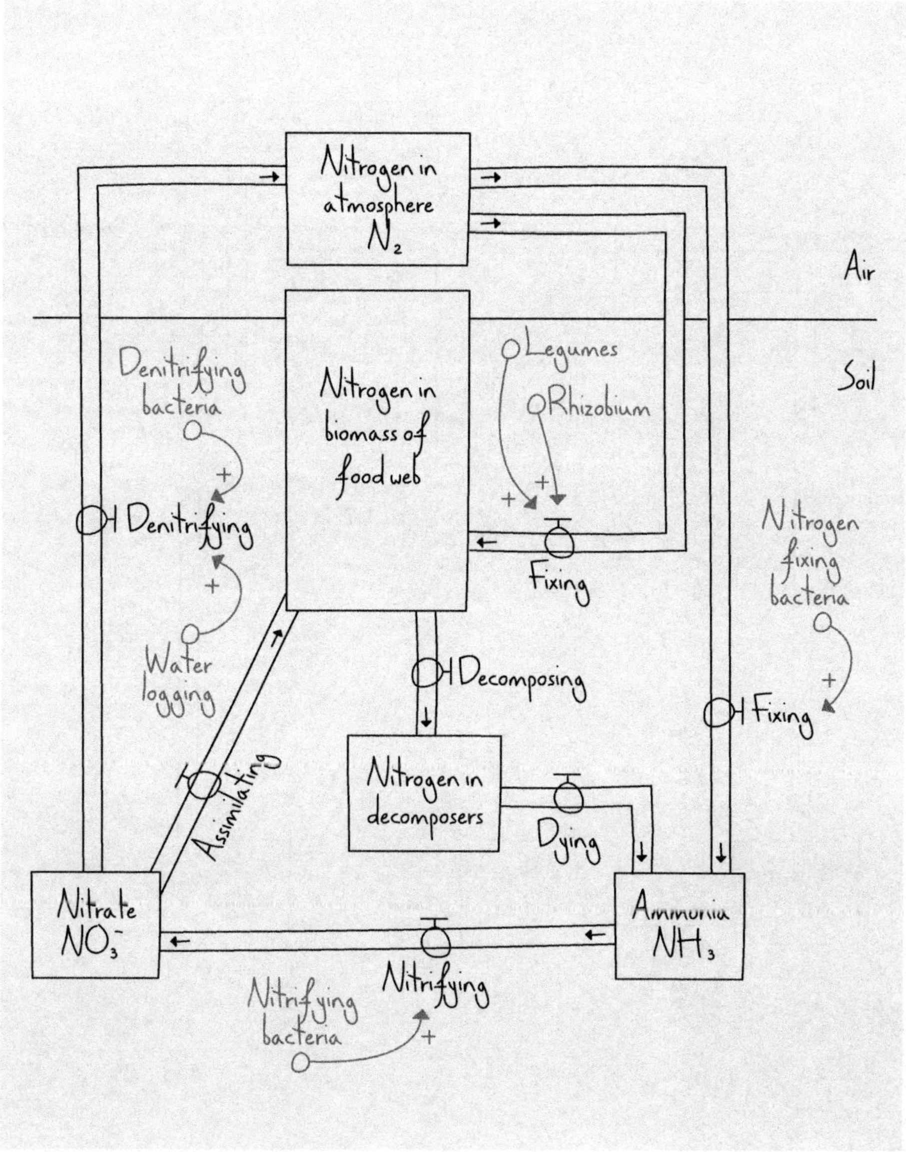

27. Nitrogen cycle: simple

Age of students I have used this model with: 14–16

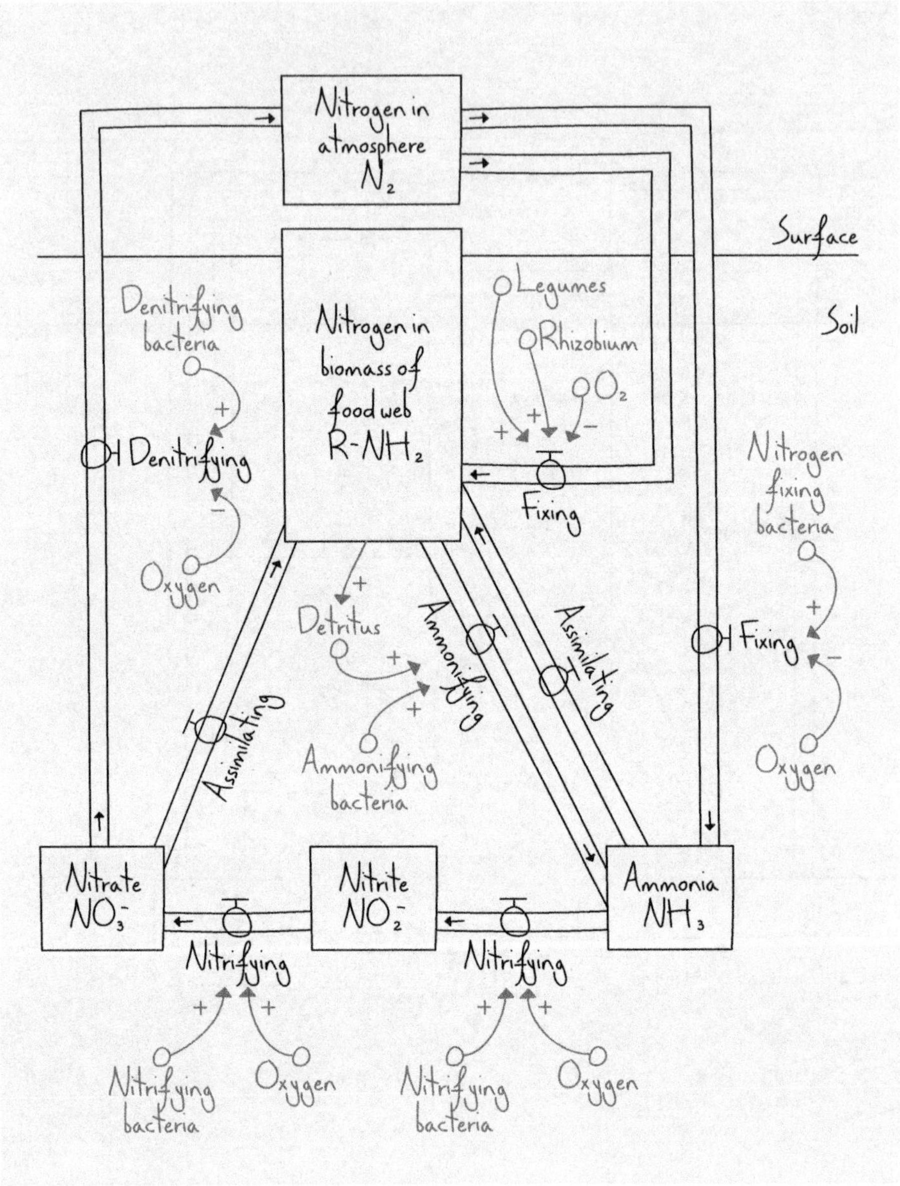

28. Nitrogen cycle: advanced

Age of students I have used this model with: 16–18

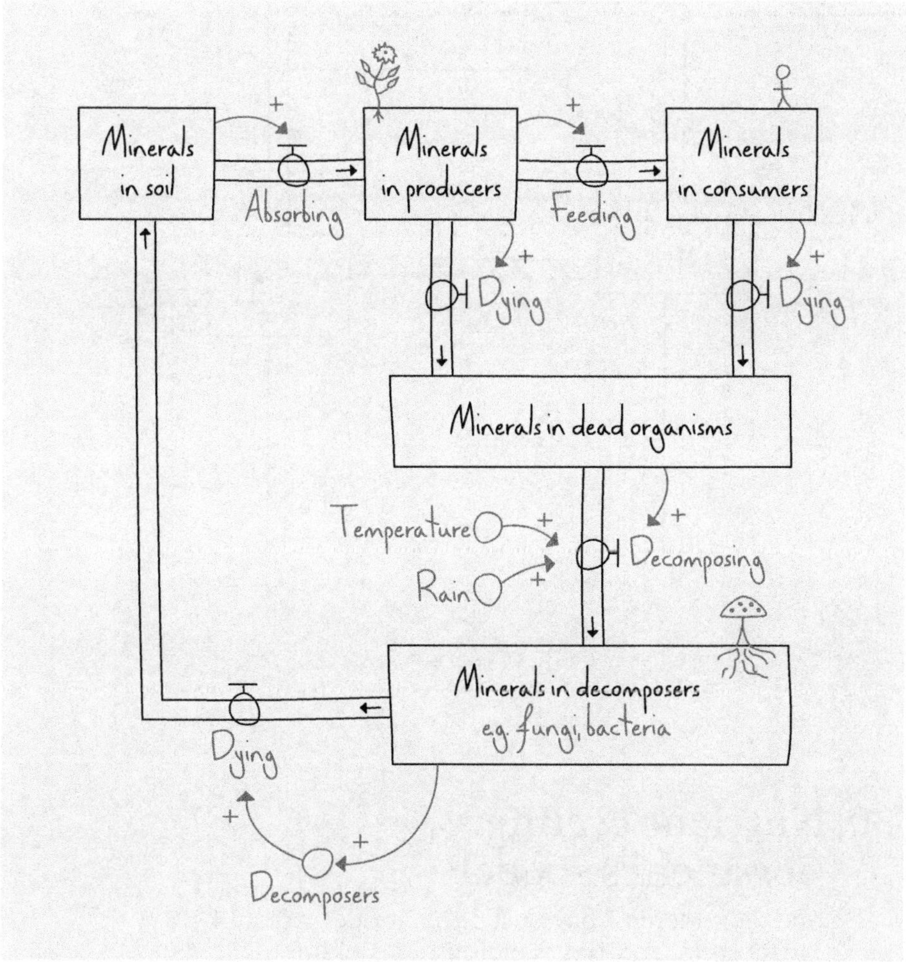

29. Nutrient cycling and role of decomposers

Age of students I have used this model with: 11–14

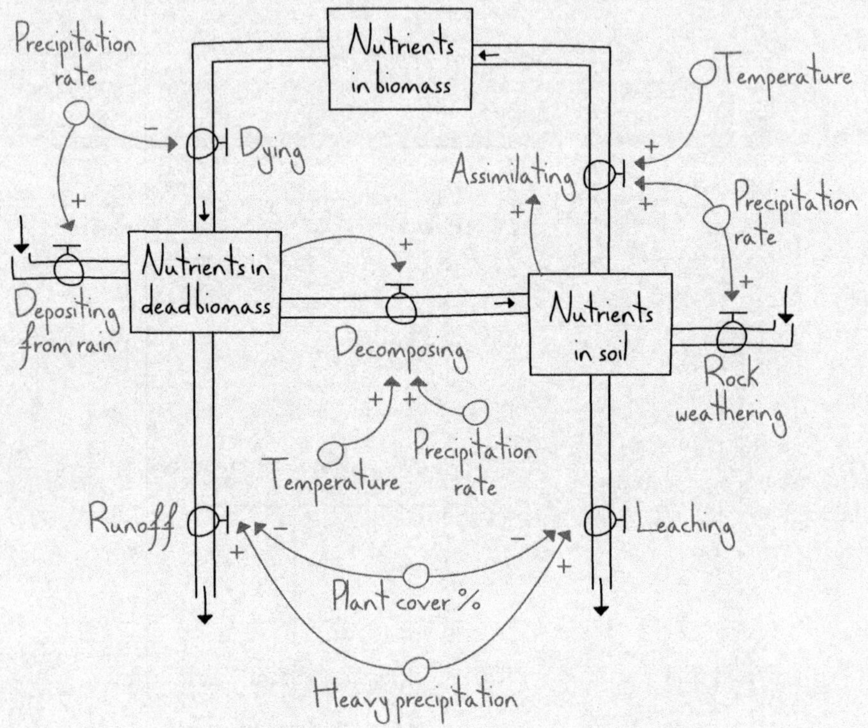

30. Nutrient cycling: Gersmehl's model

Age of students I have used this model with: 14–18
This a stock and flow version of a Gersmehl diagram (1976).

31. Predator-prey

Age of students I have used this model with: 11–12

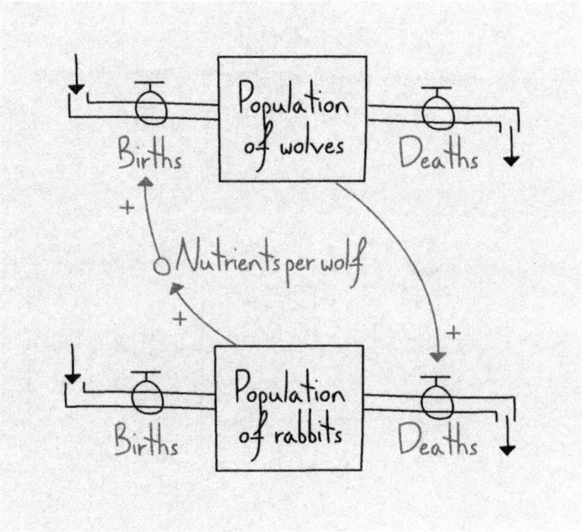

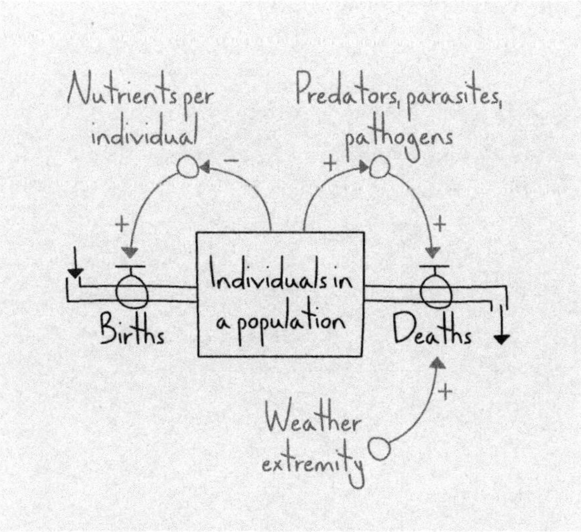

32. Population size: simple

Age of students I have used this model with: 11–16

33. Population size: advanced

Age of students I have used this model with: 16–18

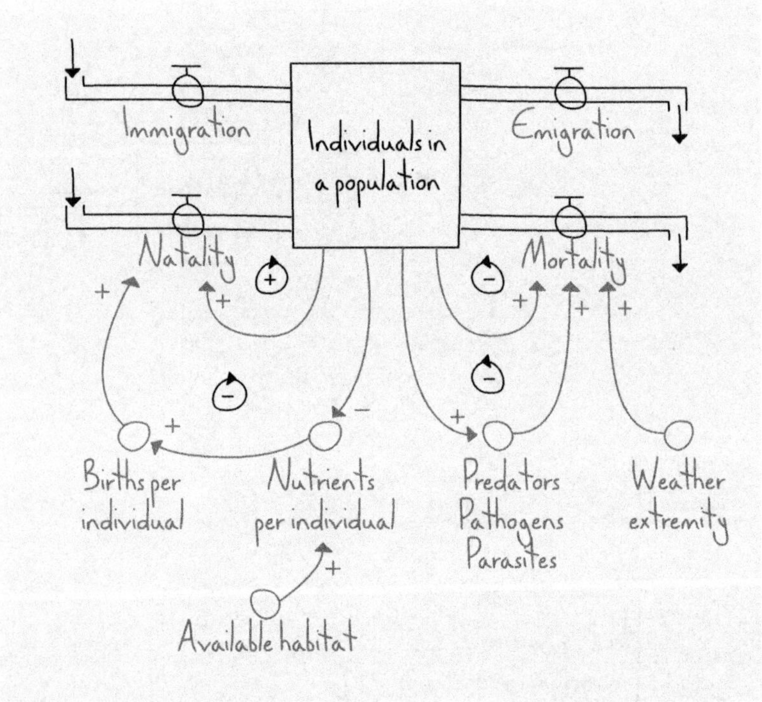

Models of Evolution

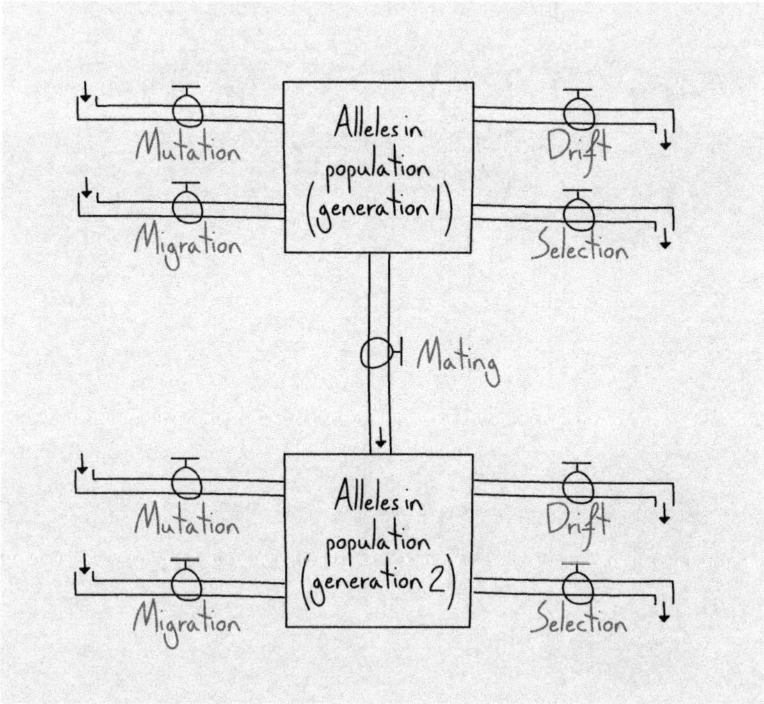

34. Gene pool: factors affecting allele frequencies

Age of students I have used this model with: 16–18

35. Gene pool: Hardy-Weinberg equilibrium

Age of students I have used this model with: 16–18

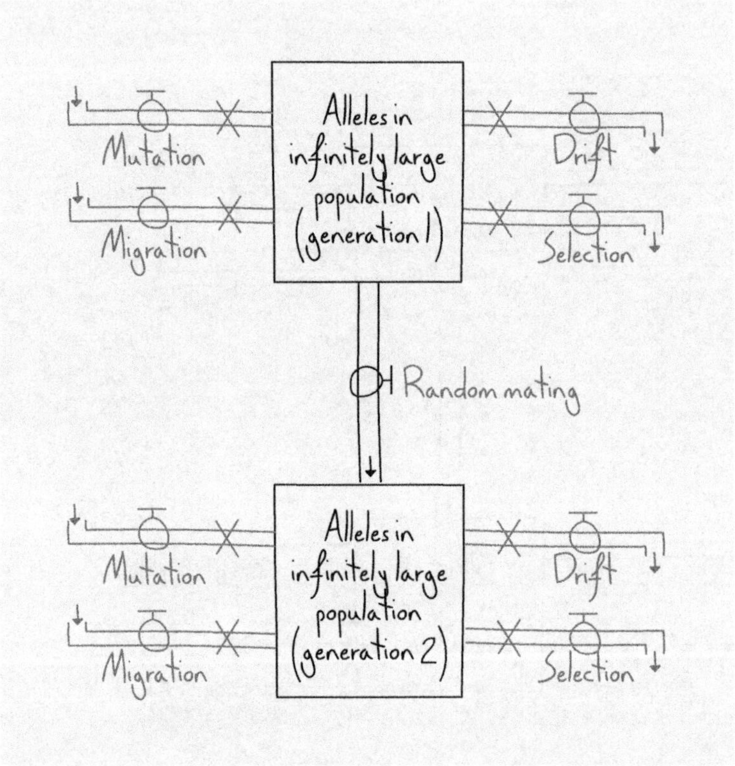

36. Natural selection

Age of students I have used this model with: 14–18

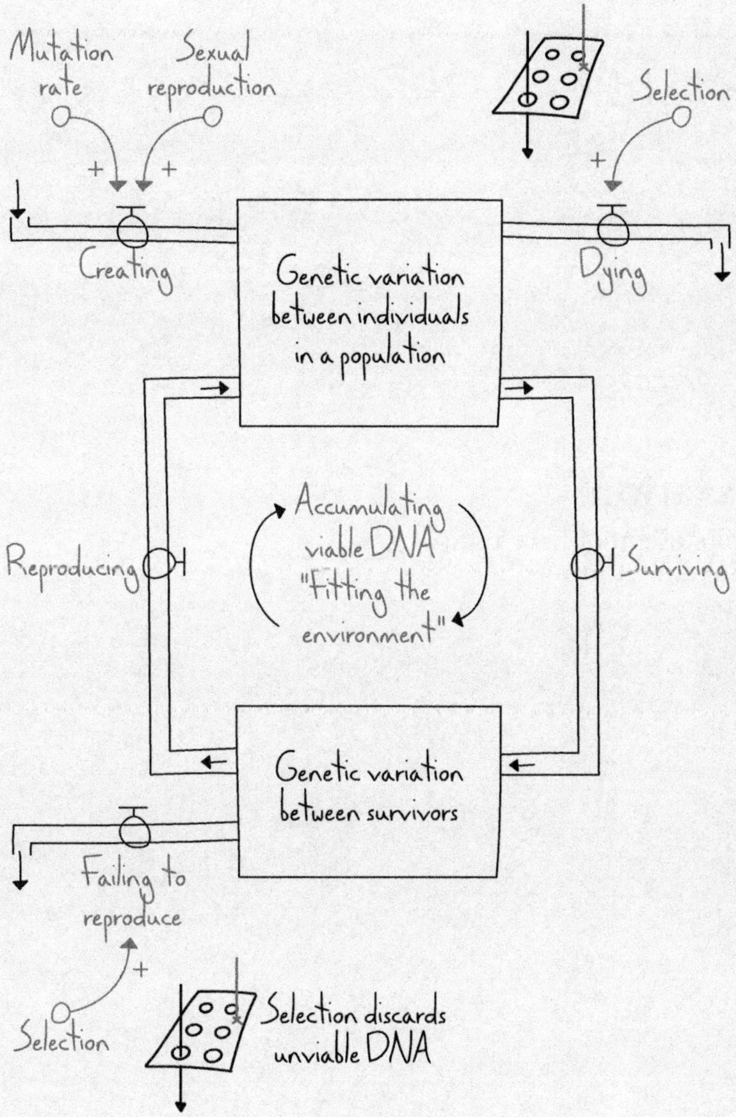
Mutation rate
Sexual reproduction
Selection
Creating
Dying
Genetic variation between individuals in a population
Accumulating viable DNA "Fitting the environment"
Reproducing
Surviving
Genetic variation between survivors
Failing to reproduce
Selection
Selection discards unviable DNA

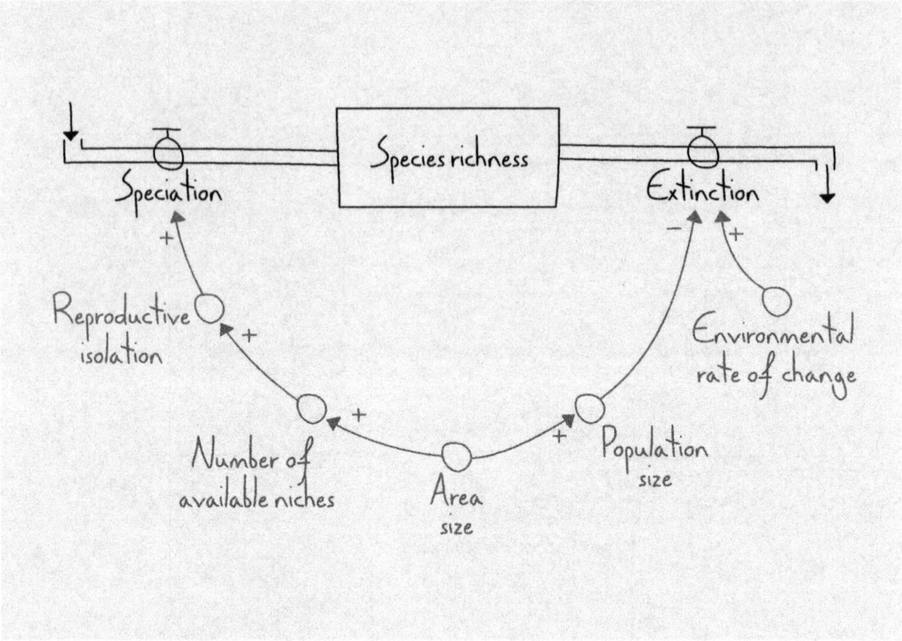

37. Speciation

Age of students I have used this model with: 16–18

ABOUT THE AUTHOR

Christian Moore-Anderson is head of biology and biology teacher of students aged 11–18 with over 15 years of teaching experience. He has published two books on biology education: Biology Made Real, and Difference Maker, and articles in the Journal of Biological Education and School Science Review. He currently teaches IBDP biology (16–18), IGCSE (14–16) biology, and general science (11–14) in mixed-attainment classes at Oak House School in Barcelona.

If you've enjoyed this book, I'd be very grateful if you left a short review. It makes a big difference. Otherwise, you can find posting updates at @CMooreAnderson on social media, and my blog: Teaching Biology.

Books by Christian Moore-Anderson:

ACKNOWLEDGEMENTS

Where would this book be without the multitude of people provoking me to think and act? I thank the cyberneticians for giving me rich ideas. But, more than anything, I recognise that the practical ideas in this book are the fruit of my interactions with my students. I thank them for constantly being frank with me about the ideas and activities I give them.

Finally, I thank those who've listened and responded with care and attention to my emerging ideas. Those who've read drafts of this book and helped me shape it into what it is. These people have left their mark on its form. Firstly, I thank those whose input has been significant: Alex Sinclair, Dan Rosen, Lee Bates, and Blanca Martínez (my wife, who designed this beautiful book). My thanks go to others who have also left their mark, whether that be in ideas, or the writing style: Juan Fernández, Alistair Hamill, Mike Goves, Gareth Bates, Michael Reiss, Jon Darkow, Paul Ganderton, Mark Enser, David Didau, Oli Caviglioli, Peps Mccrea, Sarah Cottinghatt, Tom Millichamp, Gwen Osbaldeston (my mum). I'd also like to thank Paul Pangaro for checking that my writing on cybernetics was accurate. And I thank many more who've interacted with me and nudged my thinking.

BIBLIOGRAPHY

Allen, B., Evans, M., & White, B. 2021. *The Next Big Thing in School Improvement.* Ebook Edition: John Catt.

Ashby, W.R. 1948. "Design for a Brain." *Electronic Engineering* 20: 379–383.

Ashby, W.R. 1952/1960. *Design for a Brain.* John Wiley & Sons.

Ashby, W.R. 1956. *An Introduction to Cybernetics.* New York: Wiley.

Ashby, W.R. 1958. "Requisite variety and its implications for the control of complex systems." *Cybernetica* 1 (2): 83-99.

Atkins, P. 2007. *Four Laws that Drive the Universe.* UK: Oxford University Press.

Bartlett, F.C. 1932. *Remembering: A Study in Experimental and Social Psychology.* USA: Cambridge University Press.

Bateson, G. 1972. *Steps to an Ecology of Mind: Collected Essays in Anthropology, Psychiatry, Evolution, and Epistemology.* USA: Jason Aronson Inc.

Bateson, G. 1979. *Mind and Nature: A Necessary Unity.* New York: Dutton.

Beer, S. 1972. *Brain of the Firm.* UK: The Penguin Press.

Boisot, M., & McKelvey, B. 2011. "Complexity and Organization–Environment Relations: Revisiting Ashby's Law of Requisite Variety." In *The Sage Handbook of Complexity and Management*, edited by Peter Allen, Steve Maguire, & Bill McKelvey, 279-298. London: Sage.

Booth, S. 1992. *Learning to Program: A Phenomenographic Perspective.* Göteborg: Acta Universitatis Gothoburgensis.

Brothy, J. 2006. "Graham Nuthall and social constructivist teaching: Research-based cautions and qualifications." *Teaching and Teacher Education* 22: 529–537.

Chaney, A. 2017. *Runaway: Gregory Bateson, the double bind, and the rise of ecological consciousness.* USA: University of North Carolina Press.

Churchill, W. "We Shape Our Buildings and Afterward Our Buildings Shape Us." Speech, House of Commons, October 28, 1943.

Clarke, B. 2020. *Gaian Systems: Lynn Margulis, Neocybernetics, and the End of the Anthropocene.* London: University of Minnesota Press.

Clarke, S. 2021. *Unlocking: Learning Intentions: Shifting From Product to Process Across the Disciplines.* Ebook Edition: Corwin.

Coe, R., Rauch, C., Kime, S., & Singleton, D. 2020. *Great Teaching Toolkit: Evidence Review.* UK: Evidence Based Education in partnership with Cambridge Assessment International Education. Available at: https://www.cambridgeinternational.org/Images/584543-great-teaching-toolkit-evidence-review.pdf

Conant, R., & Ashby, W. R. 1970. "Every Good Regulator of a System Must Be a Model of that System." *International Journal of Systems Science* 1 (2): 89-97.

Davis, B., Sumara, D., & Luce-Kapler, R. 2015. *Engaging Minds: Cultures of Education and Practices of Teaching*, third edition. UK: Routledge.

Donald, M. 1991. *Origins of the Modern Mind: Three Stages in the Evolution of*

Culture and Cognition. USA: Harvard University Press.

Dykstra, D.I., Boyle, C.F. & Monarch, I.A. 1992. "Studying conceptual change in learning physics." *Science Education* 76 (6): 615–52.

Ellison, P.T. 2001. *On Fertile Ground*. London: Harvard University Press.

Engelmann, S., & Carnine, D. 1991. *Theory of Instruction: Principles and Applications*. USA: NIFDI Press.

Fiorella, L., & Mayer, R.E. 2016. "Effects of observing the instructor draw diagrams on learning from multimedia messages." *Journal of Educational Psychology* 108: 528–546.

Foerster, H.von. 1969/2003. "What Is Memory that It May Have Hindsight and Foresight as well?" In *Understanding Understanding: Essays on Cybernetics and Cognition*, edited by Heinz von Foerster, 101–132. USA: Springer-Verlag.

Foerster, H.von. 1970a. "Laws of Form. Review of Laws of Form, by George Spencer-Brown." *Whole Earth Catalog*: 14.

Foerster, H.von. 1970b/2003. "Thoughts and Notes on Cognition." In *Understanding Understanding: Essays on Cybernetics and Cognition*, edited by Heinz von Foerster, 169–189. USA: Springer-Verlag.

Foerster, H.von. 1971/2003. "Perception of the Future and the Future of Perception." In *Understanding Understanding: Essays on Cybernetics and Cognition*, edited by Heinz von Foerster, 199–210. USA: Springer-Verlag.

Foerster, H.von. 1972/2003. "Responsibilities of Competence." In *Understanding Understanding: Essays on Cybernetics and Cognition*, edited by Heinz von Foerster, 191–197. USA: Springer-Verlag.

Foerster, H.von. 1973/2003. "On Constructing a Reality." In *Understanding Understanding: Essays on Cybernetics and Cognition*, edited by Heinz von Foerster, 211–228. USA: Springer-Verlag.

Foerster, H.von. 2002. *Understanding Systems: Conversations on Epistemology and Ethics*, edited by Bernard Poerksen. New York: Kluwer Academic/Plenum Publishers.

Foerster, H.von. 2003. *Understanding Understanding: Essays on Cybernetics and Cognition*. USA: Springer-Verlag.

Foerster, H.von. 2014. *The Beginning of Heaven and Earth Has No Name: Seven Days with Second-Order Cybernetics*. Edited by A Müller and K.H. Müller, Translated by: E Rooks and M Kasenbacher. Ebook Edition: Fordham University Press.

Foerster, H.von., & Maturana, H. 1998. *Future to be Determined: Concerns for Education. A conversation between Heinz von Foerster and Humberto Maturana*. Recorded by American Society for Cybernetics and Change Management Systems, directed by Pille Bunnell.

Forrester, J.W. 1961. *Industrial Dynamics*. Cambridge: MIT Press; Currently available from Pegasus Communications: Waltham, MA.

Forrester, J.W. 1968. *Principles of Systems*. USA: Wright-Allen Press.

Gersmehl, P. 1976. "An Alternative Biogeography." *Annals of the Association of American Geographers* 66 (2): 223–241.

Glasersfeld, E.von. 1980. "Viability and the Concept of Selection." *American Psychologist* 35: 970–974.

Glasersfeld, E.von. 1995. *Radical Constructivism: A Way of Knowing and Learning*. London: Routledge Falmer.

Glasersfeld, E.von. 1996. "Cybernetics and the Art of Living". *Cybernetics and Systems* 27 (6): 489–497.

Glasersfeld, E.von. 1999. "How Do We Mean? A

Constructivist Sketch of Semantics." *Cybernetics and Human Knowing* 6 (1): 9–16.

Glasersfeld, E.von. 2003. "The Constructivist View of Communication." In *An unfinished revolution*, edited by Müller A. & Müller K. H, 351–360. Vienna: Edition Echoraum.

Glasersfeld, E.von. 2007. "Cybernetics and the Theory of Knowledge". In *Key Works in Radical Constructivism*, edited by Marie Larochelle, 153–172. Rotterdam: Sense Publishers.

Günther, G. 1962. "Cybernetic Ontology and Transjunctional Operations," in *Self-Organizing Systems*, edited by Marshall C. Yovits, George T. Jacobi, and Gordon T. Goldstein, 313–392. Washington, D.C.: Spartan Books.

Harlen, W., et al. 2010. "Principles and Big Ideas of Science Education." *Association of Science Education*. https://www.ase.org.uk/bigideas

Harlen, W., et al. 2015. "Working with Big Ideas of Science Education." *Association of Science Education*. https://www.ase.org.uk/bigideas

Harries-Jones, P. 1995. *A Recursive Vision: Ecological Understanding and Gregory Bateson*. Toronto: University of Toronto Press.

Harries-Jones, P. 2016. *Upside-Down Gods: Gregory Bateson's World of Difference*. Fordham University Press: New York.

Heylighen F. 1992. "Principles of Systems and Cybernetics: an evolutionary perspective." In *Cybernetics and Systems*, edited by R. Trappl, 3-10. Singapore: World Science.

Hoverstadt, P. 2022. *The Grammar of Systems: From Order to Chaos and Back*. Ebook Edition: SCiO Publications.

Kampourakis, K. 2020. "Students' teleological misconceptions in evolution education: why the underlying design stance, not teleology per se, is the problem." *Evolution: Education and Outreach* 13: 1.

Kauffman, L.H. 2016. "Cybernetics, Reflexivity and Second-Order Science." *Constructivist Foundations* 11 (3): 489–497.

Kauffman, L.H. 2017. "Foreword: Laws of Form." *Cybernetics and Human Knowing* 24 (3-4): 5–15.

Kemp, W.M., & Boynton, W.R. 2004. "Productivity, trophic structure, and energy flow in the steady-state ecosystems of Silver Springs, Florida." *Ecological Modelling* 178: 43–49.

Krickel, B. 2024. "Different Types of Mechanistic Explanation and Their Ontological Implications." In *New Mechanism. History, Philosophy and Theory of the Life Sciences*, edited by Cordovil, J.L., Santos, G., Vecchi, D, 9–28. Cambridge: Springer.

Krippendorff, K. 2009. *On Communicating: Otherness, Meaning and Information*. New York: Routledge.

Kullberg, A., Ingerman, Å., & Marton, F. 2024. *Planning and Analyzing Teaching: Using the Variation Theory of Learning*. UK: Routledge.

Lax, W. 1993. "Symposium on Family Therapy." Annual Meeting of the American Society for Cybernetics (Philadelphia).

Lenton, T., et al. 2021. "Survival of the Systems." *Trends in Ecology and Evolution* 36 (4): 333–344.

Likourezos, V., Kalyuga, S., & Sweller, J. 2019. "The Variability Effect: When Instructional Variability Is Advantageous." *Educational Psychology Review* 31 (2): 1–19.

Lo, M.L. 2012. *Variation Theory and the Improvement of Teaching and Learning*. Sweden: Gothenburg University.

Margulis, L. 1998. *Symbiotic Planet: A New Look at Evolution*. New York: Basic Books.

Margulis, L., Sagan, D. 1995. *What is Life?* New York: Simon & Schuster.

Margulis, L., Sagan, D. 1997. *Microcosmos: Four Billion Years of Evolution from Our Microbial Ancestors.* London: University of California Press.

Marton, F. 2006. "Sameness and Difference in Transfer." *The Journal of the Learning Sciences* 15 (4): 499–535.

Marton, F. 2015. *Necessary Conditions of Learning.* London: Routledge.

Marton, F., & Booth, S. 1997. *Learning and Awareness.* New York: Routledge.

Marton, F., Runesson, U., & Tsui, A. 2004. "The Space of Learning." In *Classroom Discourse and the Space of Learning*, edited by F. Marton and A Tsui, 3–42. USA: Lawrence Erlbaum Associates.

Maturana, H. 1987. "Everything Is Said By An Observer." In *Gaia, A Way of Knowing: Political Implications of the New Biology*, edited by William I. Thompson, 67–84. USA: Lindisfarne Press.

Maturana, H. 2011. *From Being to Doing: The Origins of the Biology of Cognition.* In conversation with Bernhard Poerksen. 2nd Edition. Ebook Edition: Carl-Auer Verlag, 2004.

Maturana, H., & Varela, F. 1980. *Autopoiesis and Cognition: The Realization of the Living.* Dordrecht, The Netherlands: Reidel.

Maturana, H., & Varela, F. 1992. *The Tree of Knowledge: The Biological Roots of Human Understanding*, revised edition. USA: Shambhala Publications.

Maturana, H., & Verden-Zöller, G. 2008. *The Origin of Humanness in the Biology of Love.* Ebook Edition: Imprint Academic.

Meadows, D.H. 2008. *Thinking in Systems: A Primer*, edited by D. Wright. USA: Chelsea Green Publishing.

Misak, C. 2004. *The Cambridge Companion to Peirce.* USA: Cambridge University Press.

Mobus, G., & Kalton, M. 2015. *Principles of Systems Science.* Ebook Edition: Springer Complexity.

Modell, H.I. 2000. "How to Help Students Understand Physiology? Emphasize General Models." *Advances in Physiology Education* 23 (1): S101–S107.

Moore-Anderson, C. 2023. *Biology Made Real: Ways of Teaching that Inspire Meaning Making.* Independently published.

Nachmanovitch, S. 1982. "Gregory Bateson: Old Men Ought to Be Explorers." *CoEvolution Quarterly* (Fall): 34-44.

Nuthall, G. 2007. *The Hidden Lives of Learners.* New Zealand: Nzcer Press.

Pang, M.F., Bao, J., & Ki, W.W. 2017. "'*Bianshi*' and the Variation Theory of Learning." In: (eds) *Teaching and Learning Mathematics through Variation*, edited by Huang, R., Li, Y, 43–67. Rotterdam: SensePublishers.

Pask, G. 1975. *Conversation, Cognition and Learning.* Amsterdam: Elsevier.

Pask, G. 1976. *Conversation Theory: Applications in Education and Epistemology.* Amsterdam: Elsevier.

Pask, G. 1980. "The Limits of Togetherness." In *Information Processing*, edited by S. H. Lavington, 999–1012. Amsterdam: North Holland Publishing.

Pickering, A. 2010. *The Cybernetic Brain: Sketches of Another Future.* London: University of Chicago Press.

Potochnik, A. 2017. *Idealization and the Aims of Science.* Chicago: University of Chicago Press.

Razeto-Barry, P. 2012. "Autopoiesis 40 years Later. A Review and a Reformulation." *Origins of Life and Evolution of Biospheres* 42: 543–567.

Richmond, B. 1994. "Systems Thinking/System Dynamics: Let's Just Get On With It." *System Dynamics Review* 10 (2-3): 135–155.

Rid, T. 2016. *Rise of the Machines: The Lost History of*

Cybernetics. Ebook Edition: Scribe.

Rosenblueth, A., Wiener, N., & Bigelow, J. 1943. "Behaviour, Purpose, and Teleology." *Philosophy of Science* 10 (1): 18–24.

RSB 2021. *Evolving 5–19 Biology: Recommendations and framework for 5-19 biology curricula.* Available at: https://www.rsb.org.uk/images/Evolving_5-19_Biology.pdf

Russell, B. 2009. *The Philosophy of Logical Atomism.* UK: Routledge Classics.

Schein, E. 1996. "Kurt Lewin's Change Theory in the Field and in the Classroom: Notes towards a model of management learning." *Systems Practice* 9 (1) 27–47.

Schmidt, R.A., & Bjork, R.A. 1992. "New conceptualizations of practice: Common principles in three paradigms suggest new concepts for training." *Psychological Science* 3: 207–217.

Scott, B. 2021. *Cybernetics for the Social Sciences.* Boston: Brill.

Scott, E.E., Cerchiara, J., McFarland, J.L., Wenderoth, M. P., & Doherty, J.H. 2022. "How students reason about matter flows and accumulations in complex biological phenomena: An emerging learning progression for mass balance." *Journal of Research in Science Teaching* 1–37.

Shannon, C. 1948. "The Mathematical Theory of Communication." *Bell Systems Technical Journal* 27: 379–423 & 623–656.

Siegler, R., 1995. "How Does Change Occur: A Microgenetic Study of Number Conservation." *Cognitive Psychology* 28 (3): 225–273.

Siegler, R. 2002. "Microgenetic studies of self-explanation." In *Microdevelopment: A Process-Oriented Perspective for Studying Development and Learning*, edited by N Garnott, & J Parziale, 31–58. Cambridge, UK: Cambridge University Press

Spencer-Brown, G. 1979. *Laws of Form.* 2nd ed. USA: E.R Dutton.

Sterman, J. 2000. *Business Dynamics: Systems Thinking and Modeling for a Complex World.* USA: McGrawHill.

Stoltzfus, A. 2021. *Mutation, Randomness, and Evolution.* UK: Oxford University Press.

Sweller, J. 2011. "Cognitive Load Theory." *Psychology of Learning and Motivation* 55: 37–76.

Sweeney, L.B., & Sterman, J.D. 2000. "Bathtub dynamics: Initial results of a systems thinking inventory." *System Dynamics Review* 16 (4): 249–286. https:// doi.org/10.1002/sdr.198

Tan, Y.S.M., & S.M. Nashon. 2013. "Promoting Teacher Learning through Learning Study Discourse: The Case of Science Teachers in Singapore." *Journal of Science Teacher Education* 24 (5): 859–877.

Tan, Y., Johnstone Amiel, J., & Cheng, C. 2020. "Theorizing variation theory – a case of collaborative action research involving science teacher candidates." *Educational Action Research* 28 (3): 443–461.

Thompson, E. 2010. *Mind in Life: Biology, Phenomenology, and the Sciences of Mind.* Ebook Edition: Harvard University Press.

Tsui, A. 2004. "The Shared Space of Learning." In *Classroom Discourse and the Space of Learning*, edited by F. Marton and A Tsui, 165–186. USA: Lawrence Erlbaum Associates.

Tsui, A., Marton, F., Mok, I., Ng, D. 2004. "Questions and the Space of Learning." In *Classroom Discourse and the Space of Learning*, edited by F. Marton and A Tsui, 133–137. USA: Lawrence Erlbaum Associates.

Varela, F. 1979. *Principles of Biological Autonomy.* New York: Elsevier North-Holland.

Varela, F. 1987. "Laying Down a Path." In *Gaia, A Way of Knowing: Political Implications of the New Biology*, edited by William I. Thompson, 50–66. USA: Lindisfarne Press.

Varela, F. 1991. "Organism: A Meshwork of Selfless Selves." In *Organism and the Origin of Self*, edited by A Tauber, 79-107. Dordrecht: Springer.

Varela, F., Thompson, E., & Rosch, E. 2016. *The Embodied Mind: Cognitive Science and Human Experience*. Revised Edition. Ebook edition: MIT Press.

Wiener, N. 1954. *The Human Use of Human Beings*. New York: Houghton Mifflin.

Wiener, N. 1961. *Cybernetics: or Control and Communication in the Animal and the Machine* (Reissue of 1961 second edition). Cambridge, Massachusetts: M.I.T. Press.

Wittgenstein, L. 1922. *Tractatus Logico-Philosophicus*. Section 4.0621. London: Kagan Paul.

Wong, A., Leahy, W., Marcus, N., & Sweller, J. 2012. "Cognitive load theory, the transient information effect and e-learning." *Learning and Instruction* 22 (6): 449–457.

Woodwell, G.M. 1970. "The Energy Cycle of the Biosphere." *Scientific American* 223 (3): 64–77.

Printed in Great Britain
by Amazon

63141400R00127